100 HIKES in™

OREGON

Mount Hood • Crater Lake • Columbia Gorge • Eagle Cap
Wilderness • Steens Mountain • Three Sisters Wilderness

Second Edition

Rhonda & George Ostertag

THE
MOUNTAINEERS

Published by
The Mountaineers
1001 SW Klickitat Way, Suite 201
Seattle, WA 98134

First edition, 1992. Second edition, 2000.

Published simultaneously in Great Britain by Cordee, 3a DeMontfort Street, Leicester, England, LE1 7HD

Manufactured in the United States of America

Project Editor: Dottie Martin
Editor: Doris Cadd
Designer: Jennifer LaRock Shontz
Mapmaker: George Ostertag
Photographer: George Ostertag

Cover photograph: *Rogue River Trail, Rogue River National Forest*
Frontispiece: *Head of Metolius, Metolius Wild and Scenic River, Deschutes National Forest*

Library of Congress Cataloging-in-Publication Data
Ostertag, Rhonda, 1957-
    100 hikes in Oregon : Mount Hood, Crater Lake, Columbia Gorge, Eagle
Cap Wilderness, Steens Mountain, Three Sisters Wilderness / Rhonda & George
Ostertag ; [maps by George Ostertag ; all photographs by George Ostertag unless
noted otherwise].— 2nd ed.
        p.   cm.
    Includes index.
    ISBN 0-89886-619-7 (pbk.)
    1. Hiking—Oregon—Guidebooks. 2. Oregon—Description and travel. I.
Title: One hundred hikes in Oregon. II. Ostertag, George, 1957- III. Title.
GV199.42.O7 O844 2000
917.9504'3—dc21
                                                                    99-050629
                                                                    CIP

CONTENTS

ACKNOWLEDGMENTS

We would like to acknowledge the many people who helped bring this book to its conclusion: the staff at The Mountaineers Books, the personnel at the managing agencies who fielded our many inquiries, and the people we met along the way who shared their experiences, aided our travels, and suffered our requests for photos. Our thanks.

Rhonda and George Ostertag

PREFACE

While exploring Oregon, we found no shortage of interesting trails. The passages offered all kinds of adventures in all kinds of terrain. As with the previous edition, the challenge was to select a representative mix that hailed the diversity and spotlighted the unique yet dispersed visitor stress from the popular.

As hikers and environmentalists, we face a dilemma: the use of an area is often our strongest voice for ensuring its protection, yet that same use may threaten or degrade the very qualities in which we rejoice. However, with responsible use of all our wild areas and a tempered use of our most sensitive, most frequented lands, we can mitigate this dilemma.

We appreciate past individuals, both private citizens and agency personnel, who carried the banner for recreation and for the protection of our natural resources. Now, we must rise to the challenge and build on that legacy. Besides lobbying for adequate budgets to maintain, improve, and add to our recreational facilities comes a call to volunteer. It is a system that works and helps all trail users.

Our land-management agencies must demonstrate a genuine commitment from the top down—with lands, money, and personnel dedicated to the creation, overseeing, and protection of both natural and recreation lands. Without this commitment, the willingness heard at agencies' local levels is crushed out.

Today, more than ever, a cooperative spirit among recreationists, land stewards, and developers is needed. In Bend, Oregon, that spirit led to the creation of Newberry National Volcanic Monument—just think what other great things could be in store for the state of Oregon.

Wyethia, Ochoco National Forest

Sitka spruce

Map Legend

Interstate	95	Town	◯	
U.S. Highway	101	Wetland		
State or County Road	2	Campground	▲	
Forest Service Road	7745	Picnic Area		
Paved Road		Dam		
Gravel Road		Bridge		
Unimproved Road		Building	■	
Trailhead/Parking	℗	Summit	▲ 2,477 ft	
Described Trail		Mine/Quarry		
Alternate Trail		Viewpoint	⊙	
Creek		Point of Interest	★	
River		Pass/Saddle		
Body of Water		Lookout Tower		
Waterfall		Spring		

HIKE LOCATIONS

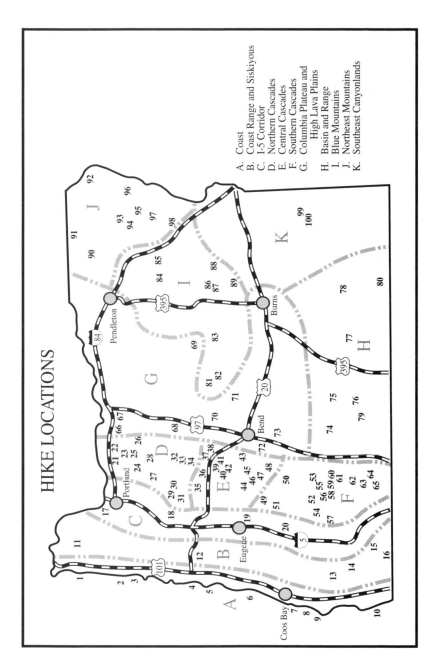

A. Coast
B. Coast Range and Siskiyous
C. I-5 Corridor
D. Northern Cascades
E. Central Cascades
F. Southern Cascades
G. Columbia Plateau and
   High Lava Plains
H. Basin and Range
I. Blue Mountains
J. Northeast Mountains
K. Southeast Canyonlands

INTRODUCTION

This guidebook features a statewide sampling of both backpack- and day-hike-length trails that challenge, excite, and engage hikers. Oregon is a vast state celebrating a diverse terrain, open expanse, and natural splendor. Within its borders, Oregon houses prized beaches, rich forests, mountain ranges of distinct character, deserts, lava lands, and canyon country. In many of these areas, state and nationally protected waterways serve as natural discovery corridors.

Limited to 100 hikes, this book can only brush the possibilities. While some trails unveil prized destinations, others are passageways to discovery and adventure. For year-round hiking, the mix includes both high-country and low-elevation routes.

USE OF THE BOOK

We have structured the book to aid in the trail selection process. First, the trails are grouped by geographical region. Second, to discover the trail character at a glance, each write-up features a summary panel identifying distance, elevation change, degree of difficulty, seasonal considerations, maps, and sources for additional information. The following explanations of some terms used in the summary lists are provided to avoid any misinterpretation:

Distance measures represent pedometer readings of round-trip distance, with the exception of the one-way, car-shuttle hikes, which are clearly specified. For the most part, backpacking excursions—sometimes dictated by distance, sometimes by attraction—are left to the hiker's judgment.

The elevation change notes the difference between the elevation extremes, providing a clue to the minimal demands of the trail.

The classification of the trails as easy, moderate, or strenuous is subjective. Easy hikes are generally short (under 5 miles), and have an elevation change less than 500 feet. Moderate hikes usually fall within the distance range of 5 to 12 miles and carry a maximum elevation change of 1,500 to 2,000 feet, and strenuous hikes are all those with a distance exceeding 12 miles and carrying an elevation change greater than 2,000 feet. Overriding considerations to these general guidelines include trail condition and grade, obstacles, and, to a lesser degree, exposure to the elements.

Summary lists do not include estimations of hiking times because personal health and physical condition, party size, the interest of the trail features, and weather and trail conditions all may influence the time spent on the trail. Hikes and trail lengths should be personalized for individual interest and physical ability.

Following the summary, the selling points of each trail are introduced: what makes the trail special, the natural history, seasonal surprises, and the rewards and disappointments. From this, hikers can determine whether the trail matches their present interests and time considerations, and they can make comparisons and selections when multiple trails bid for their attention.

Next come detailed directions to the trailhead, followed by a description of the trail's progress, which draws attention to special features and alerts hikers to obstacles and potentially confusing trail junctions. Using the given directions in conjunction with the appropriate agency map(s) is the best bet for a "no-fuss" trip to the trailhead.

The introductory map shows the eleven geographical regions defined by terrain and natural history that give structure to the book. The code numbers identify the general locations of the trailheads within those eleven regions and are relative to key routes and towns.

The maps included within the text are not intended to replace the more detailed area maps.

OUTDOOR PRIMER

For most people, wilderness trekking is a revitalizing experience, but for a few, it is an ordeal. Adequate preparation makes the difference.

Sun, wind, rain, dust, insects, steep terrain, and brush exact a toll. Prepared hikers learn to anticipate such conditions and take measures to eliminate or minimize their effects. Learning and heeding the regulations for backcountry use, becoming familiar with the area and its maps, and properly equipping for the demands of the trail and the climatic conditions will smooth the way to a pleasurable outing, as will matching the hike to the willingness and ability of the hiking party.

Hikers must show responsibility for both themselves and the environment. The following "basics" lay the cornerstones to that end.

Preparation

Outdoor experts have assembled a list of Ten Essentials for meeting and surviving the challenges that nature and the unexpected may hold for the backcountry traveler. Attending to these items provides a head start to a safe and rewarding outdoor adventure:

1. Extra Clothing—more than is needed in good weather
2. Extra Food—so that something is left over at the end of the trip
3. Sunglasses—especially important for alpine and snow travel
4. Knife—for first aid and emergency fire building (making kindling)
5. Firestarter—a candle or chemical fuel for starting a fire with wet wood
6. First-aid Kit—the hiker should also have basic first-aid knowledge, with cardiopulmonary resuscitation (CPR) skills a plus
7. Matches—in a waterproof container
8. Flashlight—with extra bulb and batteries
9. Map—the right one(s) for the trip
10. Compass—with knowledge of how to use it

Upper McKenzie Wild and Scenic River, Willamette National Forest

Clothing. The amount and the types of clothing worn and carried on a hike depend on the length of the outing, the weather conditions, and personal comfort requirements.

Layering is the important concept to remember when selecting clothes. Wool is the fabric of choice for cold or wet weather and for changeable weather conditions. It serves the hiker by retaining heat even when wet. Some of the new polar-fleece products, however, can be a good substitute. Cotton is the choice for warm summer days.

Hats are lightweight and provide a major service. In the summer, they shield the eyes, face, and top of the head from the sun's intensity. In winter, wool ones preserve body heat. In much of Oregon, a good suit of rainwear—jacket and pants—is a clothing necessity.

Footgear. Sneakers are appropriate for short hikes on soft earthen trails, if conditions are dry. For long hikes and hikes on uneven terrain, boots are preferred for both comfort and protection.

Sock layering, with a light undersock worn next to the foot and a second, ragg wool sock worn atop, helps prevent rubbing, provides cushion to the sole, and allows for absorption of perspiration. Avoid buying and wearing ragg socks with a large cotton content, as they are cold when wet and slow to dry.

Food. Food helps fend off fatigue, a major contributor to accidents on the trail, so the guideline is to pack plenty. Strive to maximize the energy value of the food for its weight, particularly when backpacking. With Oregon's wet weather, it is also a good idea to select foods that come in moisture-resistant wrappers or repackage food items in reusable plastic bags.

Equipment. The quantity and variety of equipment carried in addition to the Ten Essentials depend on the length and nature of the hike and on the season, but a good pack for transporting that gear is a must. A day pack with padded straps, a reinforced bottom, and side pockets for water bottles is appropriate for the short outing. For backpacking, it is important to select a pack that carries the weight without taxing the hips and shoulders or creating a strain on the neck.

As backpacks represent a major investment, we recommend that newcomers first try renting a backpack. One cannot adequately evaluate a pack in the store with only a few sandbags for weight. A trail test delivers a better comfort reading, plus it demonstrates how well the unit packs with one's personal gear. If your backpacking store has a rental program, check to see if the store will allow the charge of one rental to be applied to the purchase price of a new pack.

Map and Compass. Taking the time to become familiar with maps and their reading in conjunction with a compass will increase one's enjoyment of the outdoors. Maps provide an orientation to the area, suggest alternative routes, present new areas to explore, and aid in the planning and preparation for the journey.

Several maps serve the outdoor enthusiast, each with its own mix of useful information:

1. United States Forest Service (USFS) maps
2. United States Geological Survey (USGS) topographic maps (or topos), which come in two sizes: the 7.5-minute series and the 15-minute series
3. Privately produced trail or regional maps
4. The Bureau of Land Management (BLM) Blue Line Quads
5. Park brochures

As a reminder, for proper map reading, a magnetic declination of the compass is necessary, as true north does not equal magnetic north. For

Oregon, the mean declination is 20 degrees east. For specific locales, the declination may vary one to two degrees. Most topos indicate the declination on the map's bottom border.

Taking to the Trails

Reaching the Trailhead. Backcountry roads demand greater respect than city roads, where services and assistance are readily available. Keeping the vehicle in good repair; topping off the gas tank before entering the backcountry; and carrying vehicle emergency gear (jack, usable spare, tire inflator, jumper cables, and chains—for foul weather), basic survival gear for the unexpected (water, blanket, food, matches, first-aid kit, and a flashlight), and maps for the area you are visiting all promote safe backcountry travel.

Pacing Yourself. Adopting a steady walking pace allows the logging of distances with greater comfort, and taking short rests at moderate intervals helps guard against overexhaustion.

Crossing Streams. A dry crossing is preferred, but when stream conditions prohibit it, stage the crossing at the widest part of the watercourse, where the current is slower and the water more shallow. Sandy bottoms suggest a barefoot crossing, while fast, cold waters and rocky bottoms require a surer footing and call for boots. Depending on the number of stream crossings, carrying a pair of sneakers for the purpose of wading may be justified.

Hiking Cross-country. Cross-country excursions, save for short distances, are not for the beginner. Steep terrain, heavy brush, and the many downfalls tax hikers both physically and mentally, increasing the potential for injury. This, of all hiking, should not be attempted alone. Even know-how and preparation cannot fully arm one against hiker fallibility and the unpredictability of nature.

Beach Hiking. Before taking a long hike, study the tide tables to learn the times of high and low tide. To avoid the danger of becoming stranded, make sure there's adequate time or adequate beach property to complete the hike or reach safety before the incoming tide. Also, "sneaker" waves—those unexpected, irregular-sized waves that can knock you off your feet—occur along the Oregon Coast. Beware: Drift logs do not provide a safe haven from incoming waves. The force of the surf can shift, roll, and lift a log, tumbling, striking, and even crushing the unsuspecting rider.

Wilderness Courtesy

Trails. Keep to the path, as shortcutting, skirting puddles, walking two abreast, and walking along the bench of a recessed trail all contribute to erosion.

Permits and Fees. Where wilderness permits are in effect, they are generally required Memorial Day weekend (the last weekend in May) through

October 31. Presently, backcountry users can secure these permits at the ranger stations, visitor centers, or trailheads; no fee applies.

Access to a few sensitive areas, such as the Pamelia Lake Area in the Mount Jefferson Wilderness, is by a limited-entry permit only. This management policy restricts user numbers and requires application for the permit directly from the ranger district (Detroit, in the case of Pamelia) before hiking.

Currently, most of the national forests in the state are collecting trailhead fees through the Trail Park Pass Program. The monies generated from this program go directly to trail improvement. Passes are required at most major trailheads within the participating forests. Purchase these day or annual passes at ranger stations or at selected area stores before setting out.

Increasingly, day-use fees are becoming more common at state parks and at federal recreation lands other than the national forests. Visitors should come ready to purchase passes. Having a supply of single dollar bills is recommended because several sites have dollar-fed permit machines.

Party Size. When planning a backcountry outing, particularly to any wilderness, keep your party size small and adhere to any regulations restricting party size. If you are unfamiliar with an area's rules and policies or if you haven't visited an area for some time (regulations may have changed), contact the managing agency for this information before a visit.

Pets. Owners should strictly adhere to posted rules for pets. Controlling animals on a leash is not just a courtesy reserved for times when other hikers are present; it is a responsibility to protect the wildlife and ground cover at all times.

Camping. Low-impact camping should be the goal of every hiker. Wherever possible, select an established campsite and don't rearrange it by removing ground cover, bringing in logs for benches, banging nails into trees, or digging drainage channels around the tent. The clues that a hiker passed this way should be minimal.

Reduce the number of comforts (as opposed to necessities) ported into camp. Carry a backpacker's stove for cooking. When a campfire is necessary, keep it small, and heed the regulations on campfires and wood gathering. Wood collection is limited to downed wood. Snags and live trees should never be cut.

If there are no preestablished campsites, select a site at least 200 feet from the water and well removed from the trail. Delicate meadow environments should be avoided.

Sanitation. Use toilets where provided. Where this is not possible, select a site well away from the trail and at least 300 feet from any watercourse for the disposal of human waste. There, dig a hole 6 to 8 inches deep for burying the waste. If the ground resists digging, dig as deep as possible and cover well with gravel, bark, and leaves.

Unless in bear country, tissue (and women's monthly protection) should be packed out in a zip-seal bag. Should packing out these items, however, pose a danger, safely burn the soiled items.

For health protection, antibacterial solutions should be carried for use after each sanitation stop and before handling food.

Litter. "Pack it in, pack it out" is the rule. Any litter that does not completely burn should be carried out. Disposable diapers, aluminum foil, cans, orange peels, and peanut shells are all pack-it-out garbage. Burying garbage is not a solution.

Washing. Bathing and the washing of dishes should be done well away from lake or stream. Water should be carried to the washing site and biodegradable suds used sparingly. Whenever possible, select a rocky wash site, removed from vegetation.

Noise. Nature's quiet and the privacy of fellow hikers demand respect.

Safety

Backcountry travel entails unavoidable risks that every traveler assumes and must be aware of and respect. The fact that an area is described in this book does not mean that it will be safe for you. Nature is continuously evolving, and humans are fallible. Likewise, each hiker possesses a different set of skills and abilities that can change with time. Independent judgment and common sense remain the hiker's best ally.

Water. Water is the preferred refreshment for the hiker. Drinks with caffeine or alcohol are diuretics, which will dehydrate and weaken the hiker.

All drinking water taken from lakes, streams, and other natural sources should be treated. Today, even clear, pulsing streams in remote reaches may contain *Giardia*, a protozoan that causes stomach and intestinal discomfort.

Bringing water to a full boil for ten minutes or using water purification systems that remove both debris and harmful organisms offers the best protection. Although water purifiers are by far easier to transport and use, their filters vary. Make certain the selected system strains out the harmful organisms. Iodine tablets offer protection against *Giardia* if used appropriately, but they are not considered safe for pregnant women.

It is best to carry some drinking water on all excursions, as sources can dry up or become fouled. Even on short nature hikes, water is a good companion.

Getting Lost. Because becoming stranded or injured in the wild poses a great problem, it is critical to notify a responsible party of your intended destination and time of return before any outdoor adventure. Notifying the informed party upon your return completes the safety procedure.

If lost, it is best to sit down and try to think calmly. There is no immediate danger, as long as one has packed properly and followed the notification procedure. If hiking with a group, all should stay together.

Conducting short outward searches for the trail and then returning to an agreed-upon, marked spot if unsuccessful are generally considered safe. Aimless wandering would be a mistake. If the search meets with failure, whistling or making loud noises in sets of three may bring help. (Combinations of three are universally recognized as distress signals.) If it is getting late in the day, efforts are best spent preparing for night and trying to conserve energy.

Normally, unless one has good cross-country navigational skills, conserve energy, aid the rescuers by staying put, and hang out bright-colored clothing.

Hypothermia. Hypothermia is the dramatic cooling of the body that occurs when heat loss surpasses body-heat generation.

Cold, wet, and windy weather command respect. Attending to the Ten Essentials, eating properly, avoiding fatigue, and being alert to the symptoms of sluggishness, clumsiness, and incoherence among hiking party members remain the best protection. Never underestimate the unpredictability of weather.

Should a party member display the symptoms of hypothermia, it is critical to stop and get the member dry and warm. Dry clothing, shared body heat, and hot fluids all help restore body temperature.

Heat Exhaustion. The strenuous exercise of hiking combined with summer sun can lead to heat exhaustion, an overtaxing of the body's heat regulatory system. Wearing a hat, drinking plenty of water, eating properly (including salty snacks), and avoiding fatigue are the safeguards against heat exhaustion. Hiking in the early morning and evening hours with midday rests also helps avoid the problem.

Poison Oak and Ivy. To avoid contact, learn what they look like and in what environments they grow. A good plant-identification book will supply this information.

Immediately rinse off after any contact with the plant to remove or reduce oils, and then avoid scratching, which can spread the oils. Launder clothing as soon as possible upon returning home, because oils transported on the fabrics can also irritate skin. Creams that inhibit the plants' poison are available in both precontact and postcontact applications.

Stings and Bites. The best armor against stings and bites is, again, knowledge. It is important to become aware of any personal allergies and sensitivities and to become knowledgeable about the habits and habitats of snakes, bees, ticks, and other "menaces" of the wild and how to deal with the injuries they may cause. In the case of a tick bite, after removing the tick, watch for signs of redness and swelling, which could be an early indication of Lyme disease.

Consult a physician whenever wounds show signs of infection or you experience unexplained pains or symptoms of illness. Do not delay, and be forthcoming with the doctor about recent outdoor activities to speed diagnosis.

Bears. In dealing with bears, use basic sense. Food should not be stored near camp and especially not in the tent. If clothes pick up cooking smells, they should be suspended along with the food from an isolated overhanging branch well away from camp.

Sweet-smelling creams or lotions should be avoided. During menstruation, women should play it safe and avoid bear country.

Trailhead Precautions. Hikers are vulnerable. Their vehicles (and frequently their valuables) are left unattended for long periods of time in remote trailhead parking areas.

As a safeguard, heed the following precautions:

- Whenever possible, park away from the trailhead at a nearby campground or other facility. A car left at the trailhead parking area says, "my owner is gone."
- Do not leave valuables. Carry keys and wallet, placing them in a remote compartment in the pack where they won't be disturbed while on the trail.
- Do not leave any visible invitations to the thief. Whenever possible, stash everything in the trunk.
- Be suspicious of loiterers at the trailhead. Some thieves, with a pack in tow, sit at the trailhead, presumably waiting for a ride. This allows them to observe the unloading, the storing of items in the trunk, and the hiding of valuables. It also allows them to engage hikers in conversation, learning where they are going and when they'll return.

For more detailed information about outdoor preparedness, there are many good instructional books and classes on outdoor etiquette, procedure, and safety. Even the outdoor veteran can benefit from a refresher.

A Note About Safety

Safety is an important concern in all outdoor activities. No guidebook can alert you to every hazard or anticipate the limitations of every reader. Therefore, the descriptions of roads, trails, routes, and natural features in this book are not representations that a particular place or excursion will be safe for your party. When you follow any of the routes described in this book, you assume responsibility for your own safety. Under normal conditions, such excursions require the usual attention to traffic, road and trail conditions, weather, terrain, the capabilities of your party, and other factors. Keeping informed on current conditions and exercising common sense are the keys to a safe, enjoyable outing.

The Mountaineers

1 | TILLAMOOK HEAD NATIONAL RECREATION TRAIL

Distance: 6 miles one way
Elevation change: 1,200 feet
Difficulty: Easy to moderate
Season: Year round
Map: Ecola State Park
For information: State Parks, North Coast Area

This national recreation trail (NRT) follows a historic Indian route across the headland. In 1806, an Indian youth guided William Clark and twelve others from the Lewis and Clark Expedition along this route—the first white men on record to visit Tillamook Head.

Clark named Ecola (Whale) Creek for a nearby beached whale—the quest of this particular journey. Blubber and oil were needed for the expedition's return east.

Today, this trail is part of the greater Oregon Coast trail system. It travels a mostly forested inland route and offers views of Seaside, Cape Disappointment in Washington State, the mouth of the Columbia River, and the offshore 1880s-built Tillamook Lighthouse—a high seas- and weather-wrought rocky outpost, now abandoned to time and the will of the sea.

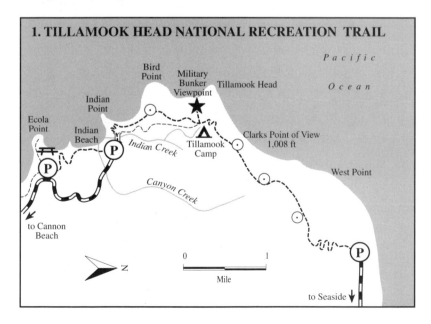

1. TILLAMOOK HEAD NATIONAL RECREATION TRAIL

Coastal forest

The northern trail terminus is found at the south end of Seaside. From South Holladay (US 101), turn west onto Avenue U, crossing the Necanicum River. At the northwest end of a golf course, turn south (left) onto Edgewood, which turns into Sunset Boulevard. Continue south to the end of Sunset for the marked trailhead.

Ecola State Park holds the southern terminus. At the north end of Cannon Beach, turn west off US 101, following the signs for the state park. Locate trailheads at Indian Beach parking or at Ecola Point parking (the southernmost area), adding 1.3 miles to the hike. The trail leaves from the north end of each parking area.

From the trailhead off Sunset in Seaside, the route journeys south through the Elmer Feldenheimer Forest Preserve before entering Ecola State Park. The gradually climbing trail tours a rich forest of western hemlock and Sitka spruce with an understory of mixed ferns, salal, and *Maianthernum* along with salmonberry, thimbleberry, and huckleberry.

Between 0.6 and 1.2 miles, switchbacks advance the trail. Marshy areas dot the route even in early summer. The climb eases where the trail passes beneath an alder canopy. In an area long ago logged, salmonberry bushes hug the path.

By 2 miles, the trail settles into an easy rolling course, passing through a forest of midsized hemlock with a few old-growth Sitka spruce. The trail then travels a corridor with alder and clearcuts on one side and ocean cliffs and limited vistas on the other.

At the 2.4-mile mark, the trail affords an open ocean vista of the headland and Tillamook Rock and Lighthouse; tree-filtered views follow. Less than a mile farther is the 60-foot detour to Clarks Point of View—the standout vista of the trek. It presents a long-distance view to the north. Beyond the vista, choked forest and salmonberry thickets frame the trail's descent.

The trail next arrives at Tillamook Camp, an open-area hiker camp with covered tables and a pit toilet, at 4.4 miles. A detour west from the camp leads to a World War II gun-encampment bunker that requires a flashlight for inside exploration. West of the bunker is a coastal vista with Tillamook

Rock and Lighthouse, a black sandy beach far below, and the offshore rocks where seabirds nest.

Forgoing the detour, the NRT continues its descent from Tillamook Camp, passing through forest, dense coastal thicket, a fern meadow marked by large alders, and a Sitka spruce forest close to the ocean cliffs.

Approaching Indian Creek, the trail offers a view of Indian Beach, an inviting strand cupping a large cove. Offshore rocks punctuate the sea off Ecola Point to the south; wind-whipped trees top the point. The headland trail then crosses Indian Creek and descends to Indian Beach parking. A side trip to the beach finds shell mounds, evidence of the early Indian occupancy of this area.

An alternative descent from Tillamook Camp is to follow the service jeep track through forest to the Indian Beach parking lot. It remains inland from the coastal cliffs and offers a fast walk downhill if daylight is waning.

From Indian Beach parking, hikers may continue south along the Oregon Coast Trail (Ecola Trail) to Ecola Point and to Crescent Beach still farther south.

2 | BAYOCEAN PENINSULA HIKE

Distance: 7.4-mile loop
Elevation change: None
Difficulty: Easy to moderate
Season: Year round
Map: None
For information: Tillamook County Parks

Bayocean Peninsula parts the Pacific Ocean from Tillamook Bay, a national estuary project. The peninsula was the site of a bustling beach community of the early 1900s until the ocean reclaimed the town about midcentury. A few clues still remain to the human presence, but mostly the legacy is erased and natural offerings reign supreme.

The spit is wild enough to have played host to a rare migrant. In 1997, a snowy owl escaping a harsh Arctic winter and a shortage of food took refuge here. Birding is always popular, though, with Tillamook Bay, the ocean beach, the surf, and Bayocean Peninsula's Cape Meares Lake all located here. The inland trees, dense shrubs, and seasonal wetlands create habitat and cover. Binoculars and bird identification guidebooks earn their weight on this beach-to-bay tour.

The spit is open to hiking and horseback riding. Tides and seasons vary impressions and sightings.

To access the spit, from US 101 in Tillamook, turn west on 3rd Street/

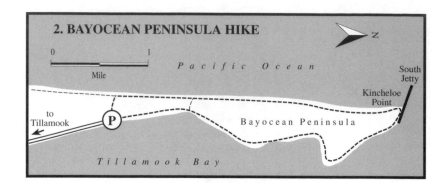

Netarts Highway for Three Capes, go 1.8 miles, and turn north on Bayocean
Road. Continue on Bayocean Road for 5 miles, skirting the bay to reach
the one-way loop road out to Bayocean Peninsula on the right. Follow the
lower peninsula road north (the dike holds the exit), to reach the gate and
parking area in 0.9 mile. A chemical toilet is the lone amenity at the gravel
parking area; there is no overnight parking.

Begin by rounding the gate and hiking the initial open aisle west through
the scotchbroom, shore pine, and Sitka spruce to the beach. Although
the hike can be reversed ending via the beach, the search for an open, dry
passage back through the inland tangle to return to the parking lot is
complicated by false paths, seasonal wetlands, and no beach landmarks
to signal the return.

After following the sandy track west through vegetation and over a rolling dune plain, descend a seaward dune to the beach at 0.4 mile. There,
turn north for a coastal stroll to the tip of the spit and South Jetty.

The spit rolls out a pleasant family beach backed by grass-capped dunes
along with a taller hill cloaked in conifer at 2 miles. The width of beach
varies drastically with the tide. The upper beach has looser sands strewn
with drift logs and tide-carried debris; the lower beach is compressed for
easier walking. Gulls, shorebirds, cormorants, and scoters are common
companions and sightings, with bald eagles or peregrine falcons highlight-
ing a tour.

Views north are of South Jetty, while looks south include Cape Meares
and Three Arch Rocks. At 3.5 miles, the rocky tongue of South Jetty juts
into the sea and captures a broad fan of clean sand, showing few footprints
and ideal for sunning. Across the inlet water is the mirror extension of the
earlier-built North Jetty.

The hike now turns inland (east) along the jetty channel, coming upon
an old roadway or fire lane in 0.1 mile, which conducts the remaining tour.
The lane crosses a rolling dunegrass plain dotted by small conifer and
scotchbroom. Seals or the sleek-headed sea lions sometimes pass through
the channel.

Tillamook Bay

After 4.3 miles, the trail drifts from the channel to pass a pair of pit toilets (a convenient wayside stop) and then a monument rock indicating "South Jetty–Tillamook Bay and Bar" before swinging south along the open bay. In another 0.1 mile, keep to fire lane trail, bypassing a spur to the right to a single picnic table.

Tillamook Bay is a large, circular, scalloped open water. Herons, loons, grebes, kingfishers, geese, and mergansers along with bald eagles, hawks, and ospreys add to sightings. An abrupt bank, a ring of rock and drift logs, and a muddy beach at low tides separate the trail from the bay. For a lengthy spell, conifer and alder screen bay views and partially shade the way.

A few paths, both true and false, branch west toward the beach through the tight shore pine–shrub setting. Towhees scratch in the ground cover as other woodland birds decorate branches. At 6.6 miles, round a second gate and continue south on the fire lane to return to the trailhead parking at 7.4 miles. Open bay viewing concludes the tour, with the Coast Range cutting a ragged eastern skyline.

3 | NETARTS BAY SPIT HIKE

Distance: 10 miles round trip
Elevation change: None
Difficulty: Easy
Season: Year round
Map: None
For information: Cape Lookout State Park

This hike explores the uninterrupted sandy beach of 5-mile-long Netarts Spit, journeying from the base of the 400-foot Cape Lookout headland north to the tip of the spit. An isolated harbor seal haul-out rests on the northern extent of the bay shore; keep a wary distance and avoid disturbing the animals. Oceanscapes and coastal dunes frame travel, with the bay shore just a short but leg-working trek across the dunes. A forested headland and a cedar swamp expand the discovery at this popular state park.

From US 101 in Tillamook, turn west on 3rd Street/Netarts Highway and follow the signs for Three Capes Scenic Loop and Cape Lookout to reach the park 12 miles southwest of town. Locate the beach access at the day-use picnic area at the south end of the park; day-use fees are charged.

At the base of the headland some rocks and tidal discovery await. This hike journeys north along the broad beach, passing below the developed park with its line of wind-shaped Sitka spruce. Cape Meares and Three Arch Rocks National Wildlife Refuge are visible throughout the hike.

Northward, vegetated dunes with eroded faces and a protective rock base edge the beach for the first 1.25 miles. Afterward, the rock corridor dies, leaving a drift-log debris below a string of more natural dunes. By this point, hikers typically have left behind the beach-going crowd and can relish in wilderness strolling.

The beach serves up a smooth, sandy strand with deposited shell fragments recording the last tideline. Shorebirds gather and disperse, feeding in the just-washed sands of the retreating tide and staying ahead of approaching hikers. Across the dunes, Netarts Estuary hosts some 154 bird species.

Digressions to the tops of the seaward dunes add overlooks of the bay, vegetated spit, and coastal mountains and hold chance sightings of wildlife. By 2.5 miles, the dunes seclude areas of Sitka spruce and shore pine, and by 3.25 miles the abutting dunes become low and rolling. Seasonal ponds trapped by the sands create habitat for ducks and other waterfowl.

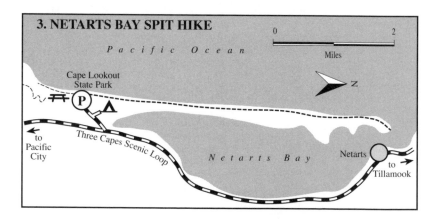

3. NETARTS BAY SPIT HIKE

Pacific Ocean

0 _____ 2

Miles

Cape Lookout
State Park

P

N

to
Pacific
City

Three Capes Scenic Loop

Netarts Bay

Netarts

to
Tillamook

On approach to the mouth of Netarts Bay and the end of the spit, travel quietly because harbor seals frequently claim the bay shore for sunning. They may number 40 or 50 strong and are exceedingly wary of foot travelers. To admire the beasts, carry binoculars and keep a respectable distance—one that does not alarm the seals or alter their behavior.

Return as you came, with Cape Lookout now your guiding landmark.

4 | SOUTH BEACH HIKE

Distance: 9 miles one way
Elevation change: None
Difficulty: Easy to moderate
Season: Year round
Map: None
For information: State Parks, South Central Coast Area

This central Oregon Coast trek offers ample opportunity for the solitary appreciation of surf and sand. The hike travels between Yaquina Bay's South Jetty and Seal Rock, interrupted by Beaver Creek near Ona Beach.

The 0.5-mile long, 1880s-built South Jetty features views of the Yaquina Bay Bridge, the fishing boats exiting the bay, and the year-round channel residents: gulls, grebes, sea lions, and seals. Near the hike's start, the Oregon State University Marine Science Center invites a detour with its displays and information on marine life, coastal geology, tides, and estuaries.

The cliffs of Seal Rock Head put an imposing "stop sign" on the journey. Here, too, a ledge of partially submerged rocks parallels the coastline; the highest rises 20 feet above the water. In the late 1800s, these rocks attracted great numbers of seals and sea lions, hence the site's name.

Multiple access points just off US 101 serve the hiker. At Newport, from the south end of the Yaquina Bay Bridge, take the turn marked for the Hatfield Marine Center–South Jetty and follow 26th Street west to the Jetty Road or park at Bridgehead Day Use, and walk to the jetty. South Beach, Lost Creek, and Ona Beach State Parks likewise offer easy access to this beach route.

Beginning a north-to-south tour, hikers find sands from the dunes have drifted against and over the top of South Jetty. Sandpipers and gulls are commonly viewed, with wintering loons less so.

At 1 mile, a broad break in the foredune signals the arrival at South Beach State Park. The passage provides access to a comfort station, picnic area, and day-use parking area.

The trek crosses four main creeks en route to Lost Creek State Park; most are easily negotiated via rock hops or easy wades as they fan out to

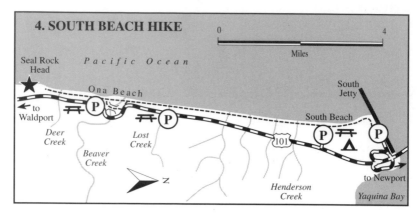

4. SOUTH BEACH HIKE

0 ————————————— 4
Miles

Seal Rock Head
Pacific Ocean
Ona Beach
← to Waldport
Deer Creek
Beaver Creek
Lost Creek
101
N
Henderson Creek
South Jetty
South Beach
to Newport
Yaquina Bay

the ocean. Henderson Creek, at 1.5 miles, marks the transition between the dunes and the 20- to 30-foot-high bluffs.

At 2.6 miles, a dark, eroding sandstone cliff with embedded fossils fronts the sandy avenue. Where the route rounds a small point, especially high tides may turn back hikers or suggest a wading. Over-the-shoulder views find Yaquina Lighthouse.

At 3.5 and again at 5 miles, patches of beach gravel can stall agate collectors. From the second gravel patch, the fence to Lost Creek State Park is visible atop the bluff ahead; Seal Rock Head rises to the south.

At 5.25 miles, a 0.1-mile path ascends a coastal-scrub corridor to the Lost Creek picnic area. Across the rocky drainage, the beach trek proceeds south traveling the wide strand below an orange-hued sandstone cliff. Wind-sculpted spruce and pine accent the top. Dunes replace the bluffs as the hike arrives at the shore of Beaver Creek (6.75 miles).

The tour's continuation usually requires a detour to US 101 and into Ona Beach State Park for a footbridge crossing of Beaver Creek to pick up the beach trek on the opposite shore. Fordings are possible when creek and tides are low.

By 7.25 miles, occasional rock outcrops punctuate the strand, followed by a chain of bedrock tidepools where some eye-catching round boulders are revealed at lowest tides. At 8 miles, the trail passes a small beach access at the community of Seal Rock. Afterward, the route crosses tiny Deer Creek.

From 8.5 miles to 9 miles, low tides and the parallel, sometimes water-isolated rock ledges create a snug cove leading up to Seal Rock Head with its surf-carved hollows. Beware of the tide when exploring this arm of beach; it is a steep climb up the cliff to safety.

Although an unauthorized footpath does grade to Seal Rock Wayside atop the headland, return to the public access 1 mile north to spare the cliff from further erosion.

Boulders revealed at low tide near Seal Rock

5 | CAPE PERPETUA COAST TRAILS

Distance: 6.7 miles maximum combined distance
Elevation change: 800 feet
Difficulty: Easy to moderate
Season: Year round
Map: Cape Perpetua Scenic Area's Hiking Trails handout
For information: Waldport Ranger District, Cape Perpetua
Interpretive Center

This hike unites six short trails of the Cape Perpetua trail system for a stunning introduction to the area's wild coastline, ancient trees, and prominent headland. The trails—Captain Cook, Cape Cove, Restless Waters, Giant Spruce, St. Perpetua, and Whispering Spruce—permit the tour to be shortened into its components for easier walks. Cape Perpetua summit is a drive-to destination, should you wish to eliminate most of the elevation change.

On March 7, 1778, Cape Perpetua received its name from Captain James Cook in honor of the feast day of St. Perpetua. At the time of Cook's visit, Indians occupied the area, subsisting on shellfish. Shell mounds along the coastal trails record the Native American past.

Start the hike at the Devils Churn View Point Parking, west off US 101,

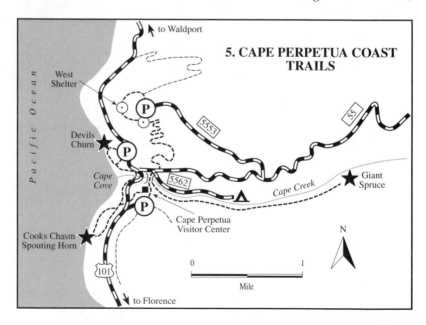

Cape Cove

10.6 miles south of Waldport; 2.3 miles south of Yachats. The paved **Trail of Restless Waters** descends from the seaward side of the lower parking level.

This trail switchbacks downhill beneath wind-shaped spruce to reach the spur to Devils Churn in 0.1 mile. To the right, stairs descend to the water-and-rock attraction; to the left is the main tour. Devils Churn is a long, narrow lava chasm, churning foam and shooting spray.

The journey south along the main trail travels past scalloped coves and ragged tongues of basalt encrusted with barnacles and mussels and containing catchpools of water and life. Before the trail approaches the protected concave of Cape Cove, a stairway descends to the lava shores and the tidepool menagerie. If you choose to explore the pools, there is no collecting and keep an eye on the waves.

Just ahead, where the Trail of Restless Waters loops back to the left, keep right now on the **Cape Cove Trail** to continue the tour. This trail cups the scenic, sandy beach of Cape Cove.

At 0.4 mile, a spur descends to the beach, while the primary tour climbs away for Spouting Horn. This section of the tour is unsurfaced and fairly steep, but it introduces an ancient forest of stout and contorted spruce. Where the trail pinches to US 101, follow the guard rail south to resume the hike past a small interpretive turnout.

At 0.6 mile, a tunnel leads to the visitor center, the noted big spruce, and the headland trails, but keep south to first round-up the coastal offering. Once again, the tour is on paved trail.

In 100 feet is the loop junction for the **Captain Cook Trail;** bear right to enjoy coastal overlooks. The trail bypasses spurs to a shell midden and a tidepool overlook of the protected marine garden. Upon emerging from a salal corridor, the trail ascends to travel above the ragged lava shore.

At 0.9 mile is the overlook landing for Cooks Chasm and Spouting Horn. Here a sea finger penetrates the land, and waters mount in a sea cave beneath the basalt ledge only to be forced up through an aperture in an exciting spout.

As the loop swings back north passing through coastal forest, keep left; spurs to the right lead to parking areas. On the return to the tunnel at 1.2 miles, pass under US 101 and follow the signs for Captain Cook Trail to reach the visitor center. The trail bypasses the site of the Cape Creek Civilian Conservation Corps (CCC) Camp and plant identification plaques.

At the center, films, guided nature walks, and natural history exhibits may invite you inside 9:00 A.M. to 5:00 P.M. daily in summer; 10:00 A.M. to 4:00 P.M. weekends in winter. The next leg of travel heads north from the visitor center entry plaza and descends toward the campground and the spruce and headland trails. Where the path approaches Cape Creek, bear right for an upstream journey on the **Giant Spruce Trail;** the footbridge spanning the creek starts the headland tour, which will be added later.

The quiet beauty of Cape Creek complements the Giant Spruce Trail, which journeys upstream edging the attractive creek-valley campground to pay homage to a record-size Sitka spruce at 2.2 miles. Giant Spruce is 500 years old and boasts a height of 190 feet. A gallery of big trees precedes the reigning spruce, while a lush understory of flora pleases.

From the spruce, backtrack to the junction with the **St. Perpetua Trail** (2.9 miles) for the real workout of this trek—the scaling of the 800-foot promontory of Cape Perpetua. Upon crossing the valley campground and FR 55, the trail is well paced with switchbacks, zigzagging up the grassy south face of the headland.

At the upper headland reaches, be sure to scan the waters for the spouts or glassy footprints of gray whales. The whales linger year-round, but the late November–December and March–April migrations increase chances for a sighting.

Atop the headland (4.3 miles), the **Whispering Spruce Trail** takes the baton. This 0.25 mile loop crowns the headland, linking Parapet and West Shelter. The tour reveals a coastal expanse stretching some 150 miles from Cape Foulweather to Cape Blanco. The stone outposts of Parapet and West Shelter were built by the CCC and are highlights in their own right.

Where the Whispering Spruce Trail loops back to the St. Perpetua Trail, backtrack down to the visitor center and retrace the way to the US 101 underpass. Upon emerging from the tunnel at 6.1 miles, turn north to retrace the Cape Cove Trail to the loop junction of the Trail of Restless Waters. There, bear right for a shady inland return to the trailhead parking lot (6.7 miles).

6 | THREEMILE LAKE–TAHKENITCH DUNE LOOP

Distance: 6.5-mile loop
Elevation change: 400 feet
Difficulty: Easy to moderate
Season: Year round
Map: USFS Oregon Dunes National Recreation Area
For information: Oregon Dunes National Recreation Area

This circuit presents a snapshot of the 32,000-acre national recreation area (NRA): a playground of "living" sands, freshwater lakes, a dune-transition conifer forest, and open beach. The dunes and most of the beach portion of this hike offer exploration that is closed to off-highway vehicles. But, if you do venture south from loop on the beach, you could encounter some vehicle use.

Threemile Lake is a long, isolated freshwater lake pinched at its middle. The trail approaches but does not suggest a lakeshore access, which is left to the hiker's device. Although no formal backcountry camps exist, no-trace camping is allowed near the lake.

The open dunes between the lake and the beach and along the Tahkenitch Dune Trail farther north offer natural fun and discovery. The transition forests house the greatest variety of NRA wildlife—some 145 species. Hummingbird, towhee, woodpecker, varied thrush, and olive-sided flycatcher are commonly spied. The area's older forests shelter deer, coyote, and eight species of salamander, as well as red-legged frogs, a sensitive species.

To reach the trail, on US 101 travel 7.7 miles north from the US 101–OR 38 junction in Reedsport or 12.5 miles south from Florence and turn west for Tahkenitch Trailhead parking. It is south of the Tahkenitch Campground turnoff.

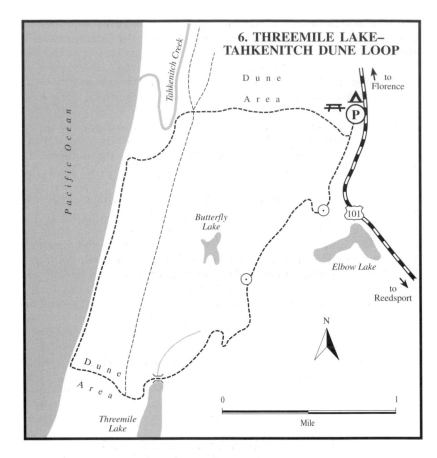

**6. THREEMILE LAKE–
TAHKENITCH DUNE LOOP**

A wide trail of easy grade ascends a corridor of thick coastal vegetation to reach the 0.25-mile trail junction. A clockwise loop begins via the lake trail, which wraps around and over the rolling terrain passing through forests of second-growth western hemlock, young Douglas fir, and classic choked, second-growth Sitka spruce.

At 0.5 mile, a bench overlooks Elbow Lake, a large, bowed coastal lake. Soon after, the trail crosses the slip face of a U-shaped dune with its loose, wind-deposited sands. It then returns to forest. A bench at 1.4 miles offers a forest-gap view of the advancing surf, the wide beach, and Tahkenitch Creek mouth.

At 3 miles, spring-fed rills announce Threemile Lake, and a quarter mile beyond the inlet footbridge, the lake trail ends on the crest of a vegetated dune. From here, overlook the lake, dunes, beach, and ocean.

For the next 0.5 mile, the circuit follows the blue-banded cedar posts west across the open dune. At the deflation plain, hikers may choose to continue west to the beach and hike it north to Tahkenitch Creek or follow the less-traveled deflation-plain trail north through the coastal scrub. For the latter, cedar posts, segments of path, and lingering footprints help guide hikers. This inland route shaves 0.5 mile from the total distance.

Opting instead for the beach route, tag the coastal shore and hike 1.25 miles north. (Beach hikers walking the loop in reverse can look for the large sign marking the inland turn to Threemile Lake.)

At 5 miles, where the dune border flattens before reaching the Tahkenitch Creek mouth, keep a sharp eye for the blue-banded post on the rise to the east; it signals the Tahkenitch Dune Trail and the continuation of the loop. Before heading inland, though, hikers may wish to visit Tahkenitch Creek, a good place to view both shorebirds and songbirds. During the snowy plover nesting restriction, March 15 to September 15, it is probably best to opt for a direct return inland. Heed posted restrictions.

Soon after heading inland, the deflation-plain spur enters from the south in 0.5 mile, and in another 0.2 mile, the hike bypasses a roped-off snowy plover nesting area. Then, in a matter of strides, the Tahkenitch Creek Trail branches left (north), journeying 2 miles to the Tahkenitch Creek Trailhead on US 101 north of the campground. Stay on the dune trail.

The dune trail continues east through the shore pine–scrub to travel the open sand at the south end of a major dune ridge that stretches north. As the trail enters the forest, a bench affords a farewell look at the dunes and beach.

Noise from US 101 then intrudes as the loop comes to a close at the initial trail junction. Return downhill.

7 | SOUTH SLOUGH NATIONAL ESTUARINE RESEARCH RESERVE

Distance: 3.8 miles round trip
Elevation change: 300 feet
Difficulty: Easy to moderate
Season: Year round
Map: Down to the Slough trail brochure
For information: South Slough National Estuarine Research Reserve

A southern extension to Coos Bay, this drowned river mouth is home to the nation's first ever estuarine reserve—South Slough. Established in 1974, it houses 4,700 acres of natural laboratory. The estuary habitat (where fresh and salt water merge) is among the world's most vital and productive, nourishing vast fisheries and wildlife populations.

Much estuary wetland has been filled in, drained, or otherwise claimed. South Slough itself has been used for logging, ranching, and farming. By the 1930s, though, this estuary had begun its return to nature's hand.

Today, the reserve's goals of research, education, stewardship, and low-impact recreation serve the naturalist well. The sanctuary is open year-round. Except holidays, its center is open 8:30 A.M. to 4:30 P.M. weekdays (daily in summer). Films, displays, self- and interpreter-guided walks, and a canoe trail introduce the slough's features. Trail and slough brochures are readily available and the routes marked.

From North Bend–Coos Bay on US 101, go west on Cape Arago Highway toward Charleston. At the east end of Charleston, turn south on Seven Devils Road (a sign indicates this route to the reserve). The visitor center is in 4 miles.

At the interpretive center hilltop, the 10-Minute Nature Trail introduces a recovering coastal forest community and launches the Down to the Slough Trail—a self-guided interpretive route that introduces the slough habitats.

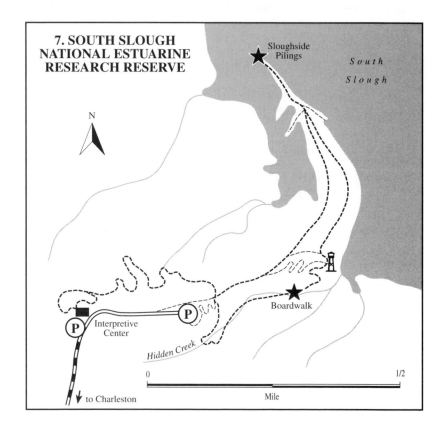

About midway through the nature trail a marked spur descends the canyon hillside for the Sloughside Pilings. It tours a scrub corridor of salal, waxmyrtle, and huckleberry; a choked second-growth forest of hemlock and cedar; and a more open, mixed forest.

At 0.75 mile arrive at a narrow dirt road (the loop junction for the slough tour). Cross over it, and hike 30 strides on a short tie trail to meet the Hidden Creek Trail between interpretive stops B and C. Turn left to continue the descent toward the slough; a detour right picks up the first two interpretive stops within 0.25 mile.

Alternatively, hikers can start the hike at the Hidden Creek Trailhead (take the spur road off the visitor center parking entrance). This saves 0.5 mile of hiking each way, reduces the elevation change, and allows you to follow its interpretive segment in order.

The Hidden Creek Trail descends the upper canyon slope overlooking the drainage of Hidden Creek, which was once harvested but is now thick with growth. Where the trail contours the slope along the alder-lined creek and crisscrosses its water via footbridges, interpretive signs introduce stream habitats. Skunk cabbage, salmonberry, mosses, and fern contribute to the canyon mosaic. Keep right at 1.25 miles for the Skunk Cabbage Walk to Sloughside Pilings.

The elevated boardwalk of the Skunk Cabbage Walk is highly scenic with its network of loops. The cabbage's yellow bloom and pungent scent herald spring, and its leaves can measure up to 4 feet long.

Ahead stretches a second boardwalk. It meanders across a salt-marsh meadow and serves up glimpses of the slough off in the distance. A couple of gentle uphill switchbacks then lead through a mature stand of spruce, cedar, and fir to the salt marsh and slough observation tower at 1.4 miles. This post holds the nicest overlook of the slough mudflats, open water, and rimming forest—a picture that changes with the tide.

At the four-way junction near the tower, the slough tour proceeds forward, while the handicap-accessible Big Cedar Trail heads left, allowing hikers to shorten the tour. Where it comes out at a parking area, bear left to follow the narrow, limited-access road uphill to return to the junction where forks lead to either the interpretive center or the upper reaches of the Hidden Creek Trail.

For the full hike, proceed forward and bear right at the next junction to follow the Tunnel Trail; to the left is a tie to the Timber Trail. The Tunnel Trail wiggles up a hillside to arrive at Slough Overlook (1.8 miles), which extends only a strained look at the slough. A nonflush toilet is found nearby.

From the vista, descend to reach the Timber Trail near the spur to Rhode's Dike. Going right leads to the Sloughside Pilings and the end of the trail at 2.2 miles. The boardwalk of Sloughside Dike delivers an up close look at the slough, which features mudflats, tidal channels, and saltwater marsh. The pilings record the former railroad-logging days and serve as roosts for gulls, herons, and other birds. Animal tracks and otter slides may be spied as opportunities for nature study and relaxation abound.

To return to the center, backtrack to the junction at Rhode's Dike and follow the Timber Trail away from the slough. Trail highlights include a brief leafy tunnel and a patch of sundews—insect-eating plants. Keep right at the junctions to emerge at a handicap-access parking area for the Big Cedar Trail at 3 miles. A peek in the door at this trail (on the left as you arrive) finds a scenic woods passage with rhododendron 20 feet tall.

For the primary tour, though, hike the limited-access road away from the parking area to the slough loop junction in another 0.1 mile. Turn right to ascend the hillside back to the interpretive center plateau; to the left is the tie to Hidden Creek Trail and Trailhead for hikers who started there. Upon meeting the 10-Minute Trail, follow the unwalked leg of its loop to return to the interpretive center at 3.8 miles.

8 | BULLARDS BEACH– FIVEMILE POINT HIKE

Distance: 14.8 miles round trip *(9.6 miles when Cut Creek is high)*
Elevation change: None
Difficulty: Moderate to strenuous
Season: Year round
Map: Unnecessary
For information: Bullards Beach State Park

This hike explores a wonderfully little-tracked beach stretching north from the jetty at Bullards Beach State Park past Cut Creek and Whisky Run to Fivemile Point. Built in 1896, Coquille River Lighthouse launches the tour from its original location, Rackleff Rock, once isolated from the mainland except for a boardwalk, now linked by the jetty. From Memorial Day (the last weekend in May) through September, volunteer interpreters staff the restored lighthouse; all other times, the lighthouse is open daylight hours, with old photographs telling its tale.

The southern beach is open to hikers and horses; the northern hike segment is open to vehicles but receives minimal motorized use. Cut Creek at 4.8 miles signals a convenient turnaround point for shortening the tour and when waters are high may dictate the tour's end.

The southern terminus and start for this hike, Bullards Beach State Park, is west off US 101, 2 miles north of Bandon. At the park, follow the road indicated for the lighthouse, parking, and beach access to begin near Coquille River Lighthouse.

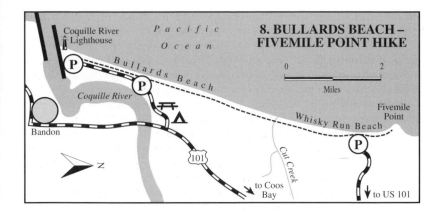

Undeveloped Whisky Run Beach signals the northernmost access. For a shuttle hike, it is reached off Seven Devils Road (turn west off US 101, 1.9 miles north of Bullards Beach and follow the signs to Whisky Run to arrive at beach parking for up to 10 vehicles in 4.3 miles).

The hike starts next to the Coquille River mouth and Coquille River Lighthouse and proceeds north from the jetty. Dunegrass, gorse, and shore pine vegetate the broad dune abutting the beach. Sneaker waves can be troublesome, especially when offshore storms stir up the ocean, and tides and season can determine the amount and character of the beach.

At 0.8 mile, spurs branch to parking areas within the park. At 1.6 miles, bypass the main beach access with a restroom facility beyond the dune. In another 0.3 mile, a spur leads to the horse camp and the Cut Creek Trail, a parallel horse trail through the dunes. Throughout, the 15- to 20-foot dunes isolate the beach from the inland world.

At 2 miles, journey past a drift-log graveyard. By 2.6 miles, the beach opens up. Northern views are of Cape Arago; southern views, the jetty and offshore rocks of Bandon.

Afterward, the tour settles into a mesmerizing walk. Telltale tracks reveal where shorebirds have excavated for food. By 3.8 miles, a few seasonal streams can pierce the dunes.

The change from abutting dune to bluff signals the breach of Cut Creek at 4.8 miles. The creek is generally crossed with an easy wade or log negotiation, but in winter and early spring, it may turn back hikers. Initially a golf course sits atop the bluff.

The bluff continues with a low frontal dune, while the beach extends a broad, flat, hard-packed avenue for comfortable strolling. This segment of beach may have an occasional vehicle or lingering tracks but generally keeps its natural aspect.

Red, buff, or gray sandstone terraces may be exposed in the eroding cliff. Side drainages cut across the strand, fanning out in broad, glassy sheets. Fivemile Point now looms to the north, with Cape Arago and its offshore rocks in the distance.

By 5.3 miles, the frontal dune becomes a disorganized chain. A lone grove of wind-sculpted trees and snags graces the bluff skyline. At 6.6 miles comes the crossing of Whisky Run, generally an easy wading. The cliffs of Fivemile Point are now the focal point of the tour.

Fivemile Point is a two-pronged extension, with the first point at 7 miles and the second 0.4 mile beyond. An attractive concave beach separates the two, but tides may halt hikers at the first extension. Know the tide schedule before rounding the first point and time a safe return.

The gray rock of the point reveals eroding concretions, honeycomb patterns, and a balanced rock atop an isolated pillar. Surf fishermen and agate hunters favor this coastal corner. The return is as you came.

9 | NEW RIVER BEACH– BANDON STATE BEACH HIKE

Distance: 2 up to 32 miles round trip
Elevation change: None
Difficulty: Strenuous
Season: Year round; March 15 to Sept. 15 stay below
    high-tide line to protect nesting snowy plovers (New
    River Spit)
Map: Unnecessary
For information: Coos Bay District BLM

This hike incorporates two fine strips of coastal beach—New River Spit, arguably Oregon's wildest stretch of beach, and Bandon State Natural Area. The whim of ocean, river, and creek determines how the tours link and where hikers may be called to a stop.

The winter of 1999 caused a breach at the New River–Floras Creek confluence, truncating the spit hike north from Floras Lake and making the northern extent of the spit all the more remote. Presently, the northern spit is only accessible by hiking the state beach south and staging a fording at the New River mouth when water levels allow a safe crossing. It remains to be seen whether the breach will eventually heal, restoring the spit to its full 10-mile length.

Created by pioneers to make pastureland and less than 100 years old, New River along with its coastal spit, drained floodplain, and sandy meadow is returning to a viable coastal dune–estuarine ecosystem. An Area of Critical Environmental Concern, New River supports a wildlife diversity that includes both threatened and endangered species: the western

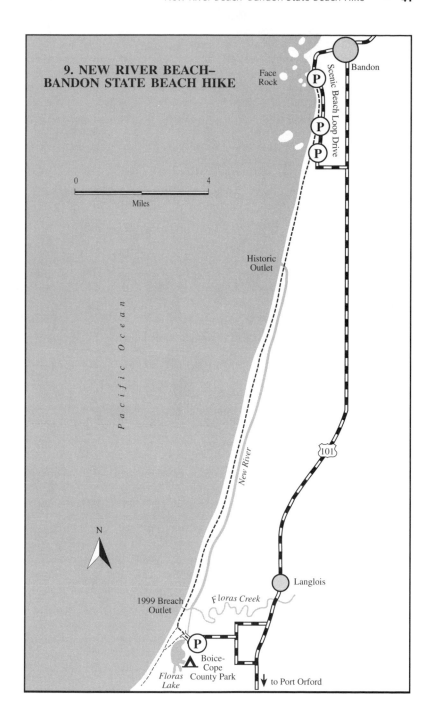

9. NEW RIVER BEACH–
BANDON STATE BEACH HIKE

Face
Rock

Bandon

P

Scenic Beach Loop Drive

P

P

0 — 4

Miles

Historic
Outlet

Pacific Ocean

New River

{101}

N

Langlois

1999 Breach
Outlet

F loras Creek

P

Boice-
Cope
Floras   County Park
Lake

to Port Orford

snowy plover, American and Arctic peregrine falcons, the Aleutian Canada goose, and the bald eagle.

Bandon State Natural Area stretches 6.5 miles north from the New River mouth to Face Rock Viewpoint and offers comfortable strolling on wave-compacted sands. It is the more civilized and accessible of the two beaches, with its southern extent open to vehicles but only lightly traveled. Views bring together a stunning series of near and off-shore rocks.

The state beach accesses lie off the Scenic Beach Loop Drive, which can be reached within Bandon, but requires negotiating a series of residential streets. For direct access to the loop, drive 3.5 miles south on US 101 from the Old Town Bandon gateway. Then, go west on Scenic Beach Loop Drive, reaching the southernmost beach access in 1 mile, Face Rock Viewpoint in 3.3 miles. Additional state park accesses lie in between for varying the length of the tour.

To reach the New River access at Boice-Cope Curry County Park, from downtown Bandon, go 14.2 miles south on US 101 and turn west on Floras Lake Loop Road. After 1.1 miles, turn right on Curry County 136 and follow the signs for a boat ramp. In another 1.3 miles, bear left, go 0.1 mile,

Coquille River Lighthouse

and turn right on Boice-Cope Road. Park near the boat ramp at road's end in 0.3 mile; a county day-use fee is charged.

To tour New River Spit from Floras Lake, cross the footbridge over the Floras Lake outlet at Boice-Cope Curry County Park and follow the trail stakes that point out sanctioned routes across the coastal plain and over the dunes to the beach. Map boards identify the beach-access options, which measure between 0.5 and 1 mile. Fencing also helps keep hikers in the proper area. Because New River Spit hosts nesting snowy plovers, heed the access restrictions posted at the bridge and elsewhere in this sensitive area.

Floras Lake is a large, blue coastal water body that spans between the county park campground and the coastal dune and beach. The lake attracts migrating birds and appeals to windsurfers. Wintering swans may grace the pool, while marsh hawks (northern harriers) may patrol the grassy rim.

Although the primary beach hike normally journeys 10 miles north to the river mouth, the present northbound tour is limited to 0.5 mile to the site of the 1999 river breach. The beach shows a marked slope and dark, loose sand; to the east rises a 10-foot-high dune ridge. From March 15 to September 15, keep to the wet sand and leave pets at home.

At the breach, view an impressive cut with deep-carved eroding banks. If the breach has healed or the water is low enough to allow a safe crossing, hikers may continue north. If not, backtrack to Floras Lake.

To the lake's south stretches another length of beach that is walkable only at low tides. However, be alert to its danger: it is bordered by scenic eroded cliffs with deep-cut coves, chasms, and canyons where hikers can become trapped, and the cliffs allow no escape from the incoming water. Sneaker waves lap at the feet, and again the beach is sloped. Views are of the sculpted rock, Blacklock Point, and Cape Blanco Lighthouse. Do not dally if you decide to go, and again, know and heed the tides.

To stroll the Bandon State Natural Area beach and perhaps cross New River to the northern spit, select one of the signed beach accesses off the Scenic Beach Loop Drive and hike south. From the southernmost access stretches the shortest option, a 4-mile hike to the New River mouth. The creek crossing near the start signals the demarcation for beach driving: vehicles are allowed south but not north of the creek and not on the dunes.

Despite possible tire tracks, the tour is nicely isolated and tranquil. Dunes back the beach, flattening after a couple of miles. Tides can swell the creek at 3 miles, necessitating a wading or an upstream crossing. Drift-log corrals or shelters sometimes mark the foot of the dunes. Fires are not allowed.

At 4 miles is the river mouth. When the water is low, consider adding a tour of the northern spit to the outing. Looks north find Bandon Rocks, south Blacklock Point, and Cape Blanco. The spit's loose sand stretches south 9.5 miles to the site of the breach. With nature's rewrite, the isolated tip offers a wonderful deserted isle. The return is as you came.

10 | OREGON COAST TRAIL, SAMUEL BOARDMAN SEGMENT

Distance: 10.3 miles one way
Elevation change: 400 feet
Difficulty: Strenuous
Season: Year round
Map: USGS Brookings, Carpenterville; USFS Siskiyou
For information: State Parks, South Coast Area

This snatch of the extensive Oregon Coast Trail provides an encapsulated look at the offerings of this premier trail system: rugged headlands, secluded beaches, shifting sands, ocean and shoreline vistas, and coastal wildlife sightings. The trail tours meadow, thicket, alder grove, and Sitka spruce forest, as it dips deep into canyons and marches sharply up the headlands. Brief US 101 interruptions punctuate the route.

Gulls, storm petrels, murres, auklets, and puffins nest on the offshore rocks, part of Oregon Islands National Wildlife Refuge. Natural bridges, arches, and blow holes are among the scenic rock features.

Multiple day-use picnic and parking areas west off US 101 access this trail. Points of entry begin 4 miles north of Brookings and 15 miles south of Gold Beach, providing hikers with numerous short or hopscotch-shuttle hike options.

Cape Ferrelo, at the southern end of the trail, invites a headland detour before the journey north. Hiking south 0.5 mile across the grassy summit meadow finds a vista overlooking Lone Ranch Beach and spanning the coastline north to south from Natural Bridges to Goat Island—an oceanscape of coves, beach parcels, headlands, offshore rocks, and ceaseless blue water.

The main tour of the Oregon Coast Trail heads north, passing through coastal meadow and scrub and touring forest to find tree-rimmed House Rock Viewpoint in 1.3 miles; finer views await. At 1.9 miles, a rocky ridge affords a northward-looking view of the ragged shore, Whalehead Cove, and distant Humbug Mountain.

Soon, the trail bears west leaving a section of old abandoned road to switchback down a grassy headland to arrive at the beach at 2.5 miles. Posts mark the trail. The route then continues north on a boulder-strewn beach isolated by a vegetated, spruce-topped cliff. Past the Bowman Creek crossing, the cliff reveals a narrow cave hollow.

By wading Whalehead Creek, hikers will find the Whalehead Beach Picnic Area at 3.3 miles. Alternatively, they may follow a bypass trail that travels upstream along the creek to the picnic area, but when it is most needed, the path is mired with mud and standing water.

The often-photographed Whalehead Island occupies center stage offshore.

Whalehead Cove

This rocky islet is so dubbed because a hollow on its seaward side and a hole in its top create the effect of a whale spout when the surf is just right.

The trail resumes near the picnic area restroom, ascending east through a magical Sitka spruce forest and meadow to head north across the Whalehead Beach entrance road at US 101. It then continues its headland climb through a shady Sitka spruce forest.

At 3.5 miles, a side trail leads onto an open headland arm, a quiet retreat with a grand north–south coastal vista. Ahead, the main trail unfolds views of rocky channels, islands, and surging water.

At 4.5 miles, the trail tags the edge of Indian Sands, a bluff outcrop of both compacted and shifting sands, which drops to the ocean in steep cliffs. Where the forest meets the sands, trail posts guide hikers northward. Thomas Creek Bridge commands the view.

Next, the trail circles a loose-sand bowl behind a tree island and overlooks a fingery cove to the north before descending into the dramatic, squeezed canyon. The stark, eroding cliff of the opposite wall contrasts with the scrub-vegetated wall traced by the trail. A steep ascent to US 101 and a short trail segment follow, before the Thomas Creek Bridge crossing.

En route to China Creek Beach, the trail drops into a dark, choked forest of Sitka spruce. At 6.7 miles, it arrives atop the grassy bench overlooking the wilderness strand.

China Creek Beach then takes the trail north. Deep drainage furrows mark the vegetated slope, and the offshore rocks create a natural sculpture garden. Low tides allow a rounding of the cliff (7.1 miles) to Spruce Creek Cove; a zigzag trail then connects Spruce Cove to US 101.

Still more US 101 trail interruptions occur near Horse Prairie Creek Canyon. A longer coastal forest tour precedes the overlook of Natural Bridges Cove (8.3 miles), where natural gateways in a rock-arm extension of the cliff admit the sea to the cove in wondrous display.

Farther north, the trail extends multiple looks at Thunder Rock, a similar rock outcrop with arch openings. After a forest and thicket tour comes Miner Creek Cove (9.2 miles), with its small beach looking out at a magnificent collection of bare and tree-capped offshore rocks.

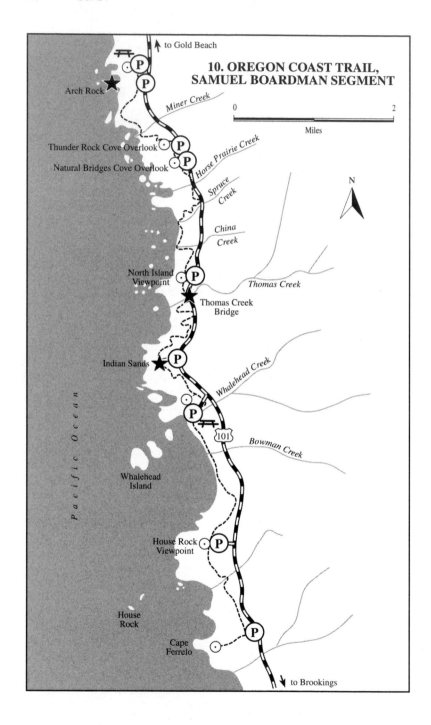

to Gold Beach

10. OREGON COAST TRAIL, SAMUEL BOARDMAN SEGMENT

Arch Rock

Miner Creek

0   2
Miles

N

Thunder Rock Cove Overlook

Natural Bridges Cove Overlook

Horse Prairie Creek

Spruce Creek

China Creek

North Island Viewpoint

Thomas Creek

Thomas Creek Bridge

Indian Sands

Whalehead Creek

Whalehead Island

101

Bowman Creek

Pacific Ocean

House Rock Viewpoint

House Rock

Cape Ferrelo

to Brookings

More coastal views cap the tour as it draws to a close at Arch Rock Picnic Area (10.3 miles).

11 | SADDLE MOUNTAIN TRAIL

Distance: 5.9 miles round trip *(with spur)*
Elevation change: 1,600 feet
Difficulty: Strenuous
Season: Spring through fall
Map: USGS Saddle Mountain
For information: State Parks, North Coast Area

Bald-topped Saddle Mountain (elevation 3,283 feet) affords one of the best vistas in Oregon's North Coast Range, spanning Oregon and Washington and featuring the Northwest volcano chain. Mounts Rainier, Saint Helens, Adams, and Hood punctuate the east. To the west, a clear day holds views of the Pacific Ocean, Astoria, and the Columbia River mouth.

Although the vista is the primary draw, Saddle Mountain is also a noted botanical area, boasting some 300 flora species, including the rare crucifer, Saddle Mountain saxifrage, and Saddle Mountain bittercress, which grow only in this limited province. More common species include Oregon iris, cinquefoil, nodding onion, and yellow fawn lily. Saddle Mountain is one of three "islands" in the North Coast Range secluding rare alpine flora; the other two are nearby Onion Peak and Sugarloaf Mountain.

From the US 101–US 26 junction, south of Seaside, travel 10 miles east on US 26. Turn north at the sign for Saddle Mountain State Park and proceed 6.9 miles on winding, paved road to the park at road's end.

Saddle Mountain

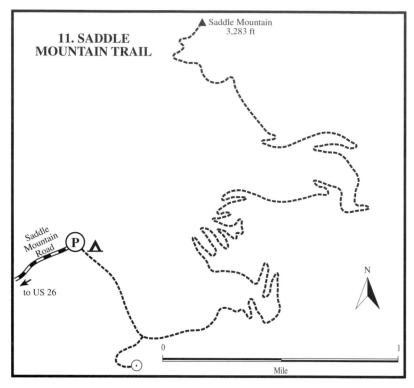

On summer weekends, spillover parking lines the road entering the park—a testament to the trail's popularity. Midweek and off-season visits promise a more peaceful encounter with the mountain.

Departing from the east side of the parking area, the trail begins as a wide, paved swath eventually becoming a foot trail. In 0.2 mile, a side trail branches to the right for a nice 0.25-mile side jaunt to an outcrop affording the first vista of the journey: a good look at Saddle Mountain, its pronounced volcanic dikes (raised rock veins), and surrounding Coast Range.

Past the 0.2-mile junction, the main trail remains mostly shaded. Second-growth fir and alder stands reign above a varied undergrowth of cow parsnip, maidenhair fern, false Solomon's seal, vine maple, and thimbleberry.

At 1.1 miles, the trail pulls into the open. Shade now is prized; carry plenty of water. The trail becomes gravelly and riddled by shortcuts. Keep to the trail to protect vegetation and avoid adding to the problem of erosion.

The trail tops the ridge at 2 miles, offering views to the north. Its open, thin-soiled meadow parades prairie smoke, Siskiyou fritillary, Indian paintbrush, and monkey flowers. The steep south-facing slope of Saddle Mountain houses a rare rock-garden community.

Unstable, crumbly rock slows and confounds the final 0.7-mile charge to the summit. Although the trail has undergone repairs to stabilize its bed, this stretch is not for the sneaker wearer; it is easy to lose your footing or twist an ankle.

The summit view rewards the effort. The grandeur of the volcano and ocean vistas is mediated only by broad sweeps of clearcut and the mostly denuded Humbug Mountain (save for the part that belongs to Saddle Mountain State Park).

Return as you came, allowing adequate time for the first precarious leg of the descent. Do not stray from the path for better footing; the summit plant life is fragile and must be protected.

12 | HORSE CREEK TRAIL

Distance: 5.5 miles one way *(when Drift Creek can be forded)*
Elevation change: 1,200 feet
Difficulty: Moderate
Season: Year round
Map: USFS Drift Creek Wilderness
For information: Waldport Ranger District

This 5,800-acre wilderness represents one of the last bastions of untouched, ancient rain forest in the Coast Range. It seduces with old-growth tranquillity and the rushing beauty of Drift Creek. The rich multistory forest is an orchestration of texture, shape, color, and lighting. Douglas fir and western hemlock dominate the forest, red alder and bigleaf maple reign creekside, and everywhere cascading greenery dresses the forest floor.

Forest management practices spared this area by first designating it as a primitive area (not for development), then as a roadless area, and finally in 1984, as a wilderness area. The trail bears the unlikely name "Horse Creek Trail," because it is a fragment of the old forest-management trail of that name.

The normally driving waters of Drift Creek isolate the north and south fragments of the Horse Creek Trail; only during late summer does Drift Creek allow their linkage. During low waters, an alternative hike also presents itself, joining Horse Creek Trail (North) and the Harris Ranch Trail. Each of these three interlocking trail fragments offers a slightly different window to the wilderness.

To reach the northern trailhead, from US 101 near Ona Beach State Park (8 miles south of Newport), turn east onto North Beaver Creek Road (County 602). After going 3.8 miles, turn right onto North Elkhorn Road, FR 51; look for the turn just past the Beaver Creek crossing.

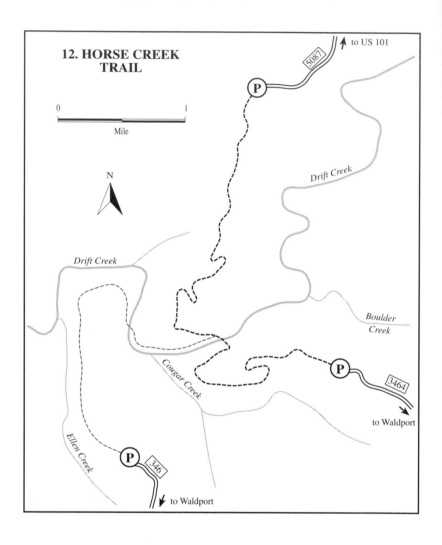

Continue east on FR 51 for 5.8 miles to where the road comes to a T. There, turn left onto FR 50. At the trail sign in 1.3 miles, turn right onto FR 5087 (an improved-surface road easily passable for conventional vehicles). The marked trailhead is in 3.4 miles.

Entering from the south, from the US 101–OR 34 junction in Waldport, head east on OR 34 for 7.3 miles. After the Alsea River crossing, turn left onto Risley Creek Road, FR 3446, and continue another 7.3 miles. At the trail sign, turn left onto FR 3464. The trailhead is at the end of the road in 1.6 miles.

When hiking north to south, the trail begins with an even grade, working its way along a ridge; the thick forest denies vistas. Elk usage of the trail shows in the breaking away of the soft shoulders and the occasional ruptures in the trail bed itself.

By 1.2 miles, the trail has abandoned its even course for a zigzagging one down the south flank of the hillside. Well-designed switchbacks slow descent, without introducing tiresome, unnecessary distance.

At 2.5 miles, a steep, unmaintained side trail branches right to meet the north end of the Harris Ranch Trail at Drift Creek. Keeping to the main trail finds the next junction at 3 miles. Harris Ranch Trail (North) is to the right. Going left leads to a creekside camp, the end of Horse Creek Trail (North), and the beckoning (or forbidding, depending on water level) trail sign for the hike's continuation on the opposite shore.

After a Drift Creek fording on the Horse Creek Trail, hikers come upon a well-trampled angler path that leads upstream 0.1 mile to a large tree-sheltered campsite. The main path of Horse Creek Trail (South) quickly pulls away from Drift Creek for a comfortable ascent. Small drainages mark the bottom half of the climb. Elsewhere, the tall, straight Douglas firs contrast the understory chaos of greenery. At 5.5 miles, the hike ends at the trailhead on FR 3464.

For the alternative Horse Creek Trail (North)–Harris Ranch Trail hike, turn right at the 3-mile junction to walk the northern segment of the Harris Ranch Trail. For 0.7 mile, it follows a bench dressed in alder, bigleaf maple, and salmonberry to meet the bank of Drift Creek.

When Drift Creek permits fording, the southern portion of the Harris Ranch Trail continues on the opposite shore, touring meadow and climbing through wilderness forest to reach the trailhead on FR 346 for a 6.2-mile shuttle. (From OR 34, east of Waldport, turn north onto Risley Creek Road and travel 4.1 miles. At the sign for Harris Ranch Trail, turn left. Go 0.7 mile on FR 346 and bear left for the trailhead.)

13 | ROGUE RIVER TRAIL

Distance: 47 miles one way
Elevation change: 700 feet
Difficulty: Strenuous
Season: Year round
Map: USFS Kalmiopsis/Wild Rogue Wilderness
For information: Gold Beach Ranger District, Medford
District BLM

This rolling, 47-mile (42 miles per U.S. Forest Service) national recreation trail journeys alongside 40 miles of the Rogue Wild and Scenic River, a captivating waterway. It travels a former mining trail and passes Zane Grey's Cabin and two National Historic Places: the Rogue River Ranch and Whisky Creek Cabin. The trail boasts exciting river views of narrow gorges, white water riffles, and yawning passages; crosses scenic creeks with beckoning swimming holes; and offers great wildlife viewing with deer, otter, osprey, blue-tailed skink, salmon, ring-tailed cat, mink, and bear (so exercise proper care with food).

Along the north canyon wall, the trail alternately tours high above and right next door to the river, offering various impressions of the Rogue. It traverses steep forested flank, leafy woodland slopes, and river bench and bar.

The trail is accommodating to backpackers. Shuttle services for rafters also serve hikers, allowing a one-way tour of the trail without a second vehicle. The river corridor holds plentiful campsites and rest stops, and hikers even have the luxury of buying iced drinks at Paradise Bar Lodge. The BLM sells a helpful Rogue River Trail booklet, which relates much of the river area history.

Grave Creek is the gateway. From I-5 north of Grants Pass, take the Merlin exit (Exit 61), head northwest into Merlin, and turn left onto Merlin–Galice Road. At 22 miles, cross the Grave Creek bridge, and turn left for the boat ramp and trailhead. Overnighters must park along the road.

The trail begins rounding the north canyon wall well above the river; mixed conifer and deciduous trees shade its path. At 2.1 miles, a side trail descends to Rainie Falls.

From Whisky Creek bridge, a 100-yard side trail leads to Whisky Creek Cabin with its abandoned apple orchard and the rusting remnants from its heyday. The river trail continues its rolling, slope-wrapping course passing through mixed forest for the next 20 miles; beware of poison oak.

At 8.7 miles, the trail overlooks Slim Pickens, a river narrow. At 17.5 miles, Kelsey Creek beckons with its deep swimming holes. At the trail split beyond the creek, take the branch leading to the river.

Preceding Ditch Creek, the trail winds through an ash- and oak-studded grassland right above the river. Because the next trail stretch is often hot and dry, be sure to top the water jugs. By 20 miles, the steep, unstable canyon slope forces the trail uphill around slide areas.

At Quail Creek, a sandy bar on the river suggests a stop to cool the feet. After crossing the creek, follow the trail branch heading toward the river. At 23.7 miles, the trail enters Quail Creek fire zone, where, in 1970, fire jumped the river, burning 2,800 acres.

At the Rogue River Ranch, the path bearing left leads to campsites and Mule Creek; the uphill fork to the right leads to the publicly owned ranch and the trail's continuation. Top the water jugs at Mule Creek.

Past the ranch, at 27.7 miles, the trail meets and bears left on an open road for 2 miles; a 2.5-mile-long basalt bench next carries the tour. Here, a churning Coffeepot—the narrowest passage on the Rogue—catches

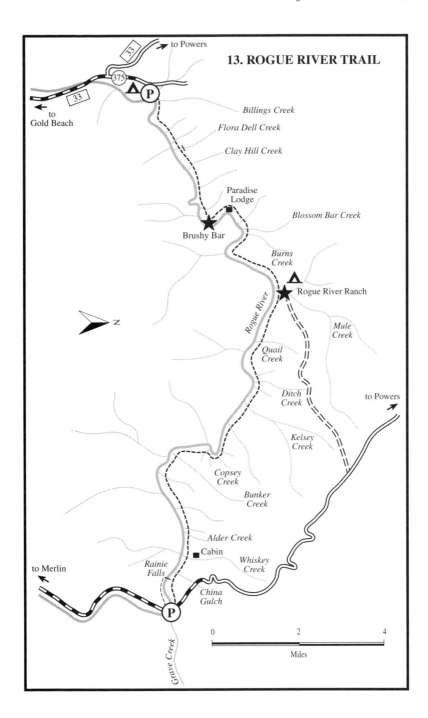

to Powers

33

375

33

to
Gold Beach

13. ROGUE RIVER TRAIL

Billings Creek

Flora Dell Creek

Clay Hill Creek

Paradise
Lodge

Blossom Bar Creek

Brushy Bar

*Burns
Creek*

Rogue River Ranch

*Mule
Creek*

Rogue River

*Quail
Creek*

*Ditch
Creek*

to Powers

*Kelsey
Creek*

*Copsey
Creek*

*Bunker
Creek*

Alder Creek

Cabin

*Whiskey
Creek*

to Merlin

*Rainie
Falls*

*China
Gulch*

Grave Creek

N

0   2   4

Miles

hikers' attention. Although the elevated bench holds grand vistas, the heat-radiating rock can be unpleasant. At 32.5 miles, alder-lined Blossom Bar Creek with its deep, shimmery pools proves a siren.

From Paradise Bar Lodge (33.8 miles), the trail heads uphill, passes through a gate, and travels the length of a grassy runway to resume its downstream trek well above the river. Later, it follows a rocky cliff nearer the river to reach the woodland flat of Brushy Bar, which has campsites but an unreliable creek.

From the bar, the trail climbs past the marker for Captain Tichenor's defeat and skirts gravel mounds from the placer mining era. Near Clay Hill Creek private residences dot the route. After an open trail segment on an oak-grassland hillside, Flora Dell Creek at 42.5 miles beckons with its 30-foot falls and shady setting.

The summer sun takes a harsher toll on the creeks along the final leg of the tour. While there's water for topping the jugs, the tempting pools are gone, and river access is limited. The trail concludes touring the open field of Big Bend Pasture to reach Foster Bar Trailhead.

Because the shuttle services generally park all vehicles at the Foster Bar boat launch, from the end of the trail, hike downstream via FR 3700.300 and County 375 and turn left for the launch, reaching the parking area and your vehicle in about 0.3 mile.

14 ILLINOIS RIVER– BALD MOUNTAIN LOOP

Distance: 24 miles round trip
Elevation change: 3,100 feet
Difficulty: Strenuous
Season: Spring through fall
Map: USFS Kalmiopsis/Wild Rogue Wilderness
For information: Galice Ranger District

This hike samples a portion of the Illinois River National Recreation Trail, offering overlooks of and access to the Illinois Wild and Scenic River. The hike's loop visits a beautiful riverside grassy bench (the former Weaver Ranch site) and tags a false summit below Bald Mountain. It also applauds the floral diversity of the Siskiyous, which surpasses that found in any U.S. mountain range other than the Great Smokies of Virginia. Along the way, the trail crosses York Creek Botanical Area, which holds some rare *Kalmiopsis leachiana,* in bloom from April to June.

From US 199 at Selma, turn west onto the Illinois River Road (County 5070/FR 4103), heading toward Store Gulch. It begins as a two-lane, paved,

Weaver Ranch artifact

and winding road and becomes a one-lane gravel road with some rough stretches (pickup or four-wheel-drive vehicle recommended). In 16.7 miles, stay on FR 4103 to reach the Briggs Creek Campground and Trailhead in 1 mile.

The river trail (#1161) tours a transition forest of ponderosa and sugar pines, cedar, fir, madrone, and oak. Near its start, spurs branch to the river. After entering the Kalmiopsis Wilderness, the trail wraps around the rugged north canyon wall, finding open views of the Illinois—flowing wide, clean, and crystalline. Slides mar the steep mountainsides.

Hayden Creek marks the entry into the small York Creek Botanical Area. From 3.25 miles to the ridge at 5.25 miles, the trail tours a richer, mixed forest secluded from river views. Beside tumbling Clear Creek (4.5 miles) is a restful campsite.

At the ridgetop junction at 5.25 miles, the Illinois River Trail to Bald Mountain journeys slightly uphill to the right. However, for a clockwise

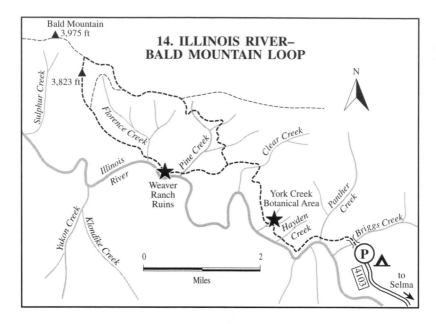

loop, follow the Pine Flat Trail (#1219) straight ahead for a steep, switchbacking descent on a wooded slope to the river bottom. Where the trail forks on the rocky, oak-fern flat, bear right and cross Pine Creek. Campsites dot the area, and a boulder-bar scramble leads to the river.

The trail now travels at the edge of the boulder bar past a reed drainage to duck into the forest near a moss-decked oak. At 6.9 miles, it reaches a beautiful homestead meadow with broken fireplace, rusting equipment, and some old cans—what was Weaver Ranch. Although the open, grassy river flat may prove inviting, pitch no-trace camps off the meadow.

Hikers and anglers find easy river access between Pine Flat and Florence Creek, as the trail rounds the slope just above the river. At 7.7 miles is the Florence Creek fording; at its bench campsite, a small sign signals the Florence Way link (#1219A) to Bald Mountain—a steep, narrow path streaking up the hill.

As it traces the ridge above Florence Creek, Florence Way, which is on an irregular maintenance schedule, offers a greater challenge with downfalls and faint or overgrown stretches in the burn areas. Where the trail fades, stop and scan the hillside to discover the next identifiable path fragment, which is never far from sight.

At 10 miles, the trail crosses an open slope offering a deep-canyon view of the Illinois far below and the Klondike and Yukon Creek drainages. Soon after, the trail travels the dividing ridge between the Florence and Sulphur Creek canyons, which is essentially a fire line.

In a brushy clearing, at the 10.7-mile junction, going right meets the Illinois River Trail 2 miles east of Bald Mountain; going straight leads toward Bald Mountain. Proceed forward for the summit ridge. At 11.5 miles, scorched bushes and trees rim the hike's false summit (elevation 3,823 feet). Views from the knob sweep the river canyon and the opposite wall.

Next follow the grassy footpath that bears left (west) away from the false summit to reach the Illinois River Trail at 12 miles. A left leads to Bald Mountain proper in shy of a mile; a right begins the homeward trek. (Counterclockwise-loop travelers on the Illinois River Trail will need to watch for this turn, because the signs face away from them.)

The closing leg of the loop travels a scorched forest for a couple of miles. On an impressively steep slope marked by cliffs, the trail offers views of the wildly rugged Silver Creek canyon.

At 16.5 miles, the trail rounds a small ridge and descends more rapidly. It crosses the forks of Pine Creek and offers views across clearings of the Illinois River canyon, before arriving at the ridgetop junction with Pine Flat Trail to close the loop (18.75 miles). From there, retrace the river trail east to the Briggs Creek trailhead.

15 | STERLING MINE DITCH TRAIL

Distance: 17 miles one way, plus access spurs
Elevation change: 800 feet
Difficulty: Strenuous
Season: Year round, except during low-elevation snows
Map: BLM Sterling Mine Trail System brochure
For information: Medford District BLM

This trail tours a remnant from Oregon's colorful prospecting era. Placer gold strikes in the early 1850s led to the founding of Jacksonville, and in 1877, miners fashioned an artificial creek to draw water from the Little Applegate River to the mineral-rich Siskiyou mountainsides. The 26.5-mile-long, 3-foot-deep ditch, completed in 6 months, remained in use until the 1930s. Now, a stream of hikers flows alongside the ditch.

The historical route passes through deciduous-evergreen transition forest and across oak-grassland hillsides. In the spring, wildflowers abound, but beware because poison oak is at its peak potency. Common wildlife sightings include deer, grouse, and ravens.

From Jacksonville, follow OR 238 west toward Grants Pass. Go 7.4 miles and turn left onto Applegate Road at Ruch. In 2.8 miles, turn left onto Little Applegate Road (a paved and gravel route). Signs indicate the way to the trailheads. Locate the easternmost one at Little Applegate Recreation Site in 11 miles; the recreation site itself is now closed.

The westernmost trailhead for the ditch trail is at Deming Gulch. From the junction of Little Applegate and Sterling Creek Roads (5.5 miles southeast of Ruch), go 2 miles north on Sterling Creek Road, and turn right onto Armstrong Gulch Road. At the road fork in 0.3 mile, bear left, and go about 0.7 mile on BLM 39-2-8 to find a direct access to the ditch trail on the right side of the road.

If time is limited, the eastern sampling holds the better offering. From the abandoned Little Applegate Recreation Site, a 0.5-mile spur accesses the ditch. Elsewhere, the access spurs measure between 1 and 1.75 miles long. The multiple trailheads allow for customized hikes; a 4-mile loop knits together the Tunnel Ridge, Sterling Mine Ditch, and Bear Gulch trails with the help of a brief road segment.

The east-end spurs ascend moist gulch drainages and white oak hillsides to reach the primary ditch trail. Early views feature the Little

Upper Applegate River Valley

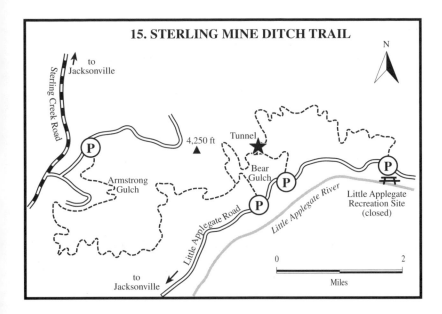

15. STERLING MINE DITCH TRAIL

N

to Jacksonville

Sterling Creek Road

4,250 ft ▲

Tunnel ★

Bear Gulch

P

P

P

P

Armstrong Gulch

Little Applegate Road

Little Applegate River

Little Applegate Recreation Site (closed)

0   2

Miles

to Jacksonville

Applegate Valley with its alternating oak and evergreen slopes. In the distance, the river rushes.

Touring the levee above the ditch, the trail is mostly flat. Where the ditch passes through private properties, the trail charges up and around the private holdings.

Despite the passage of time, the ditch remains defined but not detractive. Small bushes and grasses have softened its banks and invaded its bottom. The wooden retaining walls, many now in disrepair, and the 30-foot-long, 3.5-foot-high tunnel that passes through the ridge 5 miles west of the ditch's east end testify to the construction feat.

The trail segment between Wolf Gap and Armstrong Gulch includes a 4-mile stretch through a recovering fire zone. Views of Little Red Mountain, Sevenmile Ridge, and Yale Creek drainage invite the eyes to stray from the scorched forest.

On either side of the burn is thriving transition forest. Heading west, the trail unfolds views of Negro Ben Mountain, Mount Baldy, Burton Butte, and Little Applegate and Applegate river valleys, before entering a moister mixed forest on its way to Armstrong Gulch. Along the final trail leg to Deming Gulch, the surrounding clearcuts steal from both the shade and view.

Seasonal changes alter the look of the trail and bring their own unique pleasures, but whatever the season, the trail's usual flatness welcomes a leisurely study of all its offerings.

16 | BIGELOW LAKES– BOUNDARY TRAIL (SOUTH)

Distance: 18.6 miles round trip to Swan saddle
Elevation change: 1,000 feet
Difficulty: Strenuous
Season: Spring through fall
Map: USFS Siskiyou, Illinois Valley Ranger District (topo)
For information: Illinois Valley Ranger District

The Boundary Trail component of this hike won national recreation trail distinction in the 1980s. It snakes along the outreaches of Oregon Caves National Monument and crisscrosses the border between Siskiyou and Rogue River National Forests, before dipping into the Red Buttes Wilderness. The secluded off-trail beauty of Bigelow Lakes introduces and closes this hike.

The trail takes the hiker on a roller-coaster trek, over saddles and ridges and through valleys. Among the sidelights is Denman Cabin, a one-time line shack for livestock management, now a rustic spot for a midday meal.

Vistas are obtained throughout the journey, but an off-trail excursion to the top of Craggy Mountain unfolds a first-rate spectacle: a 360-degree introduction to the neighborhood with Little Craggy Peak; Swan Mountain; the Sucker Creek drainage; and Elijah, Lake, and Grayback Mountains. Piercing the horizon are Mount McLoughlin and California's Mount Shasta and Pyramid Peak.

To reach this trail from the junction of US 199 (Redwood Highway) and OR 46 (Oregon Caves Highway) in Cave Junction, take OR 46 east, following the signs to Oregon Caves National Monument. After 13.5 miles, turn left (north) onto FR 4613, a good gravel road. After 6.6 miles, turn right onto Bigelow Lakes Road (FR 070).

The road is marked "Limited Maintenance, Not Suitable for Low Clearance Vehicles" but remains fine for 0.7 mile. Park near the junction there, and bear right, walking the remainder of FR 070 to the actual trail. Up ahead, a road collapse makes the remaining distance impassable for vehicles.

The narrowed, abandoned section of existing road offers a fast, pleasant walk to the historic trailhead. After 0.8 mile, skirt the gaping hole left behind by the collapsed road, and at 1.3 miles, reach the historic trailhead on the left-hand side of FR 070. Be alert for the unlabeled, house-shaped sign that indicates the trail. A lovely alpine meadow slope claims the view.

The trail climbs in zigzag fashion between two wide sweeps of the mountain meadow. At 1.9 mile, a vacant signpost indicates a footpath striking out across the west meadow. The path fades, but by following its general course, hikers will come to a gated fence (necessary because of grazing cows), with the larger Bigelow Lake just beyond.

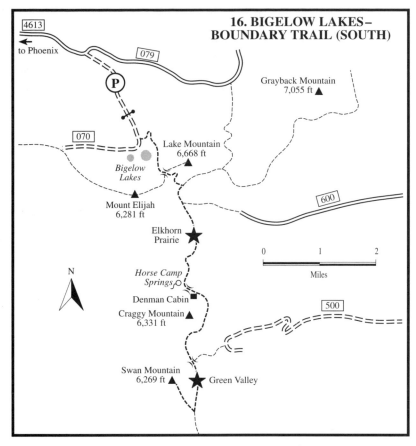

16. BIGELOW LAKES–
BOUNDARY TRAIL (SOUTH)

4613
to Phoenix
079
P
Grayback Mountain
7,055 ft ▲

070
Lake Mountain
6,668 ft ▲

Bigelow
Lakes

Mount Elijah
6,281 ft ▲

600

Elkhorn
Prairie ★

0   1   2

Miles

N

Horse Camp
Springs ○

Denman Cabin ■

Craggy Mountain ▲
6,331 ft

500

Swan Mountain
6,269 ft ▲   ★ Green Valley

The main trail continues climbing, offering overviews of Bigelow Lake, its feeding waters, and the ridges fanning to the horizon. At 2.8 miles, the trail arrives at the saddle between Lake Mountain and Mount Elijah. Again, the trail signs here are missing. The trail heading downhill connects to the Boundary Trail, while the trail striking out to the right leads to Mount Elijah and Oregon Caves. Fifty yards back on the Bigelow Lakes Trail, hikers may have noticed the unmarked spur to Lake Mountain as it angled off to the northeast.

Proceed downhill to the Boundary Trail junction and a large campsite at 3.8 miles. With a reliable spring to the northeast, this campsite is the ideal base from which to explore the Boundary Trail in either direction, but for this hike, proceed south.

From the southeast end of the campsite, the trail ascends beneath a fir-spruce canopy. Tanoak, vanilla leaf, and twisted stalk add to the understory. At 4.7 miles, the trail enters Elkhorn Prairie.

Just before the saddle, at 6 miles, is Horse Camp Springs. Upon crossing the saddle, hikers first glimpse the destinations to the east. Steller's jays, hawks, woodpeckers, and grouse abound.

A brief walk leads to the next unmarked trail junction. Uphill to the right finds the collapsing shell of Denman Cabin and an enticing, although nonpotable spring in 0.1 mile. From the cabin, a trail crosses over the spring to eventually rejoin the main trail, which rounds the east flank of Craggy Mountain.

To stage a cross-country assault on Craggy's summit, head up the south slope. On top, a prized vista awaits. Mount Shasta and Mount McLoughlin, the southern Siskiyous, and the distant Cascades display wilderness grandeur.

At 7.8 miles, the main trail meets the East Fork Sucker Creek Trail on the Craggy–Swan Mountain saddle. From here, the Boundary Trail travels through dry forest before slicing the lush meadow that earns Green Valley its name.

From Green Valley, an uphill climb leads to the Swan Mountain saddle (9.3 miles), the stopping point for this hike. The Boundary Trail, however, continues south, eventually becoming part of the Red Buttes Wilderness trail system.

As a closing destination, Swan Mountain saddle, a wind-whipped, dry meadowland, offers rewarding views of Tannen Mountain, Sucker Butte, and Red Buttes Wilderness. To achieve the summit vantage requires a half-mile cross-country effort.

The return is as you came.

Bigelow Lake

17 | WILDWOOD NATIONAL RECREATION TRAIL

Distance: 29.5 miles one way
Elevation change: 600 feet
Difficulty: Moderate to strenuous
Season: Year round; open between 5:00 A.M. and 10:00 P.M.
Map: Portland Parks Bureau trail map
For information: Portland Parks and Recreation
    Department, Hoyt Arboretum

Cached within Portland's city limits, this noteworthy metropolitan trail explores some of Forest Park's 5,000 acres of natural habitat. The national recreation trail (NRT) is ideal for times when business or homelife ties hikers to the city.

The Wildwood Trail is a family trail, one for all ages. It invites a morning jog and the exercising of leashed pets. The multiple access points to the NRT allow hikers to customize the length of their tour.

A number of side trails connect to and explore outward from this primary artery. In addition to the NRT, Forest Park offers another 15 miles of foot trail and some 30 miles of gated roadway. The junctions, for the most part, are well marked and allow hikers to navigate loops and side tours with the use of the park's trail map. Blue diamond markers or the occasional mileage marker helps travelers stay on track.

The trail crosses fire lanes and city streets and tours the natural buffers amid the area's residential tracts. For most of its nearly 30 miles, the Wildwood Trail rolls out a 3-foot-wide, leveled bed and a comfortable grade for its slope-contouring journey. During heavy rains, expect it to be muddy in a few places. Carry all drinking water for the hike.

At the southern terminus, there is ample parking near the World Forestry Center. From US 26 in west Portland, take the indicated exit for Washington Park and the Oregon Zoo and follow the well-signed route north to the World Forestry Center. Then, hike north from the center to the Oregon Vietnam Veterans Memorial and nearby trailhead.

Skyline Boulevard, a major route through Portland's northwest hills, strings together multiple signed access-spurs leading to the heart of the Wildwood Trail. Because the trail's northern terminus at N.W. Newberry Road lacks trailhead parking, the best way to sample the northern end of the trail is from N.W. Germantown Road. Take the indicated turn for N.W. Germantown Road off N.W. St. Helens Road (US 30) just north of the St. Johns Bridge. N.W. Germantown Road holds three trailheads; the marked trailhead in 1.7 miles has a parking area for up to six vehicles and offers direct access to the Wildwood Trail for tours both north and south.

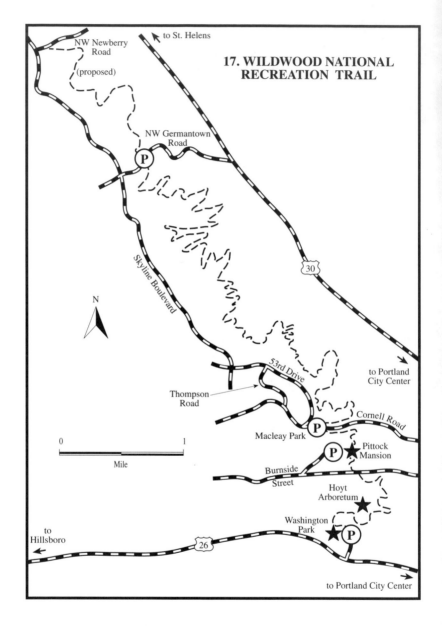

17. WILDWOOD NATIONAL RECREATION TRAIL

From south to north, when starting near the memorial, the Wildwood Trail passes through the prized parks of Portland's northwest hills for a more "civilized" tour. It ventures through broad woodland corridors and across the open lawns of the developed parks. Road noises and rooftops

Balch Creek

occasionally intrude, yet even here, pockets exist where the forest succeeds in filtering out city reminders.

Touring Hoyt Arboretum, the Wildwood Trail enters a planned forest that unites native Northwest trees, shrubs, ferns, and wildflowers with more than 900 types of trees and woody shrubs from around the world. The arboretum's own 9.8-mile trail network is organized by tree family/class; small plaques identify the species. Staying on the Wildwood Trail alone, hikers view the pine-conifer and redwood planting schemes.

Where the trail passes through woodland corridors, bigleaf maple and alder primarily comprise the overhead canopy; a few Douglas fir and western hemlock pierce the leafy roof. Vistas along the route are few. Perhaps the best is secured at Pittock Acres (3.8 miles). A short detour to the hilltop finds both the French Renaissance mansion that once belonged to newspaper magnate Henry Pittock and an overlook of the city. The grounds are open (free) to the public.

Cornell Road at 5 miles marks the dividing line between the refined tour and the more remote and wild stretches of the Wildwood Trail. Beyond Cornell Road, the route probes deep into Portland's wilderness park (Forest Park), traveling mostly through second growth. This deeper, multistory forest displays a richer texture.

The northbound tour now stays in a similar setting all the way to N.W. Germantown Road (24.6 miles) and beyond. Because of its dead-end nature, the final leg of the tour to N.W. Newberry Road is often less tracked, promising more tranquil exploration.

Whether it's for a short walk or a long-distance tour, the Wildwood Trail well serves the city-bound hiker.

18 TRAIL OF TEN FALLS

**Distance: 7.5-mile circuit with spurs and interlocking
small loops**
Elevation change: 400 feet
Difficulty: Moderate
Season: Year round
Map: State park flier
For information: Silver Falls State Park

Country roads wrap around fields, pastures, and tree farms to deliver this
surprising destination—a pocket of old-growth forest along Silver Creek
Canyon, which houses 10 major waterfalls. The falls measure between 27
and 178 feet high, with five falls plunging more than 100 feet. Headward
erosion by Silver Creek carved out this canyon showcase. Where the cliff
basalts were weakest, the water's force sculpted cavernous hollows behind
the falls and scenic amphitheater bowls. This canyon forest and watery
wonder are protected within Silver Falls State Park.

To reach this 8,700-acre Willamette Valley park, from OR 22 about 12
miles east of Salem, take the exit for Silver Falls State Park and OR 214.
Signs mark the junctions, as OR 214 twists its way northeast to the park in
15.5 miles.

Multiple trailheads found at the day-use areas and along OR 214 access
this hiking circuit (also referred to as Silver Creek Canyon Trail). Map
boards at the trailheads and at junctions along the trail aid in navigation.
Signs identify each falls and its height, while a few interpretive panels

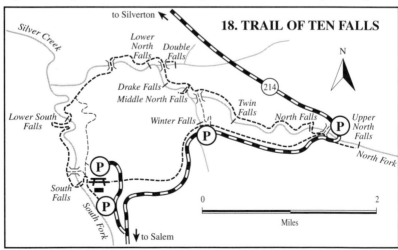

18. TRAIL OF TEN FALLS

Middle North Falls

explain area history. The park's campground offers hikers a pleasant overnight base.

From South Falls Day-Use Area "A," a paved forest path descends to South Falls, the most visited and photographed falls in the park. Before descending, hikers can overlook this falls; part way to it, a spur suggests a quick view of Frenchie Falls.

At the next junction, keep left to arrive at South Falls; a right leads to the footbridge spanning the creek below the falls. The 177-foot veil of South Falls may be examined from sides, back, and face. Where the trail passes through the cliff hollow behind the falls, hikers are treated to an unusual perspective looking through the spraying chute.

After emerging from the hollow, the Trail of Ten Falls then descends, bypassing the bridge below the falls for the full 7.5-mile loop. The bridge offers yet another camera angle on the droplet veil and a loop return back to the canyon rim for a much shorter tour.

As the trail pursues the South Fork of Silver Creek downstream, it travels a rich cedar-fir-maple canyon with cascading greenery and offers views of the clear-coursing South Fork. At 1 mile, the loop unfolds side views and outward-looking views from behind the 93-foot watery curtain of Lower South Falls.

Soon after, the trail curves away from the South Fork to follow the North Fork of Silver Creek upstream, passing Lower North, Drake, Middle North, and Twin Falls, with the option of a side trip to Double Falls at 2.3 miles. A platform extends over the steep creek-canyon cliff for a safe viewing of

Drake Falls. Double Falls is a seasonal falls with reduced waters in summer, but its cliff is the true show stopper. Middle North Falls (106 feet) is arguably the prettiest waterfall in the gallery.

At 4.3 miles, the trail delivers multiple perspectives on the 136-foot North Falls. Again, hikers may pass into the gaping mouth of the cliff to peer out through the thick, white droplet veil. As the trail climbs away from North Falls and out of the canyon, beware: the stone steps may be slippery when wet, especially when temperatures drop.

Where the trail levels out, it offers overlooks of the scenic pools and swirling cascades of North Fork Silver Creek. Over-the-shoulder looks reveal the simultaneous quick drop of both the trail and the water into canyon.

Bypassing the trail junction for the loop's canyon rim return, hikers will find a 0.2-mile upstream trail leaving the northernmost parking area. This spur probes still deeper into the moist canyon of North Fork Silver Creek, ushering hikers to an Upper North Falls vista. This broad falls enters its canyon slipping over a rocky bowl for a 65-foot drop into a circular pool.

After backtracking downstream to the junction above North Falls, hikers can then resume the loop by bearing left for the canyon rim tour. This is a fast segment with minimal grade change, touring a corridor of Douglas fir and cedar between the rim and the park road.

A switchbacking, downhill detour from the turnout for Winter Falls Viewpoint holds one final look at the plunging waters that bring this park fame. This look pairs the 134-foot shimmery streamers of Winter Falls with a bold view of the steep, moss-mantled basalt canyon wall. The rim trail proceeds back to the South Falls picnic area and the loop's ending.

The long days of summer allow for a comfortable completion of the 7.5-mile circuit, with time for detours and an unhurried appreciation of all the falls.

19 | MOUNT PISGAH SUMMIT TRAIL

Distance: 3.2 miles round trip
Elevation change: 1,000 feet
Difficulty: Moderate
Season: Year round, except during extreme fire danger
Map: Trails of the Howard Buford Recreation Area brochure
For information: Lane County Parks Division

This trail ascends a classic grassland–Oregon white oak woodland of the Willamette Valley hills to reach the summit of Mount Pisgah (elevation 1,531 feet). The broad summit overlooks the Willamette Valley floor, the Springfield-Eugene area, the Coast Range, and the near and distant Cascade peaks.

19. MOUNT PISGAH SUMMIT TRAIL

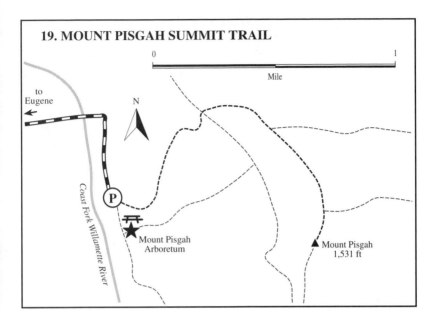

This 2,363-acre natural park houses an ecologically diverse land rising above the Coast and Middle Forks of the Willamette River. Old fire roads and footpaths lace the higher slope presenting loop-tour options.

At the base of the hill, interconnected, short trails explore the 210-acre Mount Pisgah Arboretum with its riparian, marsh, forest, and grassland habitats. Some of its oaks and maples are more than 200 years old. Trail and natural history brochures are available at the arboretum for a nominal fee.

From OR 58, 0.25 mile east of I-5, go north on Seavey Loop Road. A sign for Mount Pisgah marks the turn. At the T-junction in 1.8 miles, turn right on Seavey Way, following the brown road signs for Buford Park and Mount Pisgah Arboretum. The park lies less than a half mile ahead; the trailhead is found at the arboretum parking area at the end of the park road.

From the hiker gate above the parking area, the trail climbs, passing beneath utility lines. As it rounds a natural oak-grassland slope dotted with a few Douglas fir, it overlooks the arboretum. The former road allows for a steady climbing grade. At 0.1 mile, a footpath intersects the Mount Pisgah Summit Trail; continue forward.

Early views of the round-topped mountain soon greet hikers. Below the trail is an intermittent, gurgling creek. At 0.5 mile, a secondary trail breaks away to the left to mount and cross a nearby low saddle. A detour to this saddle finds an overlook of the farmland along the Middle Fork Willamette River and Potato Hill.

The summit trail continues its open grassland tour. Views build to include the confluence of the Coast and Middle Forks of the Willamette River, the

White oaks tower above Mount Pisgah Summit Trail.

valley fields, the Coast Range, Spencer Butte, and the Springfield-Eugene area.

At 0.8 mile, the trail crosses under the wires one last time, as it enters a turn to travel the west face of Mount Pisgah; the view now spans 180 degrees west. The trail then tops the summit ridge at 1 mile and enters an oak grove.

Where the trail forks at 1.1 miles and again at 1.2 miles, take either path as they again merge in a short distance. Boulders just off the trail invite hikers to pause and enjoy the western panorama.

Travel the ridge grove, and at 1.4 miles, take the uphill path to the right to tag the mountaintop. The summit throws open a window to the east featuring the distant snow-capped Three Sisters. Atop Mount Pisgah, a bronze monument shows the topography of the immediate area. Its carved base records the mountain's geologic evolution. Trails crisscross the broad summit to unfold a 360-degree view.

Return as you came, or chart a loop return using one of the many other park trails.

20 | MILDRED KANIPE MEMORIAL COUNTY PARK TRAILS

Distance: 2.9 miles round trip
Elevation change: 200 feet
Difficulty: Easy to moderate
Season: March 15 through Oct. 31, 7:00 A.M. to dusk
Map: Park map flier
For information: Douglas County Parks

Self-described as "her father's only boy," Mildred Kanipe worked at his elbow as a child and single-handedly kept the ranch going after his death. When she died in the early 1980s, the ranch was entrusted to Douglas County. This park honors the donor's rugged independence and her vision for the ranch, keeping its historic and natural features.

The park encompasses 1,100 rolling acres drained by Bachelor Creek. Grassland expanses interrupted by stands of oak and Douglas fir characterize its low foothills; rare Columbia white-tailed deer wander the property. Coyote, fox, beaver, nutria, blue-tailed skink, crayfish, frog, and wild turkey can also be seen. The old buildings, fence fragments, gates to be closed, grazing sheep, and open spaces keep the ranching legacy alive.

From the intersection of First and Oak Streets in Oakland, travel 3.8 miles east on Oak Street, which becomes Driver Valley Road (County 22). At the road fork, bear left on Elkhead Road (County 50) and proceed 2.9 miles to the main park entrance (0.3 mile past the equestrian entrance).

At the main day-use area, find a handicapped-accessible restroom and picnic area, but bring drinking water because the well is small and the water unsavory. Smoking is prohibited, and dogs are not allowed in the park's back reaches.

A map is generally available at the main day-use area or at the equestrian staging area, or you can request one from the county parks department. It shows the existing routes. Most are old two-tracks, some better defined than others. Plans call for an upgraded map and some signing. In the meantime, fencelines and structures provide navigational clues. Be alert for poison oak year-round.

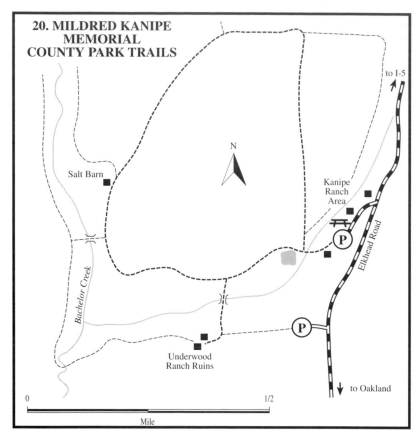

20. MILDRED KANIPE MEMORIAL COUNTY PARK TRAILS

to I-5

Salt Barn

Kanipe Ranch Area

N

P

Elkhead Road

Bachelor Creek

P

Underwood Ranch Ruins

to Oakland

0   1/2

Mile

From the main day-use, the Kanipe homestead, follow the gravel ranch road south from the end of the parking lot past the picnic area and work shed. Where the surfaced road ends at 0.1 mile, trace a line across the open lawn to a gate at the far right corner of the fenced enclosure ahead. Pass through the gate (closing it behind you) and follow the mowed track along the edge of the square stock pond. The uphill path to the right is the loop return.

From the pond, follow the grassy track to the rimming oaks at the south end of the field and pass through an opening in the fence to come out at a ranch-road junction at 0.4 mile. The left route leads to the historic Underwood Ranch and equestrian area. The primary loop veers right journeying deeper into the ranch wilds.

To view the exterior of the Underwood place (a 0.6-mile round-trip spur), hike the road to the left coming to a T-junction and there, turn right to reach the sagging, two-story Underwood home and its rustic barn on a plateau above Bachelor Creek. The location allows park overviews.

Oak

Back at the 0.4-mile junction (1 mile), the clockwise tour follows the gravel ranch road west, topping an oak-grassland rise in 0.2 mile. Wildflowers abound. As the road continues its meander among the oaks, avoid the intersecting foot trails.

Then, at the 1.4-mile junction, avoid the bridge and take the two-track to the right as it enters a stand of oaks. A snaking, thin drainage lies to the right. A steady ascent leads to the salt barn (1.6 miles), a tin-roofed, two-sided shelter with stout tree trunks for its supports.

The hike then follows the grassy track that arcs to the right past the barn for a gentle mosey up the oak-studded grassland rise. Do not take the path that rounds the barn to the left. If the loop's track has not been recently mowed and is hard to follow, turn back.

Travel is sunny as hikers now keep to the right of the drainage depression. Over-the-shoulder views present the rural countryside and Cascade skyline before the trail returns to woodland. The fence corner at 2.1 miles signals the next junction. For the loop, pass through the fence opening on the right to hike north along the west boundary fence, now climbing along the upper slope.

Tag the high point and at 2.2 miles reach a phone-cable marker next to a gate in the western fenceline; these signal the downhill return. Hike the grassy two-track to the right for a straight forward descent through rolling oak terrain. At 2.4 miles, a grassy knoll serves up open views of the ranch, rural valley, foothills, and Cascades.

Shortly after comes a steep 0.1-mile descent back to the pond enclosure. Turn right to pass through the gate at the corner of the enclosure, completing the loop at the pond, and then backtrack to the day-use (2.9 miles).

21 | GORGE TRAIL

Distance: 34.7 miles one way *(Bridal Veil to Wyeth)*
Elevation change: 1,500 feet
Difficulty: Strenuous
Season: Year round, except during low-elevation snows
Map: USFS Trails of the Columbia Gorge
For information: Columbia River National Scenic Area

The burgeoning Gorge Trail, which incorporates new and existing trails and abandoned segments of the old scenic highway, opens the door to many of the Oregon-side attractions of the Columbia River Gorge National Scenic Area (NSA). It will one day link Portland with the town of Hood River, some 65 miles east; presently, it is complete between Bridal Veil and Wyeth (east of Cascade Locks).

This main hiking artery travels just above or below the front cliffs of the gorge, stringing together a prized collection of trails. Together, they explore the drama of the Columbia River Gorge: sheer basalt cliffs carved by an ancient roiling river, the silver threads of a host of major waterfalls, temperate Douglas fir rain forests, celebrated vistas, narrow side canyons, and crystalline creeks. In addition to long-distance hiking, the Gorge Trail allows for a variety of loop hikes and provides a gateway to the Mark O. Hatfield Wilderness trails. Its lone drawback is the noise from the interstate highway, rail, and river transportation routes that likewise share the gorge.

The Gorge Trail enjoys multiple access points off the 7-mile western segment of the Old Scenic Highway (US 30). From Portland, travel I-84 east and take the Bridal Veil exit. Trailheads are found near the Bridal Veil junction, at the vista turnouts farther east, and at Ainsworth State Park. Additional access points are found at John Yeon State Park near Warrendale, at Wahclella Falls Trailhead south of Bonneville Dam, at Eagle Creek Campground west of Cascade Locks, near Bridge of the Gods in Cascade Locks, and at Herman Creek and Wyeth Campgrounds.

Beginning at the trailhead just east of the Bridal Veil junction, the Gorge Trail pursues the Angels Rest Trail uphill, touring a temperate Douglas fir–bigleaf maple rain forest on its eastward journey. At 2.2 miles, a side trail to the left leads to Angels Rest atop the gorge wall for a grand wind-swept vista looking downstream.

At 4.8 miles, the trail tags a view of the mystifying headwater springs that immediately give rise to the full-coursing Wahkeena Creek. The hike then descends along the creek, which holds a series of falls.

Farther east, the trail reaches the Multnomah Falls area. Downstream from the Multnomah Creek crossing, a short spur to the left leads to a vista

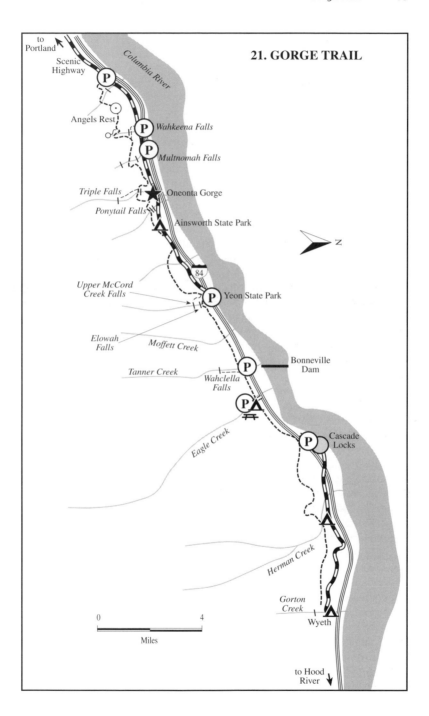

21. GORGE TRAIL

to Portland

Columbia River

Scenic Highway

Angels Rest

Wahkeena Falls

Multnomah Falls

Triple Falls

Oneonta Gorge

Ponytail Falls

Ainsworth State Park

84

Upper McCord Creek Falls

Yeon State Park

Elowah Falls

Moffett Creek

Tanner Creek

Wahclella Falls

Bonneville Dam

Eagle Creek

Cascade Locks

Herman Creek

Gorton Creek

Wyeth

N

0   4

Miles

to Hood River

platform atop Multnomah Falls. At 620 feet, Multnomah is the fourth tallest falls in the nation. The main trail switchbacks downslope to a junction at 7.6 miles. Here, the Gorge Trail proceeds east. The trail heading west leads to the popular lower-bridge vantage for viewing Multnomah Falls and to historic Multnomah Lodge—a worthwhile side trip.

For this tour though, keep to the Gorge Trail. It wraps east from the junction touring multistoried forest, rounding cliffs, and crossing over scree slopes en route to Oneonta Gorge (9.4 miles). Oneonta is an impressively narrow chasm, richly decked in mosses and ferns—a designated botanical area. A side trip uphill finds Triple Falls in 1 mile, three side-by-side 100- to 135-foot falls. Beyond Oneonta, the Gorge Trail continues its forest-and-cliff tour passing behind Ponytail Falls.

After skirting above Ainsworth State Park, the Gorge Trail reaches the old scenic highway (at about 13 miles) and follows the frontage road east to John Yeon State Park. Rock and mud slides forced the abandonment of the section trail that previously rounded the gorge wall here.

From Yeon State Park (15.3 miles), the trail heads east into a rich Douglas fir forest. In less than 0.5 mile, a right leads to Upper McCord Creek Falls, while the Gorge Trail proceeds left for Elowah Falls. It soon arrives at a footbridge vista of this pretty waterfall that spills through a cleft. After bypassing picnic sites, the trail alternately travels through forest and across scree slopes to the fording at Moffett Creek (17.4 miles).

Along the next stretch, the forest setting is pleasant, but the trail is far too close to the freeway to be completely relaxing. Utility corridors, here and elsewhere, steal from the tour. A brief stretch via an old two-track followed by a right on the downhill path finds the old highway leading to Tanner Creek and Wahclella Falls Trail at 19.1 miles. A 1-mile detour upstream from the gated road leads to this elegant falls.

Bypassing the falls trail, the Gorge Trail continues east toward Eagle Creek, traveling beneath the bigleaf maples and alders of a second-growth forest. It follows old two-tracks and crosses forest roads. Nearing the junction for Wauna View Point, the trail traverses a fern-and-scree slope. The viewpoint suggests another detour for a gorge vista.

Rich, ancient forest surrounds the hiker on the remainder of the trip to Eagle Creek. In fall, hikers can watch the salmon wriggle upstream to spawn in the clean gravels of the creek. From the day-use area (22.2 miles), the Eagle Creek Recreation Trail—the most popular entrance to the Mark O. Hatfield Wilderness and itself a waterfall showcase—may call hikers away from the front wall tour. The Gorge Trail proceeds east to Cascade Locks, often via the old highway.

From Cascade Locks (24.7 miles), the Gorge Trail pursues the Pacific Crest Trail (PCT) southbound to the Herman Bridge Trail (28.8 miles), which takes the baton for the next 1.2 miles. Upon crossing Herman Creek, the Gorge Trail then chases the Herman Creek Trail upstream for 0.6 mile before resuming solo travel east to Wyeth. Watch for this left turn at Herman Camp (the Herman Creek–Gorton Creek trail junction).

This latest stretch of the Gorge Trail unrolls a tranquil, forested, slope-contouring journey, with brief views from the interrupting tongues of talus. On arrival at Wyeth's Gorton Creek, a short scramble upstream from the footbridge finds a secluded waterfall. For now, until the Gorge Trail grows east, the hike ends at Wyeth (34.7 miles).

22 | HERMAN CREEK– WAHTUM LAKE LOOP

Distance: 26.2-mile loop, plus optional side trips
Elevation change: 4,100 feet
Difficulty: Strenuous
Season: Late spring through fall
Map: USFS Trails of the Columbia Gorge
For information: Columbia River Gorge National Scenic Area

This Mark O. Hatfield (formerly Columbia) Wilderness circuit travels mainly through forest as it ascends the canyon of Herman Creek, tags pretty Wahtum Lake, and crosses and descends the ridge housing Benson Plateau. Ancient Douglas fir forest richly woven with bigleaf maples yields to a congested forest of high-elevation firs at the upper reaches. A cedar swamp and diverse spring- and summer-flowering flora add to the journey.

Above Wahtum Lake, Chinidere Mountain beckons for a detour. This side trail travels through forest and up a talus slope to a top-of-the-world 360-degree view. The panorama applauds the Mark O. Hatfield Wilderness and offers looks into Washington State. Along the ridge, meadow openings and forest gaps bring additional views.

To reach the loop, from I-84, take Exit 44 for Cascade Locks. At the town's east end, follow Forest Lane (the frontage road along the freeway's south side) toward Oxbow Hatchery. Going 1.7 miles finds a work center and the turn for Herman Creek Campground and Trailhead. Trailhead parking lies 0.4 mile uphill. In winter, the gated road requires hikers to walk this road distance.

The hike's first 2 miles offer little but roll by quickly. After the short uphill switchbacks and the crossing of a utility-corridor road at 0.25 mile, the trail briefly enters a nice, forested stretch as it bypasses the Herman Bridge Trail.

A closed dirt road continues the hike through semiopen second growth. Marked hiker routes branch away, including the Gorge Trail at 1.3 miles,

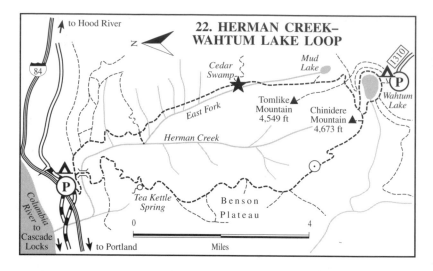

but keep to the roadway, which eventually narrows to a footpath at 1.9 miles. A fuller forest now encloses the trail.

The trail climbs and rounds past mossy rock outcrops and oak-shaded points to enter the wilderness at 2.8 miles. Cascading creeks and intermittent waters accent the trek; some require wading. Deep in the canyon flows Herman Creek.

At 4.1 miles is Casey Creek Camp. An unmarked, steeply dropping, 0.6-mile side path leads to the camp's water source—the confluence of Herman Creek and its east fork. From the camp, the trail follows the East Fork Canyon upstream.

At 7.1 miles, the route crosses a skunk cabbage bog. Beyond it, the Cedar Swamp Shelter occupies a grand ancient cedar grove. The loop then continues through moister forest to reach the East Fork crossing, followed soon after by Noble Camp. As the trail climbs, the forest shows smaller fir and hemlock as it naturally thins with the gain in elevation. Past the Mud Lake Trail Junction (9.2 miles), the hike tops out.

Several trails now work their way to Wahtum Lake. At 10.2 miles is the Anthill Trail Junction; stay on the Herman Creek Trail. In another mile, the Herman Creek Trail comes to a T-junction with the Pacific Crest Trail (PCT). Bear left to reach Wahtum Lake. A primitive, walk-in camp is above the south shore of the lake.

After rounding the lake clockwise to the Lower Chinidere Trail Junction, go right, cross the log-jammed outlet, and head uphill to again reach the PCT (13.5 miles). The loop resumes bearing left. An early detour follows the Chinidere Mountain Trail, climbing 0.3 mile and 400 feet. The summit view features the deep drainages and high ridges of the wilderness, the Wahtum Lake bowl, and Mounts Adams and Hood.

Forgoing the detour, the PCT follows the ridge, touring true fir forest and talus slopes. Openings offer views of the Eagle Creek drainage and Tanner Butte to the west; Herman Creek drainage, Tomlike Mountain, and Woolly Horn and Nick Eaton Ridges to the east.

At 15.5 miles, a side trail leads to a vista atop a cliff rim. It adds views of Mount Adams and the Columbia Gorge.

From the Eagle-Benson Trail Junction, the PCT flattens as it travels north along the eastern edge of forested Benson Plateau. By 19.2 miles, the trail steeply descends from the main plateau. Near Benson Way Junction, hole-riddled snags mark the forest, and the PCT switchbacks down to Tea Kettle Spring (20.8 miles). Campsites occupy the junction flats.

At 22.3 miles, the trail enters a steep, open wildflower meadow with limited views toward Washington. After more downhill switchbacks, the trail leaves the Mark O. Hatfield Wilderness.

At the 24.3-mile junction, the loop continues downhill to the right via the Herman Bridge Trail, passing through forest, touring below cliffs, and crossing scree slopes to Herman Creek Bridge. Upon climbing from the creek, the loop closes at the Herman Creek Trail (25.5 miles). Go left to return to the trailhead in 0.7 mile.

23 | LOST LAKE–LOST LAKE BUTTE TRAILS

Distance: 3-mile loop *(lake)*; **4.5 miles round trip** *(butte)*
Elevation change: Minimal (lake); 1,300 feet (butte)
Difficulty: Easy (lake); moderate (butte)
Season: Mid-summer through early fall
Map: USFS Mount Hood
For information: Hood River Ranger District

These two hiking trails introduce the shimmery, 240-acre blue lake at the northwestern foot of Mount Hood and its next-door butte. The lake and hilltop vantages showcase Mount Hood in its icy grandeur. The natural attributes of the area—fishing, quiet paddling, a popular forest service campground, and rustic resort—win over guests.

Lost Lake Recreation Area is about 35 miles southwest of Hood River; 22 miles west of Dee. From US 30 (Oak Street) in Hood River, go south on 13th Street and follow the signs for Odell and Parkdale. As the route weaves out of town, it becomes Tucker Road/Hood River Highway. After 3 miles the route turns left; in another 2 miles, bear right driving past Tucker Park. Where you arrive at a small village in another 2.2 miles, turn right for Dee and Lost Lake and travel another 4 miles. There, bear right at

Mount Hood over Lost Lake

the Parkdale-Dee Junction, go 0.2 mile, and then keep left to follow Lost Lake Road (FR 13) the remaining 13.4 miles to the lake area.

For the 3-mile **Lake Shore Trail**, begin at Panorama Point parking on the north shore of Lost Lake. Counterclockwise, the trail enters the woods to the west for discovery of an ancient forest of large-diameter Douglas and Pacific silver fir, western hemlock, and western red cedar. Capture views of Mount Hood through the tree cover.

At 0.6 mile, the trail tours a 0.25-mile boardwalk along the marshy area of Inlet Creek and its associated springs. The rare cutleaf bugbane grows here and nowhere else.

Rolling forest-shore travel resumes, interrupted by an open talus passage at 1.3 miles. In another 0.5 mile, the Lake Shore Trail bypasses the Huckleberry Mountain Trail to swing around the southern tip of this triangular-shaped lake. It next passes below a group shelter and family campsites.

Along the remainder of the circuit, views of Lost Lake Butte and stands of stout cedar bring pleasurable discovery. Much of the trail along the east shore is either on boardwalk or shows a wheelchair-accessible width.

Hike past the Old-Growth Barrier Free Trail, a couple of platforms for lake access at 2.1 miles, and the public boat ramp at 2.6 miles. Beyond the resort area (2.9 miles), the trail crosses the Lake Branch bridge for the

23. LOST LAKE–LOST LAKE BUTTE TRAILS

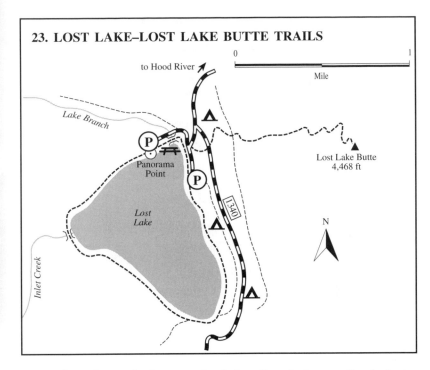

return along the north shore passing below the picnic area. It culminates with a fine panoramic view of Mount Hood and Lost Lake before following the stairs uphill to Panorama Point parking (3 miles).

For the **Lost Lake Butte Trail**, begin where the recreation area road arrives and forks at the lake. The signed trail ascends from the east side of the road to angle across the Lakeshore Express Trail at 0.1 mile and cross FR 1340 at 0.2 mile. It then swings left, contouring above the campground, before again turning uphill and crossing swords with the Old Skyline Trail (0.3 mile).

The rock-studded butte trail tours a midelevation mixed conifer forest. The trail shows a comfortable grade throughout its climb to the summit (elevation 4,468 feet).

By 0.75 mile, the trees lose stature, and huckleberries grow more abundant. At 1.9 miles attain the upper butte reaches for the first volcano views, with Mounts Adams and St. Helens to the north. In June, snow patches can linger on the trail. At the top, Mount Hood boldly salutes hikers, with Mount Jefferson seen peeking over the distant ridges. Rounding out the view are the community of Dee, the West Fork Hood River drainage, and Hickman Butte Lookout. Lost Lake shimmers in the basin below; atop the butte rest the remains of a former lookout. Return as you came.

24 | SALMON RIVER TRAIL

Distance: 14 miles one way *(wilderness permit required)*
Elevation change: 1,600 feet
Difficulty: Strenuous
Season: Summer through early fall
Map: USFS Mount Hood, Bull of the Woods Wilderness/
  Salmon-Huckleberry Wilderness
For information: Mount Hood Information Center

This scenic trail journeys up the Salmon River Canyon for a sampling of the 45,000-acre Salmon-Huckleberry Wilderness and limited views and access to the Salmon Wild and Scenic River. Although the trail strings past a series of river waterfalls, the tumbling waters remain a mystery save for their thunderous voices. Historic fires have swept the forest, but large natural trees and bottoms of spared old growth remain.

The Salmon River supports a native fishery with wild salmon and steelhead runs; fishing is catch-and-release only. Formal side trails branch north to the upper wilderness reaches, while steep secondary trails descend toward the river. Outcrops and rock features extend views and add to touring.

To reach the trail, from US 26 at Zigzag, turn south on Salmon River Road (FR 2618) and follow it for 4.8 miles to the lower river trailhead, 0.3 mile past Green Canyon Way Campground. For the upper trailhead, about 2 miles east of Government Camp, turn south off US 26 onto FR 2656 for

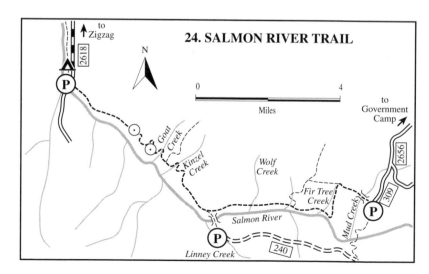

Salmon River Trail

Trillium Lake Campground and follow FRs 2656 and 309 for 5.4 miles to reach the trailhead; it is 4.1 miles past Trillium Lake.

From the lower trailhead, the trail follows the river upstream, traveling among old-growth Douglas fir and western hemlock. A plant-draped rock wall frames one side. The trail bypasses a few well-trampled river sites, and then at 1.9 miles enters the wilderness. At 2.1 miles, it bypasses Rolling Riffle Camp, a flat area on the river bench.

The trail then climbs steadily through younger forest with a few small rhododendron among the forest cover. At 3.2 miles, where the primary trail veers left through forest, a half-moon spur wraps around the nose of the ridge for a panoramic overview of the Salmon River Canyon before returning to the main trail. As fragile grasses and a natural rock garden of wild-flowers cap the protruding rock, keep to the path. A falls marks the river far below, and in early summer, hikers may spy a snowy peak beyond the immediate canyon ridges.

The river trail now unrolls a pretty brown ribbon through the verdant greenery. In under 0.5 mile, a spur tags the next grassy point for canyon and cross-canyon views. Again, sounds of a waterfall add to the experience. The creek at 3.9 miles marks the first source for water, but most of the tributaries along the trail are dependable. At 4.2 miles pass the last vista spur.

Ahead stretches a comfortable trail that alternately rounds the steep canyon wall, tours forest flat, and drifts into side drainages. After stones ease the crossing of Goat Creek (4.9 miles), a spur to the right leads to a campsite, and rhododendron pair with the main trail's climb. At 5.5 miles, a small sign indicates a designated campsite to the left.

Proceed forward at the signed junction with the Kinsel Lake Trail (5.8 miles) to cross the scenic bedrock of Kinsel Creek. The river trail next travels the divide between Kinsel Creek and the river. At 6.5 miles are more designated campsites.

By 7.4 miles, the river's roar is again strong, but the congested forest precludes views. Slowly, the trail grades toward the river, and side trails—some well trampled, others primitive—spur off for the canyon bottom. Eventually, the hike offers filtered looks at the racing river.

At the 8.5-mile junction keep left for the Salmon River Trail; the Linney Creek Trail descends to a log footbridge over the river before journeying south. A detour to the bridge offers open looks at the river, with a campsite upstream from the span.

Where the river trail makes a broad undulation, it passes old-growth survivors from long-ago fires at 8.7 miles and 9.6 miles. With the next creek crossing, the trail traverses a woods flat, once again slipping farther from the river. With a climb, the trail crosses Wolf Creek (10.1 miles).

Another flat advances travel, with the trail parting waist-high bracken ferns. At the end of the flat, the river is again within striking distance. Where the trail rounds a rock face at 10.7 miles, hikers win a river overlook. A good-sized creek that may require wading early in the year precedes the junction with the Fir Tree Trail, which heads north; keep straight ahead for the river trail.

A rough-hewn, hole-riddled boardwalk spans a skunk cabbage bog before the trail passes through an open, rocky area below an extensive talus-and-boulder slope. At 12.1 miles is the first of back-to-back stream crossings of the Fir Tree Creek forks. The climb now accelerates, turning away from the river with a switchback at 12.5 miles. Emerging from Fir Tree Canyon, the trail levels off before turning right at the 13.3-mile junction with the Dry Lake Trail.

A quick climb and descent lead to the footbridge over Mud Creek, before a final climb takes the trail to FR 309 and the end of the line at 14 miles.

25 | TIMBERLINE TRAIL

Distance: 40.7-mile loop *(wilderness permit required)*
Elevation change: 4,100 feet
Difficulty: Strenuous
Season: Midsummer through early fall
Map: USFS Mount Hood Wilderness
For information: Mount Hood Information Center

This heavy-duty hiker trail constructed in the 1930s by the Civilian Conservation Corps applauds the rugged beauty of Mount Hood. Along it, hikers dip deep into chiseled drainages, ford glacial streams, cross rocky

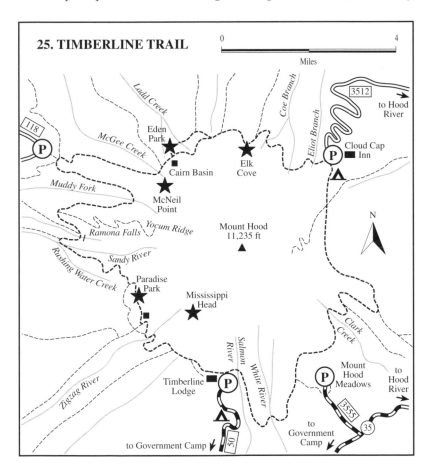

25. TIMBERLINE TRAIL

White River Canyon, Mount Hood

slopes, bypass glaciers and snowmelt falls, and tour high-elevation forest and inviting alpine meadows. In places, snowfields linger into summer. Stream crossings are best accomplished in the morning, when waters are lowest; at times, some may be impassable.

Mount Hood (elevation 11,235 feet) is a strato-volcano that had four minor eruptions in the 1800s. A buried forest along the tour hints at the mountain's explosive nature. A harsh environment of thin soils, change-able weather, and hefty winds claims the mountain. Spreading outward from the volcanic peak is the Mount Hood Wilderness Area, measuring 47,000 acres.

Mid-July and August find a wildflower showcase in the high meadows with bear grass, lupine, paintbrush, penstemon, and phlox. Vistas feature the many faces of Hood; its forested neighborhood; Mount Jefferson and Trillium Lake to the south; and Washington State's Mounts Adams, St. Helens, and Rainier to the north.

One of the most-climbed glaciated peaks in the United States, Mount Hood represents a technical climb. The Timberline Trail ties together the popular climbing routes along with two dozen side trails and welcomes both day hikers and backpackers.

This trail is most easily accessed from Timberline Lodge. From US 26 east of Government Camp, turn north onto Timberline Road and go 5.2 miles to the lodge and ski area. The Timberline Trail and Pacific Crest Trail (PCT) are one in this area; look for the trail to begin behind the lodge.

Other accesses lie off Lolo Pass Road (FR 18). Follow FRs 1825 and 1825.100 to the Ramona Falls Trailhead, or take FRs 1828 and 1828.118 to Top Spur Trailhead. For an easy access off OR 35, turn west onto Cooper Spur Road and follow FR 3512 through the Cloud Cap–Tilly Jane Historical District to the trailheads near Cloud Cap Inn.

A clockwise tour from Timberline Lodge passes beneath the ski lifts to visit alpine forest and meadow and spare, open slope. Mount Jefferson commands the view to the south. At 2.2 miles, the rollercoaster journey tops the open east ridge overlooking the rugged volcanic cut of Zigzag Canyon with Mississippi Head.

The trail then slips in and out of Zigzag Canyon, passes through Paradise Park, crosses creeks, and tags waterfall vistas. By 7.4 miles, it offers views of Slide Mountain and overlooks of Rushing Water Creek. The Sandy River crossing follows; cairns mark the route.

Approaching Ramona Falls (10.2 miles), the route briefly follows Old Maid Flat, a lahar (a ridge of rock and debris) formed during a Mount Hood eruption some 200 to 250 years ago, now clad by lodgepole pine. The falls is a beauty, broad and spreading, splashing over moss-capped basalt.

At 13.3 miles, the Muddy Fork requires two stream crossings, but the overhead view rewards with Hood, Yocum Ridge, Sandy Glacier, and McNeil Point. Much of the way, the trail tours old-growth hemlock and true fir forest with lichen-brushed tree trunks.

The trail then switchbacks below McNeil Point, gains overlooks of the Lost Lake Basin, and rounds meadow bowls and seasonal ponds. At the Cairn Basin rock shelter (19.4 miles) the trail forks: the trail to the left continues the circuit to Eden Park; the right fork shortens the hike by 0.4 mile.

Beyond Elk Cove, the creek headwaters often house broken blue-glacier chunks. Views build to feature Washington's Mounts Adams and Rainier, the Langille Glacier and Crags, a ghost forest, Barrett Spur, the Hood River Valley, and Cloud Cap Inn.

At Cloud Cap Saddle Campground (27.5 miles), fill the water jugs because water sources become few. A detour east finds Cloud Cap Inn. The

Timberline Trail resumes, bypassing a stone shelter en route to the crossing of Lamberson Spur—the highest point on the trail (elevation 7,320 feet).

The trail continues its rising-dipping course. At 38.3 miles, the water level of White River may suggest an upstream crossing. But because the washout during the 1998 spring runoff may still impact this crossing for years to come, it is a good idea to phone ahead to learn of any closures or reroutes.

Beyond the White River, the PCT (North) and Timberline Trail merge. A leg-taxing, loose sand trek follows as the trail ascends the dividing ridge between the White and Salmon river drainages. At the plateau, hikers overlook the desolate headwater bowl of White River Canyon. Here, the last eruptions some 200 to 250 years ago buried the forest. Over time, wind and rain have uncovered a few crowns and upper limbs of the historic trees.

From the ridge, the trail continues west, crossing the headwater drainages of the Salmon River, touring open, wildflower-dotted slopes and patchy, snag-pierced alpine forest to return to the lodge at 40.7 miles.

26 | BADGER CREEK TRAIL

Distance: 12.2 miles one way
Elevation change: 3,100 feet
Difficulty: Strenuous
Season: Spring through fall
Map: USFS Mount Hood, Badger Creek Wilderness
For information: Dufur Ranger Station

This popular creekside trail explores the southeast arm and heart of 24,000-acre Badger Creek Wilderness. The glacier-carved canyon boasts a transition forest, blending both east and west and high- and low-elevation species. The southeast extension of the wilderness houses a drier habitat of white oak and ponderosa and white pine with a grassy, annual-sprinkled floor. With a gain in elevation, hemlock and true fir forests command the stage. From late June through July, the wilderness meadows have colorful wildflower blooms.

Cradled in the creek's headwater bowl is Badger Lake, tree-rimmed and dammed. A slope of silver snags and scree rises above one side, but the dam steals from the natural setting.

Good roads access the southeast trailhead. From OR 35 north of Barlow Pass, turn east onto FR 48, following it toward Rock Creek Reservoir. Or, from US 197 at Tygh Valley, turn west at the sign for Rock Creek Reservoir; the county road becomes FR 48 at the forest boundary.

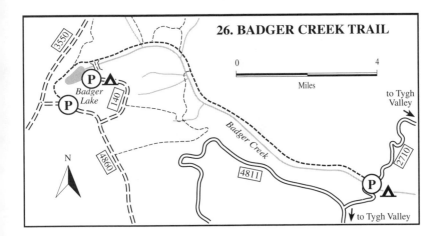

26. BADGER CREEK TRAIL

East of the reservoir, turn north off FR 48 onto FR 4810 and follow FRs 4810 and 4811 north and west to reach FR 2710 in about 3 miles. Turn right for Bonney Crossing Campground. The trail begins across from the camp, where FR 2710 crosses Badger Creek; park at the campground.

Following the north bank of Badger Creek upstream, the journey begins amid Douglas fir, oak, and pines. A rocky savanna claims the higher slope. The early miles of the journey afford the best acquaintance with Badger Creek. Upstream, the trail offers only tree-filtered views.

The 3-mile mark finds a small, lupine-dressed, creekside meadow. With uphill switchbacks, the trail tours a drier slope, and by 5 miles, the trail slips even farther from Badger Creek, losing all views of it.

The rise in elevation introduces a true midelevation Cascade forest of Douglas fir and hemlock with a few cedar, spruce, Pacific yew, and maple. At 7 miles is the Post Camp Trail Junction; the junctions are all well marked. Beyond it, the Badger Creek Trail passes a nice campsite overlooking the creek.

At 7.6 miles is the Cut-off Trail Junction; stay on the creek trail, which serves up peaceful travel. After 9.5 miles, the trail again affords limited creek views. Although the trail crosses numerous small drainages, the tour remains dry during all but the heaviest runoffs.

At 10.5 miles, a 0.1-mile side trail crosses the footbridge over Badger Creek and continues upstream to quiet Badger Camp, which is also accessed via forest road. Following the road uphill finds the main portion of the campground above man-made Badger Lake.

Bypassing the camp spur, the Badger Creek Trail ascends from the broad canyon bottom to the primary lake access at 11 miles. Beyond it, the trail travels a choked fir-spruce forest.

At 11.3 miles, a regal spruce with a split trunk marks the end to the choked forest. Gaps in the tree cover extend limited last looks at Badger Lake. By 11.8 miles, huckleberry bushes border the open-cathedral path. The trail then narrows, becoming rocky as it nears the trailhead on FR 4860 (a high-clearance-vehicle road). Round-trip hikers return as you came.

27 | CLACKAMAS RIVER TRAIL

Distance: 7.8 miles one way
Elevation change: 400 feet
Difficulty: Moderate
Season: Year round, except during low-elevation snows
Map: USGS Fish Creek Mountain; USFS Mount Hood
For information: Estacada Ranger District

The pulsing, clear waters of the Clackamas Wild and Scenic River, a side trip to an unexpected waterfall, and remnants of old-growth splendor recommend this tour. In spring, when water levels are high, kayakers and

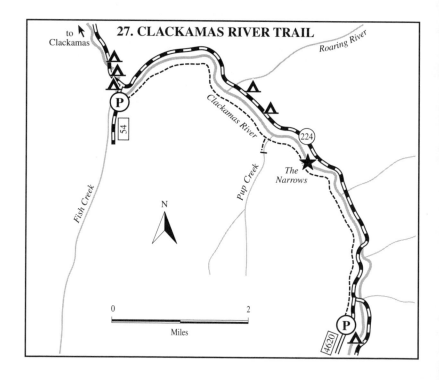

27. CLACKAMAS RIVER TRAIL

Osprey nest

rafters ride the watery trail of the river. The footpath itself is open to hikers only, closed to horse and mountain bike use.

This trail follows the southwest bank, touring a low-elevation ancient forest with brief sections of postharvest and postfire second growth and utility-corridor meadows. The rolling route alternates from the slope to the river bench, offering river overlooks and approaches. Scattered, primitive camps welcome day hikes of various lengths. Mostly, the trail escapes the intrusion of nearby OR 224.

From Estacada, go southeast on OR 224, entering Mount Hood National Forest. Near Fish Creek Campground, turn right onto FR 54 to find the marked trailhead and a large, developed parking area near the bridge. To reach the trail's southeast terminus, stay on OR 224 and turn right onto FR 4620 for Indian Henry Campground. The trailhead lies opposite the camp.

From FR 54, an upstream journey tours a mixed old-growth forest. For a brief time, the trail surrenders to an old nature-reclaimed road. Between 0.3 and 0.5 mile, the trail serves up excellent river views before entering the first climb of its roller-coaster journey.

At 1.4 miles, the trail reaches a campsite, but the noise of OR 224 intrudes. The trail is often rock studded, and a few seasonal falls streak the moss-decorated cliffs that rise above the trail. For the next mile, OR 224 remains visible. A nicer campsite occupying a beautiful river flat lies at the 2.5-mile mark. Opposite the Roaring River confluence, the trail switchbacks up the forested slope.

At 3.75 miles, nearing the descent to Pup Creek, a side trail branches to the right. This 0.25-mile footpath tours the forested bench overlooking Pup Creek before taking a switchback up the slope to a falls vista point. Pup Creek Falls captivates with its 200-foot showery drop that begins as a 100-foot veil and feeds into a tall, spreading, tiered falls and then a shorter basalt-hugging drop.

From the falls spur, the Clackamas River Trail continues upstream with a stepping stone crossing of Pup Creek; beware: the stones can be slippery when wet. For plotting round-trip day hikes, Pup Creek signals the midway point.

Past the creek, the trail traverses a long utility corridor with an open bracken fern meadow and alders at the fringe. At 4.4 miles, look for an osprey nest atop a riverside tree. Ahead stretches a nice, rolling forested tour above the river.

At 4.7 miles, a side-creek crossing leads to a pleasant campsite on a forested bench overlooking the river. Another utility corridor follows, before switchbacks descend to an overlook of the Narrows—a basalt-rimmed river channel (5.2 miles). Beyond it, a campsite welcomes a picnic lunch or a riverside stay.

The trail then passes through a mature cedar grove interspersed by fir and hemlock, a second-growth forest, and yet another utility-corridor meadow to arrive at an area of scenic cliffs and ancient forest. At 6.3 miles, the trail passes beneath a ledge and behind a ribbony intermittent falls.

Where OR 224 rounds below but out of sight of the trail, the noise from a generator intrudes. A fire-culled forest of smaller trees next claims the trail; a few charred monarchs carry the tale. After a footbridge crossing at 7.3 miles, the trail climbs and wraps around a forested slope to the FR 4620 trailhead.

28 | SHELLROCK TRAIL– ROCK LAKES LOOP

Distance: 13.8 miles round trip
Elevation change: 1,000 feet
Difficulty: Strenuous
Season: Late spring through fall
Map: USGS High Rock, Fish Creek Mountain; USFS
  Mount Hood
For information: Clackamas Ranger District

This sometimes rugged, roller-coaster trail visits mountain lakes and a high meadow and tops Frazier Mountain (elevation 5,110 feet). The mostly shaded trail tours forest of both western and mountain hemlock and Douglas and true fir.

The trail snags brief but splendid looks at Mount Jefferson; Olallie Butte; Mount Hood; and Washington's volcano line-up of Adams, St. Helens, and Rainier. Other vistas include Serene Lake and the headwater drainage of the South Fork Roaring River below Indian Ridge.

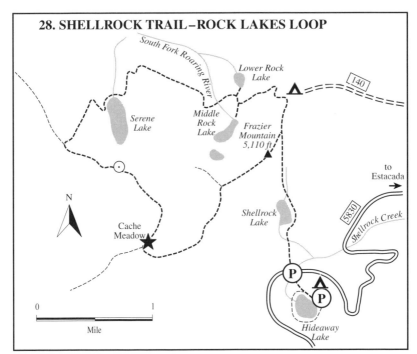

28. SHELLROCK TRAIL–ROCK LAKES LOOP

Lake basin visitors and overnighters will want to come well supplied with insect repellent, especially for trips following the snowmelt. Early season hikers may have to contend with downfalls on the route.

The trail begins at Hideaway Lake. From Estacada, go southeast on OR 224 for 25 miles and from there, take FR 57 east for 7.4 miles. Turn left onto FR 58, followed by another left in 3.1 miles onto FR 5830. In 5.3 miles, go left on the campground entrance road, FR 5830.190, to reach the camp and trailhead in 0.2 mile.

The hike rounds the northwest shore of Hideaway Lake to reach the Shellrock Trail junction in 0.2 mile. It then travels a low forested rise above the lake, skirts a meadow, and crosses FR 5830 reaching an alternative trailhead and parking area for the Shellrock Trail at 0.6 mile. A large, open harvest unit with small evergreens, bear grass, and huckleberry claims the next 0.4 mile.

The trail reenters a full forest for a short, mild descent to Shellrock Lake, a beautiful, large lake at the base of Frazier Mountain's forest-and-scree slope. Go right, crossing the outlet creek to round the lakeshore.

From the camp flat at 1.5 miles, follow the route angling uphill to the right. This steep, rugged segment, sometimes rocky and marshy, works its way up the inlet drainage. At 2.4 miles, the trail arrives at a T-junction, the start of the loop tour.

A left begins a clockwise tour along the abandoned jeep track heading toward Cache Meadow. High-elevation trees, open, rocky stretches, and volcano vistas mark the loop. By 2.7 miles, the trail begins touring a full forest thick with huckleberry atop Frazier Mountain.

At 3.25 miles, turn left for Grouse Point Trail, leaving the dirt lane. A footpath resumes with a hefty forest descent to enter moist Cache Meadow (4.25 miles). Where the meadow path fades, curve right to enter forest and find a lean-to shelter. The blazed trail then continues along the meadow's forest fringe.

At the unmarked three-way junction at 4.4 miles, take the fork to the right to continue the loop; do not cross the creek. The trail strings along the forest–meadow fringe to 4.75 miles, where it climbs away. At 5.4 miles, it tops and tours a ridge.

A detour into the small cut at 5.6 miles finds the finest vista of the hike—a four-volcano view with Mounts Hood, Adams, St. Helens, and Rainier. Deep in the basin rests oval Serene Lake; a rugged cliff outcrop towers above it. The loop skirts the cut and follows the ridge for a slow descent.

At the 6.3-mile junction, go right to enter the Serene Lake basin. In 1 mile, the trail reaches a superb lakeside campsite with a table. The loop travels left to cross the outlet. Ahead, a low rise separates the trail from the lake; spurs branch to the water.

The trail next tours a steep slope marked by forest and talus stretches. Cedars claim the moist drainages. At 9.5 miles, the trail crosses the South Fork Roaring River, a log and rock crossing.

At 9.7 and 10 miles are the short spurs to Lower and Middle Rock Lakes, respectively. Lower Rock Lake is a good-sized, shrub-and-forest-rimmed lake below Indian Ridge. The large, deep Middle Rock Lake rests below a steep, rugged flank of Frazier Mountain.

Beyond the lakes, a wider trail continues uphill to primitive Frazier Campground (11.25 miles). Tables, grills, and pit toilets serve campers and hikers. From there, the loop heads uphill to the right along the closed jeep track indicated to Cache Meadow. Where the loop closes at 11.4 miles, go left following the 2.4-mile Shellrock Trail to end the hike.

29 | TABLE ROCK WILDERNESS TRAIL

Distance: 17.5 miles round trip or a 12-mile shuttle
Elevation change: 3,600 feet
Difficulty: Strenuous
Season: Spring through fall
Map: BLM Table Rock Wilderness access map and brochure
For information: Salem District BLM

This hike explores a 5,750-acre island of protected forest on a tableland feature rising above the heavily cut Molalla River drainage. The rugged terrain, the vegetation changes, and the sharp reliefs of the basalt outcrops and crests unite to create a rewarding wilderness tour. In spring, the rhododendron blooms particularly recommend the hike.

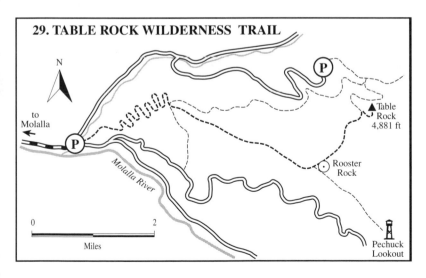

29. TABLE ROCK WILDERNESS TRAIL

N

to Molalla

Molalla River

Table Rock 4,881 ft

Rooster Rock

Pechuck Lookout

0   2
Miles

Where the trail claims the Table Rock summit (elevation 4,881 feet), views span the Cascade volcano chain from the Three Sisters in the south to Washington's Mount Rainier in the north. Far-reaching views toward the Willamette Valley and Coast Range complete the panorama.

The hike travels a segment of an old Indian-pioneer route that once linked the Willamette Valley to eastern Oregon. In recent years, the Youth Conservation Corps has rehabilitated the route. Campers should pack in stoves because open fires are strongly discouraged in this fragile wilderness.

From Molalla's city center, go east on OR 211 for 0.6 mile and turn right onto South Mathias Road. In 0.3 mile, turn left onto South Feyrer Park Road. At the T-junction in 1.7 miles, turn right onto South Dickey Prairie Road, staying on it for 5.3 miles. There, cross over the river via South Molalla Road and go 12.8 miles to reach the Middle Fork–Copper Creek Road junction.

For the lower trailhead, go right reaching the Old Bridge Trailhead in 0.1 mile. For the upper trailhead, go left on the gravel Middle Fork Road, heading uphill for 2.7 miles. There, turn right onto Table Rock Road. The trailhead is just before the rock-slide and road closure at about 4.6 miles. The upper trailhead allows for shuttle hikes and a shorter round-trip tour to the Table Rock summit (6.5 miles).

Beginning from the lower trailhead, hikers sign on for a hefty uphill haul to the summit. Initially, the trail passes through a forest of big Douglas firs with a classic low-elevation understory mix interrupted by patches of bracken fern.

By 2.5 miles, the trail is touring a drier slope. In an open meadow, hikers overlook the Molalla River drainage. The trail then crosses the "Old Jeep Road" Trail and continues climbing, returning to a richer forest.

For the most part, the grade is steady, marked by a few steeper stretches. Where the trail traces the ridgeline, thick patches of rhododendron crowd the path. At 5.3 miles, the grade eases as the trail rolls along the upper ridge, passing through forest and open, rock studded flats. Hikers obtain views of the Three Sisters and Mount Washington to the distant southeast and the Molalla River drainage below.

At 6.3 miles is an unmarked junction. The faint trail ahead continues to Pechuck Lookout. The trail to Table Rock climbs uphill to the left, crossing over the open saddle flat near Rooster Rock.

The trail then crosses to the opposite side for a steep, forest descent. Where it bottoms out in a shrubby meadow below Rooster Rock, thimbleberry, nettles, bracken fern, and false hellebore shower into the path, hiding it from view. Continue rounding to the left, traveling a line where the meadow and forest meet; the route passes a small camp flat at 6.8 miles.

The trail next climbs through forest to follow a semiopen ridge toward the base of Table Rock. By 8 miles, views of Mount Jefferson and Table Rock with its striking, vertical-ribbed basalt greet the hiker.

At the small, open camp flat at 8.25 miles, the path to Table Rock heads uphill straight ahead, while the one to the upper trailhead descends to the left. Both are unsigned.

At 8.5 miles, a grand Cascade Mountain vista begins to unfold with Mounts Jefferson and Washington, Three Fingered Jack, and the Three Sisters. As the trail tops the tableland, the crowns of Mounts Hood, Adams, and Rainier join the lineup, with Mount St. Helens completing the show.

Round-trip hikers, return as you came. Shuttle hikers, return to the camp flat at the foot of the rock and take the downhill path to the upper trailhead. The route adds new perspectives on Table Rock as it rounds the base, touring a forest-shrub corridor to pass over a rock jumble below the cliffs.

The trail next descends through forest, skirting a lower rock feature and contouring the hillside. Where it comes out at the former trailhead at 11 miles (abandoned because of the slide), follow the flagged route along road and through forest to skirt the slide and come out at the new trailhead (12 miles). Future plans call for a formal mile of trail to replace this stretch, but until then, this is the hike.

30 BULL OF THE WOODS– PANSY LAKE LOOP

Distance: 7.2 miles round trip
Elevation change: 1,900 feet
Difficulty: Moderate
Season: Late spring through fall
Map: USFS Bull of the Woods Wilderness/Salmon-
 Huckleberry Wilderness
For information: Estacada Ranger District

This trail tours an ancient forest, collects volcano and wilderness vistas en route to and while at Bull of the Woods Lookout (elevation 5,523 feet), strolls wildflower-spangled ridgeline saddles, and visits modest, shallow mountain lakes.

Use of this area dates back to the 1880s and included hunting, fishing, prospecting, and partaking of the health benefits of Bagby Hot Springs. A 75-mile trail system explores the wilderness.

From Estacada, travel southeast on OR 224 for 25 miles to the junction of FRs 46 and 57. There, follow FR 46 south for 3.4 miles and turn right on FR 63. Go 5.5 miles and again turn right, following FR 6340. Remain on FR 6340, bypassing the Dickey Creek Trailhead turn in 2.6 miles, and in another 5.2 miles, bear right onto FR 6341. The trailhead is on the left in 3.4 miles, with parking for up to ten vehicles located across the road. Much of the route is paved.

The trail enters the wilderness, touring a rich forest of Douglas and true fir and western hemlock. The good earthen path shows a comfortable, climbing grade.

Past the hiker register at 0.3 mile, the forest shows a thick midstory of rhododendron and vine maple. At 0.75 mile, the trail crosses a side creek just above a small falls.

At the nearby junction, go left for the loop. A detour downhill to the right visits Pansy Basin Camp in 0.1 mile and continues left into forest to arrive at a dry wildflower meadow and a square-on vista of a rock-slide slope on Pansy Mountain Ridge (0.25 mile).

Forgoing the detour, at 0.8 mile hikers arrive at the loop junction; climbing uphill to the left begins a clockwise tour, which crosses the often-dry drainage from Dickey Lake and steadily ascends, touring a full forest of small-diameter, high-elevation firs.

At 1.4 miles lies the 0.1-mile spur to Dickey Lake, downhill to the right. It is a scenic, green pool at the foot of Dickey Ridge. The loop continues, passing through a brief meadow patch before returning to the high-elevation forest. Quick switchbacks then lead to the trail junction at 2.1 miles. For the

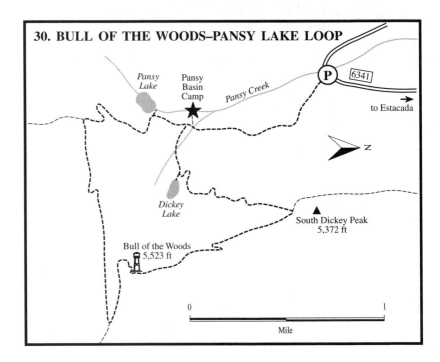

30. BULL OF THE WOODS–PANSY LAKE LOOP

Mount Jefferson vista

loop, bear right, angling uphill. Where the trail passes above talus slopes, it offers window-views of the Collawash drainage.

At 2.4 miles, the trail tops a saddle with views down the Dickey Creek drainage. A secondary spur to the left finds the first open view of Mount Hood. As the trail passes below and along the ridge, hikers snare additional looks at Hood along with Mount Jefferson—bookends to a view that includes Olallie Butte, Big Slide Mountain and Basin, and the Elk and Welcome Creek drainages.

At 3.1 miles, the trail arrives at the lookout, built in 1939. Views sweep the Mount Hood–Mount Jefferson expanse and broaden to include looks at Mother Lode, Battle Ax, Silver King, and Pansy Mountains.

The Welcome Lake Trail then continues the loop, descending through a full forest of big fir and hemlock with a huckleberry-dominant floor. At the 3.75-mile junction, the loop follows the Mother Lode Trail to the right.

The descent traces a long contour across the steep, forested slope. At 4.3 miles, some cedars enter the mix, and forest gaps offer views of Mother Lode Mountain. In 0.5 mile, the trail offers a final look at Mount Jefferson. At the Pansy Lake Junction, go right.

The trail now descends a mostly scree and talus slope into the basin. A side-arm ridge offers a Pansy Lake overlook. At 5.8 miles, going straight continues the loop; bearing left visits shallow Pansy Lake. A forest-shaded campsite sits near the outlet.

From the 5.8-mile junction, the loop continues toward FR 6341, soon returning to a full forest. Where the loop closes at 6.4 miles, retrace the original 0.8 mile to the trailhead.

31 HENLINE MOUNTAIN–HENLINE FALLS TRAILS

Distance: 5.4 miles round trip *(mountain)*; **1.6 miles round trip** *(falls)*
Elevation change: 2,700 feet (mountain); 400 feet (falls)
Difficulty: Strenuous (mountain); easy (falls)
Season: Late spring through fall (earlier for falls hike)
Map: USFS Willamette, Bull of the Woods Wilderness/
  Salmon-Huckleberry Wilderness
For information: Detroit Ranger District

These hikes of contrasting difficulty introduce two sterling features in the prized Opal Creek area, a vast uncut tract threaded by pristine blue-green waters. The mountain hike offers a rewarding climb to a false summit of Henline Mountain with views of the rugged, forested canyon. Henline Falls is a 60-foot veil on a steep side tributary that feeds into the Little North Fork Santiam. Next to the falls, a tunnel harkens to the mining history of the area.

From OR 22 at Mehama (about 25 miles east of Salem), turn northeast

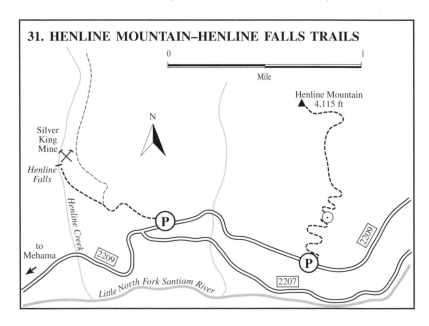

31. HENLINE MOUNTAIN–HENLINE FALLS TRAILS

on FR 2209 for the Little North Fork Recreation Area and bear left at the Y-junction at 16.6 miles to remain on FR 2209. The falls trailhead is on the left in another 0.2 mile at the barricade for FR 301 and has parking for a pair of vehicles. Proceed 0.6 mile farther on FR 2209 to find the mountain trailhead at the base of a road cut; parking is roadside.

The **Henline Mountain Trail** strikes uphill next to the trail register for a steady, sometimes rocky climb up the steep spur ridge to Henline Mountain. The hike tours an uncut, but fire-culled Douglas fir forest, hinted at by the even-sized 1- to 1.5-foot-diameter trees.

Pikas may animate the scree slope that is traced by the trail at 0.3 mile. The next scree patch serves up the first view, a look out the Little North Santiam River drainage. Afterward, switchbacks advance the tour.

Detours onto the trailside rock outcrops at 0.7 and 0.9 mile offer grand overlooks of the Little North Santiam, Elkhorn Valley, and the neighboring ridges. The headwater drainages in Opal Creek Wilderness enhance the view.

At 1.2 miles, the forest shows a more open canopy introducing a floral change, including the appearance of rhododendron, but the forest again fills out before the climb intensifies at 1.6 miles. As it rounds the ridge to the north, the trail flattens. A couple of vista openings precede the turn onto the slope above the Stack Creek drainage (2.2 miles). True fir grow along the upper trail reaches.

A rocky switchback assault then completes the climb to the crest and the former lookout site (elevation 4,115 feet). From here, the 360-degree panorama features Henline Mountain, the mouth of the Opal Creek drainage, the Little North Santiam River drainage, Elkhorn Valley, and the area's rugged slopes, deep canyons, outcrops, and cliffs. The return from the former lookout site is as you came.

The **Henline Falls Trail** begins at the barricade on FR 301. It slips into forest to bypass the barrier then pursues the former road for a gradual ascent. Where FR 301 broadens and curves at 0.5 mile, turn left off the road and proceed into forest, coming to a junction in 50 feet. Small signs mark the paths: straight ahead leads to Henline Falls; uphill to the right, the Ogle Mountain Trail climbs for 2.5 miles and 2,000 vertical feet along the canyon slope to end at the forest boundary. For the selected hike, continue forward.

An alder gateway frames this trail entering a hemlock-fir forest. Mid- to late April finds Oregon grape and lilies in bloom. The trail's climax is an exciting, up close side-vista of the multidimensional Henline Falls, where a wind-whipped droplet veil overlays the cliff-skipping waters.

Dark cliffs create a scenic corner cradling the falls, and the tunnel of the old Silver King Mine penetrates one wall. Intrepid hikers armed with flashlights may venture inside the tunnel. Expect wet feet and crickets.

Backtrack to the trailhead or check out the Ogle Mountain Trail.

32 | RED LAKE–POTATO BUTTE HIKE

Distance: 8.5 miles round trip or a 6.6-mile shuttle
Elevation change: 600 feet
Difficulty: Moderate
Season: Late spring through fall
Map: USGS Breitenbush; USFS Olallie Lake Scenic Area,
  Mount Hood
For information: Clackamas Ranger District

This hike offers a sampling of the 11,000-acre lake-peppered region along the north-central Cascade Crest known as Olallie Lake Scenic Area. It visits lakes and ponds, tours midelevation forests and prime huckleberry patches, and offers an area overlook from atop one of the low cinder buttes that contribute to the bumpy skyline of the scenic area.

With the great number of lakes, lakeside solitude is always within striking distance, but early season hikers should come prepared for mosquitos. In the fall, this hike finds favor with the berry picker. *Olallie* is an Indian word for berries.

This trail leaves from Lower Lake Campground. From OR 22 at the west end of Detroit, turn north onto FR 46 at the sign for Breitenbush, Elk Lake, and Olallie Lake. For the best route into the area, go 22.3 miles and turn right onto FR 4690 at the sign for Olallie Lake Scenic Area. At the T-junction in 7.8 miles, turn right onto FR 4220 to reach Lower Lake Campground in another 4.3 miles. A marked trailhead and day parking are found along the campground loop road. Consult the USFS map for directions to FR 4600.380, which is off FR 46, if you plan a shuttle hike.

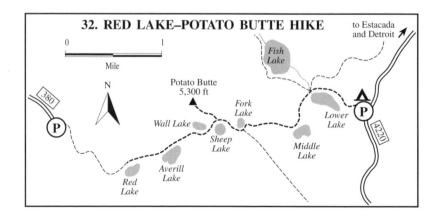

The hike begins in a forest of true fir and hemlock. At 0.25 mile is Lower Lake. This beautiful 16-acre lake with a depth of 73 feet is the deepest lake in the scenic area.

Numerous openings along the bank invite lake enjoyment and angler access. Where the trail leaves the lake at 0.5 mile is a junction: the trail to the far right leads to Triangle Lake and Olallie Meadows; the trail straight ahead goes to Fish Lake; and the one to the left finds Averill Lake and Red Lake, the hike's destination.

The open-cathedral trail to Red Lake is rock studded with rises and dips. Atop the rise at 1 mile, hikers discover Middle Lake, a small pond to the left; a talus slope rises above it. As the trail rounds Middle Lake, it offers looks across the shallow waters and up the basin at a small rocky butte.

Soon, the trail passes through a grassy meadow patch with a lily pond just beyond. At 1.8 miles is another shallow, forest-rimmed pond with a campsite near the trail. Beyond is a junction: a left leads to the Pacific Crest Trail; right continues the hike to Red Lake.

The trail to Red Lake rounds shallow Fork Lake—the first of five in a line-up of larger lakes. Along the shore of Sheep Lake (2.1 miles) is the marked trail junction to Potato Butte. This 0.75-mile spur can be added now or on the return trek.

The Potato Butte spur meanders through an open lodgepole pine forest. Because the trail hasn't been maintained in several years, hikers can expect some logs to clog the way. At 0.3 mile, the trail rounds a small, seasonal pond, after which it climbs rapidly in true "go-for-it" fashion.

Before long, small-diameter fir, pine, and hemlock rise from the butte's red cinder slope, and boulders litter the upper butte reaches. Gaps in the tree cover afford looks at Mount Jefferson to the south.

At 0.6 mile, the trail tops the mile-high feature and follows its rim to the summit vantage for a 180-degree view overlooking the forested expanse of the Breitenbush drainage to the north. Olallie Butte barely appears in the northeast corner of the vista; Sisi Butte Lookout is due north.

Forgoing the Potato Butte spur, the Red Lake trail rounds the large water body of Sheep Lake, which has a scenic peninsula and affords a view of Twin Peaks where the trail leaves the lake. Within 0.1 mile, the hike reaches Wall Lake, which rivals Sheep Lake in size. Averill Lake appears at 3.1 miles, with nice, little-used campsites along its shore.

Ahead, keep an eye out for the side trail to Red Lake on the left; it is unmarked, and the lake is well secluded by forest. Near the turn, a silver stump with a couple of protruding nails hints at a one-time marker. Although much smaller than Averill, Red Lake is an enticing hideaway, with a single-party campsite just off the spur.

Round-trippers, return as you came; shuttle hikers, continue downhill to FR 4600.380, passing through a rich forest of lichen-covered, large-diameter fir and hemlock.

33 PAMELIA LAKE–GRIZZLY PEAK HIKE

Distance: 10.4 miles round trip *(must secure a limited-entry pemit from Detroit Ranger District before arriving)*
Elevation change: 2,700 feet
Difficulty: Moderate
Season: Late spring through fall
Map: USFS Mount Jefferson Wilderness
For information: Detroit Ranger District

This relaxing, old-growth tour visits a good-sized, though shallow mountain lake and claims the summit of Grizzly Peak (elevation 5,799 feet). Grizzly Peak affords perhaps the best up close and square-on view of Mount Jefferson anywhere to be found. Views along the way include the Pamelia Lake Basin, the North Santiam drainage, Mount Hood, and Three Fingered Jack.

Even with the limited-entry permit system in place and controlling visitor numbers, hikers should still minimize the length of their stays and opt for day hikes instead of overnight outings.

From Detroit, go 11.8 miles east on OR 22 and turn left onto FR 2246, Pamelia Road. Or, from the community of Marion Forks, go 4 miles northwest on OR 22 and turn right. Follow FR 2246, a paved and gravel route, for 2.7 miles to the trailhead parking area at road's end.

Paralleling Pamelia Creek upstream, this trail travels a dark, shadowy old-growth forest, entering Mount Jefferson Wilderness at 0.25 mile. At 0.9 mile, the trail reaches a trampled bank overlooking a series of cascades and a small pool. Pamelia Creek is a clear, white-green water spilling between richly vegetated banks. Soon, more light penetrates the forest, and the buffer between the trail and the creek broadens.

A corridor of adult-high rhododendron next ushers hikers along the way, but the bushes disappear before the trail junction at 2.25 miles. Here, the path straight ahead finds the lakeshore in 100 yards, the one to the left leads to the Pacific Crest Trail, and the one to the right begins the hike to Grizzly Peak.

Opting first for a lakeside visit, hikers quickly arrive at Pamelia Lake. Rhododendron thread the forest perimeter, which is set back from the open, rocky shore. From shore, hikers secure views of Grizzly Peak and Mount Jefferson.

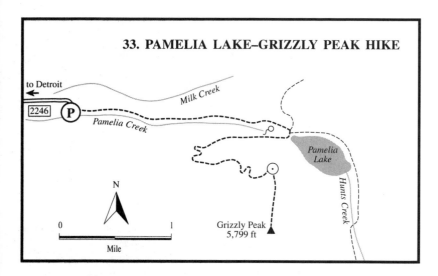

Upon returning to the 2.25-mile junction, follow the Grizzly Peak Trail as it crosses over the rocky lake outlet. The trail then swings a long, downstream switchback above Pamelia Creek before angling up the slope for a comfortable, steady climb.

Cloaking Grizzly Peak is a wonderful, multistory old-growth forest, replaced by small trees and a bounty of rhododendron at 2.9 miles. Switchbacks follow, and the setting again changes with the hike following a sunken grade through an open, high-elevation forest.

After contouring a slope with some dominant big firs, the trail takes a turn and finds an open view of Mount Jefferson and an overlook of the Pamelia Lake basin. Only a part of the lake is visible. Cathedral Rocks and a glimpse at Goat Peak complete the view.

Gaps in the tree cover extend additional looks at Mount Jefferson along with a view of the North Santiam River drainage. At the trail bend at 5 miles, the crown of Mount Hood draws attention. Afterward come limited looks at Three Fingered Jack and the Three Sisters.

From the site of the former summit lookout at 5.2 miles, a bold view of Mount Jefferson encompasses 7,000 feet of vertical relief from the Pamelia Lake basin to the summit crest. Goat Peak is fully visible, and Mount Hood rises to the north. A gap in the tree cover offers a Three Fingered Jack–Three Sisters view; another opening pinpoints Coffin and Bachelor Mountains. Although the summit mountain hemlocks deny a 360-degree vista, the vantage on Mount Jefferson excuses the shortcoming. When ready to descend, return as you came.

34 | EIGHT LAKES BASIN HIKE

Distance: 16.2 miles round trip *(wilderness permit required)*
Elevation change: 1,900 feet
Difficulty: Strenuous
Season: Late spring through fall
Map: USFS Mount Jefferson Wilderness, Willamette
For information: Detroit Ranger District

This Mount Jefferson Wilderness hike journeys to popular Marion Lake and then swings a loop through the wilderness backcountry of Eight Lakes Basin to visit a first-rate series of quiet mountain lakes. It passes through scenic old-growth stands and patches of huckleberry, bypasses freshwater springs and small wetlands, and crosses cascading streams for a fine wilderness sojourn.

From OR 22 at the community of Marion Forks (16 miles southeast of Detroit), turn east on FR 2255 (Marion Road, a paved and gravel route) to reach the trailhead in 4.5 miles. There are pit toilets at the trailhead.

The hike follows a well-trampled trail through a multistory old-growth forest for a steady ascent into the wilderness. At 1.3 miles, talus slopes carry the trail past Lake Ann; approach quietly, as waterfowl commonly hide among the lake grasses. Shore fishing is limited because of the bushy shore. Both here and at Marion Lake, respect posted camping closures.

At the 1.7-mile trail junction (the loop junction), follow the Marion Lake Trail left for a clockwise tour that arrives on the north shore between a pair of peninsulas. The return will be via the Outlet Trail. On arrival at Marion Lake at 2 miles, again keep left for Eight Lakes Basin; paths to the right lead either to campsites (no fires within 100 feet of shore) or to a tie to the Outlet Trail.

True fir and bear grass set the stage for forest travel, while the talus slope of shore extends lake views with Marion Mountain (a 2.8-mile hike from the lake), Marion Peak, and Three Fingered Jack.

As the tour continues to round the steep lake bowl some 50 feet above the shoreline, the forest grows more mixed. After cutting across a lake peninsula, the trail then arrives at the next junction (2.4 miles). Proceed forward toward the Minto Pass Trail; to the left is Lake of the Woods. Rustic signs sort out the paths.

The trail now drops steadily to arrive at the next set of Marion Lake campsites and a creek footbridge at 2.6 miles. A detour is needed to renew a lake acquaintance because the primary trail crosses the bridge and a rustic boardwalk, keeping back from shore.

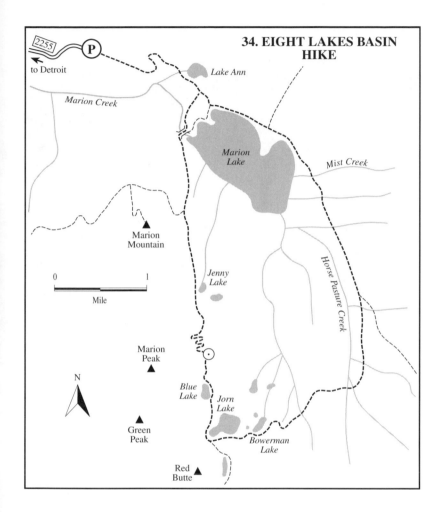

34. EIGHT LAKES BASIN HIKE

to Detroit

Marion Creek

Lake Ann

Marion Lake

Mist Creek

Marion Mountain

0   1

Mile

Jenny Lake

Horse Pasture Creek

Marion Peak

N

Blue Lake

Jorn Lake

Green Peak

Bowerman Lake

Red Butte

Additional camps and a series of springs mark off distance. At 3.4 miles comes the first of four crossings of the divided Mist Creek waters. This scenic creek descends the steep forest slope in a series of racing, white-water ribbons, and its voice well precedes a view. Planed logs span the broadest of the forks while stepping stones allow a crossing of the smaller streams. Nonetheless, some muddy strides are inevitable.

Afterward the trail rolls across an old lava flow and then swings uphill. By 4 miles, the terrain flattens with gentle forested slopes or plateaus; small boardwalks span soggy sites. At the 4.5-mile junction, follow the signed Bowerman Trail, bearing right to continue the basin loop.

The trail now rolls or climbs, with the switchback at 6.5 miles affording a look at Mount Jefferson off to the left. At 7 miles, the trail cups a small,

Marion Lake

circular, shallow pond; spurs branch to its shore. At 7.3 miles, a spur to the right leads to the one and only access to Bowerman Lake, arriving at a southern cove for a length-of-the-lake view of Mount Jefferson.

On the loop, open forest, pocket meadows with potholes, and boulder-studded fields engage travelers before the spurs break away right for Jorn Lake at 7.7 miles. It, too, showcases Mount Jefferson to the north along with a western skyline of Saddle Mountain and Marion and Green Peaks.

Above Jorn Lake at 7.9 miles, the loop veers right, following the Blue Lake Trail; the trail to the left leads to Red Butte and Mowich Lake, among other places. The loop then crosses the Jorn Lake inlet for views of the southwest arm of this lake and looks at Rockpile Mountain to the northeast before a moderate forest climb takes the trail to Blue Lake at 8.7 miles.

Here, the basin loop veers right, but the shoreline camps straight ahead beckon. Blue Lake fills the basin below Marion Peak and Saddle Mountain. A rocky point along its east shore extends views of the turquoise lake and wilderness skyline and tempts swimmers, anglers, and sunbathers.

From the lake, the trail climbs and rolls through semiopen forest, then switchbacks up the shoulder of Marion Peak to the high point of the tour. Looks at Three Fingered Jack may slow steps or suggest a detour onto a rocky knoll just off the trail.

A no-nonsense, S-bending descent follows. It begins in a windthrow area and eases by 10.9 miles where more lodgepole pines come into the forest mix. At 11.5 miles, a spur to the right leads to a meadow-ringed, shallow pond—Jenny Lake, with campsites amid the spruce; watch for the spur because Jenny Lake goes unseen from the trail. Be aware that from Blue Lake to here, the trail is dry.

Next on the loop tour, a small pond on the left heralds the 12.4-mile junction. Bear right for the downhill return to Marion Lake. Areas of talus offer rock seating, with the lake coming into view by 13.5 miles.

Cross the outlet bridge in another 0.2 mile and follow the 0.8-mile Outlet Trail downstream overlooking Marion Creek before drifting deeper into forest to close the loop. To return to the trailhead, turn left, backtracking the first 1.7 miles of the tour.

35 | COFFIN MOUNTAIN TRAIL

Distance: 3 miles round trip
Elevation change: 1,400 feet
Difficulty: Easy to moderate
Season: Late spring through fall
Map: USGS Detroit; USFS Willamette
For information: Detroit Ranger District

South of Detroit Lake, this hike climbs to the summit of Coffin Mountain. The route passes through old-growth and fire-denuded forest. In late July and early August, the summit ridge features a bear grass bloom extravaganza.

Atop the mountain stands a fire lookout tower, staffed during the summer months. The summit view sweeps the Cascade crest spotlighting Mounts Jefferson, Hood, and Washington; the Three Sisters; and Three Fingered Jack. Olallie Butte, Detroit Lake, and a neighboring former lookout site, Bachelor Mountain, add to the vista lineup. Because the trail is dry and often exposed, carry plenty of water.

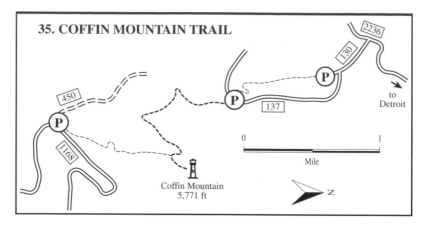

35. COFFIN MOUNTAIN TRAIL

Coffin Mountain
5,771 ft

Mile

to
Detroit

From the Detroit Ranger Station, go 7.7 miles east on OR 22 and turn south onto FR 2234. In 4 miles, turn right onto FR 1003, followed soon after by a left onto FR 2236. Go 2 miles on FR 2236 and turn left onto FR 130. Follow FRs 130 and 137 to reach the upper trailhead in about 1.5 miles. Look for the marked trailhead on the left-hand side of FR 137; parking is alongside the road.

The route to the trailhead consists of paved and good gravel surfaces. This particular hike approaches Coffin Mountain Lookout from the north. A second route arrives from the south off FR 1168.450; it involves a steeper climb on a rough trail.

Passing between two gate posts, the trail enters an old-growth stand of towering, large-diameter Douglas firs. The number of big trees quickly decreases as the forest complex shows a more mixed canopy of fir, hemlock, and spruce.

At the 0.25-mile trail junction, go left for Coffin Mountain Lookout. An unmaintained trail is visible to the right. The trail now climbs, pulling into the open where silver snags record the 1967 lightning-started Buck Mountain wildfire.

The exposed slope allows early views of the lookout and an overlook of the Blowout Creek drainage. Clearcuts mark many of the neighboring hillsides. Along the upper reaches of Coffin Mountain, mountain hemlock, noble fir, and creeping juniper frame the trail.

At the 1.25-mile junction, the path to the right journeys south across the summit ridge, before descending to the southern trailhead on FR 1168.450. A brief detour along this route finds an impressive, seasonal sea of bear grass along with southern views of the Cascade Crest. For the lookout though, go left along the ridge. Where the trail pulls into the open, the tower looms ahead.

At 1.5 miles, the trail claims the summit (elevation 5,771 feet) for a grand look at the Detroit Lake area and the Cascade volcano lineup stretching from Diamond Peak to Mount Hood. Impressive drop-away vertical cliffs claim the north and east sides of the lookout point. When ready to surrender the view, return as you came.

36 | IRON MOUNTAIN TRAIL

Distance: 3.4 miles round trip
Elevation change: 1,500 feet
Difficulty: Moderate
Season: Spring through fall
Map: USGS Echo Mountain; USFS Willamette
For information: Sweet Home Ranger District

Iron Mountain represents one of the premier wildflower showcases in the state of Oregon, bringing together ancient forest, alpine meadow, and rock ledge floral species. On July 4, the historical date marking the peak of the bloom calendar, wildflower aficionados from across the state make their annual trek to the mountain. Together with nearby Echo Mountain, this significant botanical area houses 17 species of conifer and several rare plants.

The summit (elevation 5,455 feet) affords a grand vista of the Cascade Crest and the Central Cascade neighborhood. The 360-degree view features an all-star skyline with Mounts Adams, Hood, Jefferson, and Washington; the Three Sisters; and Diamond Peak. Cone Peak, Echo Mountain, Tombstone Prairie, and Browder Ridge comprise the immediate neighborhood,

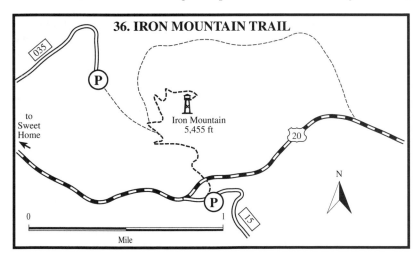

36. IRON MOUNTAIN TRAIL

035

P

to
Sweet
Home

Iron Mountain
5,455 ft

20

P

15

N

0   1

Mile

and the mountain's own rugged volcanic cliffs complete the panorama. A fire lookout sits atop the mountain. Road noise from US 20 alone disturbs the trail's tranquillity.

From Sweet Home, travel 35.6 miles east on US 20 and turn right onto FR 15 at the sign for Iron Mountain Trailhead. In 0.3 mile, an ample trailhead parking area serves hikers. The trail begins across the road from the parking area.

A forest of hemlock and true and Douglas fir with a diverse understory of bunchberry, false Solomon's seal, vanilla leaf, lupine, and huckleberry frames travel. The tall, full forest affords wonderful shade, but be careful in 0.2 mile, where the Iron Mountain Trail crosses US 20 to continue the climb.

This popular hike enjoys a wide, groomed, well-graded trailbed. The old-growth habitat engages with its big trees, jagged snags, and midstory vine maples.

At 0.4 mile, the trail rounds a large, red volcanic-rock outcrop, striking both in size and in the suddenness of its appearance. As the trail switchbacks uphill, it leaves behind many of the big trees.

At 0.7 mile, the hike draws into the open for the first view of the summit cliffs and lookout. The trail then enters a steep meadow with bracken fern and tall floral species measuring 18 to 24 inches high.

Although the slope steepens, the trail remains steady. At 0.9 mile is the Cut-off Trail junction. Here, a spur arrives from the trailhead on FR 035 (seen below and reached north off US 20 west of the main trailhead). It offers a shorter hike to the summit.

The smaller-diameter trees create an open overhead canopy. At the 1-mile junction, the Cone Peak Trail heads left and crosses over that peak's saddle. The Iron Mountain Trail heads right. Each switchback builds upon the view.

The slope grows rockier with colorful wildflower displays of larkspur, Indian paintbrush, wallflower, star tulip, lupine, columbine, waterleaf, and more. Islands of trees spot the rock and meadow slope.

At 1.3 miles, the trail swings directly toward the imposing summit cliff for a dramatic look. Where the trail enters a turn, the view features Cone Peak, Mount Jefferson's summit crown, and the lookout.

Soon, the climb adds the presence of Mount Hood along with the rounded top of Mount Adams. The 1.5-mile switchback extends a superb view of the Three Sisters overlooking Iron Mountain's ragged cliff.

Ground juniper, mountain hemlock, and small cedar hug the higher reaches. Atop the summit ridge, a detour left out onto a small point unfolds a sweeping vista of the Cascade volcano chain from Mount Adams to Diamond Peak, along with the immediate peaks and ridges and Tombstone Prairie.

The lookout affords a different perspective on the setting and the finest look at Iron Mountain's volcanic cliffs. The return is as you came.

37 | WEST BANK METOLIUS TRAIL

Distance: 14 miles round trip
Elevation change: 300 feet
Difficulty: Moderate
Season: Spring through fall
Map: USGS Whitewater River; USFS Deschutes
For information: Sisters Ranger District

This hike follows the Metolius Wild and Scenic River for an eye-engaging tour. Grassy mounds, small islands, and silvered logs accent the aquamarine water, which reveals various moods as it churns through deep trenches, riffles over stones, and slows to form deep, tranquil pools. Special fishing regulations apply to much of its length.

Along the route, hikers can tour the grounds and operations of Wizard Falls Fish Hatchery. A self-guided tour introduces the displays and holding ponds. A favorite stop is the settling pool, which collects the "escapee" fish, attracting eagles, minks, and herons.

From US 20/OR 126, 9.3 miles northwest of Sisters, turn north on County 14 toward Camp Sherman. At the junction in 2.5 miles, go left on County 1419. In another 1.3 miles, head straight on FR 1420 for Sheep Springs Horse Camp. Stay on it for the next 4 miles; the road surface becomes gravel. Turn right onto FR 1420.400 to reach Lower Canyon Creek Campground and the West Bank Metolius Trailhead in 0.7 mile. The trail leaves the end of the camp loop for a downstream tour.

The hike starts at the Canyon Creek–Metolius River confluence, a few miles downstream from the Metolius headwater. This river owes its origins to springs from deep beneath Black Butte. The water emerges at a

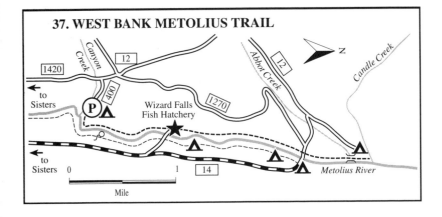

37. WEST BANK METOLIUS TRAIL

Headwaters of the Metolius

fairly constant rate of 50,000 gallons per minute, immediately launching a full-coursing river.

The hiker-only path begins along a natural stretch of the river, free from development, and closely hugs the waterway. Meadow bank; the bitterbrush-grassland slope; and ponderosa pine, fir, and western larch frame the way. On the opposite shore at 0.3 mile, a series of low, spring-launched cascades bubbles white over a mossy bank to join the river.

By 1.2 miles, a few side drainages create marshy spots that require stone-stepping negotiations, and large, vegetated islands begin to split the river's flow. Farther downstream, underwater shelves and trenches again change the river's look.

By 2.25 miles, the trail climbs toward Wizard Falls Fish Hatchery. Where the trail forks, either path leads to the hatchery parking area (2.5 miles). From there, hikers may detour for a hatchery visit, or continue the shoreline hike, which resumes just above the bridge and below the hatchery grounds.

En route to Lower Bridge (5.5 miles), the rolling trail tours a mostly dry, bitterbrush-grassland bank with some magnificent old-growth ponderosa pines. Grand river views continue.

In the fall, the rotting flesh of the spawned-out Kokanee can lend a putrid edge to the crisp morning air—part of the natural cycle. At Lower Bridge, the West Metolius Trail angles left across FR 12 and pitches down a steep slope to continue its river pursuit. The trail from here to Candle Creek is at times canted, rock studded, or eroded, causing awkward footing.

At 5.75 miles is a restful place to stop, sit on a log, and admire the water. For a brief spell ahead stretches a lusher, forested flat. In another mile, the trail arrives at a nice, fast-rushing river bend, a potential ending for the hike, but the trail continues across the Abbot Creek footbridge to Candle Creek Campground and its trailhead at 7 miles.

For a different river perspective on the return trek upstream, hikers may opt for an east-bank tour between Lower Bridge and the bridge at Wizard Falls Fish Hatchery.

38 | BLACK BUTTE TRAIL

Distance: 4 miles round trip
Elevation change: 1,600 feet
Difficulty: Easy to moderate
Season: Summer through fall
Map: USFS Deschutes
For information: Sisters Ranger District

This hike explores the prominent, symmetrical volcanic watchman overlooking the Metolius River drainage and Sisters area. The butte derives its name from its dark appearance. It is one of the most accessible summit hikes in the state, suitable for most family members. The trail is good, wide, and steady climbing with preview vistas along the way. The 1920s cupola lookout atop Black Butte (elevation 6,436 feet) is one of the few in the Northwest.

From US 20/OR 126, 5.6 miles northwest of Sisters, turn northeast on FR 11 (toward Indian Ford Campground). In 3.7 miles, turn left onto improved FR 1110, Black Butte Trailhead Road. Then, stay on it to find the trailhead and parking in 5 miles. The road is passable for conventional vehicles.

Black Butte cupola

Initially lined by a rustic, weathered-wood fence, this hiker-only trail ascends through a mixed-age pine-fir forest on the butte's west flank. Along the trail, gather tree-filtered views of Mount Washington, Three Fingered Jack, and Hayrick Butte.

Midway up, the trail travels an open shrub slope. Views to the south round up Black Butte Ranch, North and South Sister, Broken Top, Mount Washington, and Belknap, Little Belknap, and Black Craters to encourage the onward ascent.

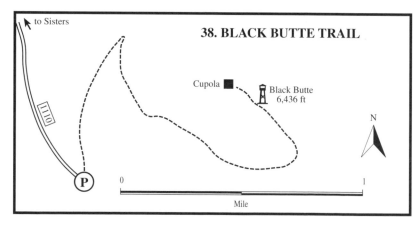

Nearing the summit, the trail enters a ghost forest recovering naturally from the 1981 lightning-fire that swept 190 acres. Here, hikers add views of the high desert plateau–Deschutes River plain and Mounts Jefferson, Hood, and Adams.

The summit ridge pulls all the vistas together and includes views of Green Ridge, Suttle Lake, and the Metolius Basin. Identification signs near the cupola introduce the key panoramic features. The return is as you came.

39 | PATJENS LAKE LOOP TRAIL

Distance: 6 miles round trip *(wilderness permit required)*
Elevation change: 500 feet
Difficulty: Easy
Season: Summer through fall
Map: USFS Mount Washington Wilderness
For information: McKenzie Ranger District

This minimally demanding trail is ideal for family hikes. The circuit passes through a semiopen forest, bypasses a couple of long, narrow meadows; and visits the shores of the three shallow lakes composing Patjens Lakes. The hike concludes along a forested bench overlooking Big Lake. Although not a vista hike, the tour does offer views of Sand Mountain, Mount Washington, the Three Sisters, and Hoodoo and Hayrick Buttes. Mostly, though, it is a relaxing, rolling, dry-forest tour.

From US 20 at Santiam Pass, turn south at the sign for Hoodoo Ski Area onto FR 2690, Big Lake Road. In 0.9 mile, turn left staying on paved FR 2690 and continue straight for another 3 miles, bypassing Big Lake Campground to reach the trailhead on the right-hand side of the road. The road ends ahead.

The hike begins paralleling FR 2690 southwest, traveling an open forest corridor to the loop junction at 0.2 mile. A counterclockwise tour begins to the right; the good earthen path shows a minimal grade. Along the tour, hikers can witness forest succession as the small firs gradually replace the lodgepole pines.

Hikers may be lured aside where the trail tours the forest fringe to a narrow, 0.4-mile-long wet meadow, which has rich, knee-high grasses, a buffer of blueberry bushes, and a cross-stitching of silver logs. Larger firs and hemlocks rise above the trail. At 1.5 miles, the trail comes to a junction: a right leads to Cayuse Horse Camp; the path straight ahead continues the loop with a climb.

Gaps in the tree cover offer looks northwest at Sand Mountain Lookout.

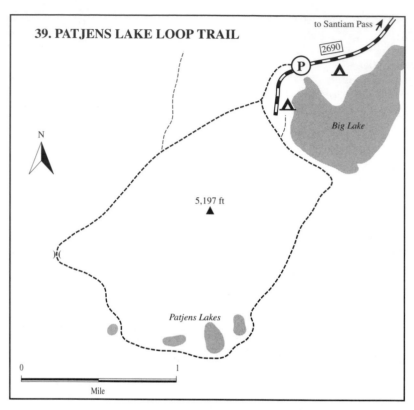

39. PATJENS LAKE LOOP TRAIL

to Santiam Pass

2690

P

Big Lake

N

5,197 ft

Patjens Lakes

0   1

Mile

At 1.75 miles, where the trail enters Mount Washington Wilderness and crosses a saddle, hikers snare quick looks at Mount Washington and the Three Sisters. The route then descends through drier forest and open bracken fern patches.

At 2.7 miles, the trail is next door to an oblong, shallow pond ringed by meadow. In another 0.5 mile, the trail rolls up to the first of the Patjens Lakes. A short spur leads to this shallow, circular lake situated at the foot of a low, unnamed, forested butte.

Tracing the forest fringe alongside another long, scenic meadow, the trail tags the second Patjens Lake at 3.5 miles. Along the west shore, a cross-lake view finds Mount Washington as it peeks over the forest rim. In another 300 yards, the path to the right continues the loop; the one to the left leads to the last of the Patjens Lakes, the smallest of the lake bodies.

A dry, mixed-forest flat next claims the trail for a semiopen tour. At 5 miles, an unmarked, although maintained, trail branches right, while the loop continues straight ahead to tour the forested bench along the southwest shore of Big Lake. Hoodoo and Hayrick Buttes overlook the lake basin, and small bays scallop the shoreline.

Big Lake and Hayrick Butte

Where the trail forks at 5.5 miles, the loop trail bears left to circle behind the shoreline rise. The downhill path to the right leads to the walk-in camp and a nice view of Mount Washington in 300 yards. A forest tour brings the loop to a close at 5.8 miles. Bear right to return to the trailhead.

40 | McKenzie River National Recreation Trail

Distance: 26.5 miles one way
Elevation change: 1,800 feet
Difficulty: Moderate
Season: Spring through fall
Map: USFS Willamette, McKenzie River National Recreation Trail brochure
For information: McKenzie Ranger District

This first-rate addition to the national recreation trail (NRT) system visits cold water springs, Clear Lake, the Upper McKenzie Wild and Scenic River, exciting river falls, ancient forest, and lava flows. Some 3,500 years ago, lava spillage from Nash Crater dammed the ancient McKenzie River and continues to influence the present-day river, a major tributary of the Willamette River.

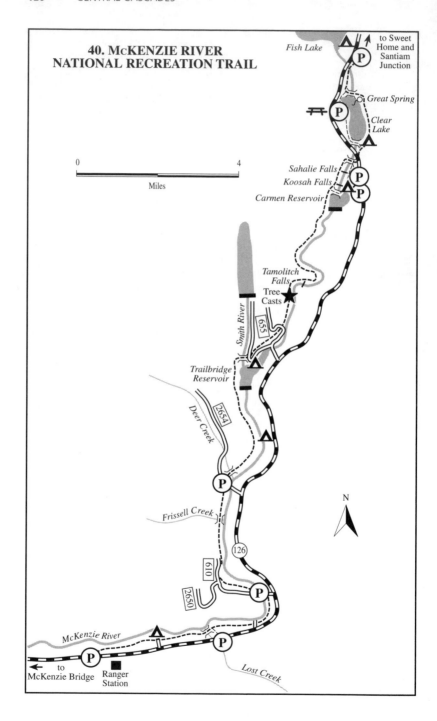

**40. McKENZIE RIVER
NATIONAL RECREATION TRAIL**

Fish Lake

to Sweet
Home and
Santiam
Junction

Great Spring

Clear
Lake

0 ——————— 4

Miles

Sahalie Falls
Koosah Falls

Carmen Reservoir

Smith River

Tamolitch
Falls

Tree
Casts

655

Trailbridge
Reservoir

Deer Creek

2654

N

Frissell Creek

126

610

2650

McKenzie River

Lost Creek

to
McKenzie Bridge

Ranger
Station

Multiple trailheads off OR 126 access this linear route for a variety of shuttle hikes. A remnant of the historic wagon road that linked Central and Eastern Oregon with the Willamette Valley in the late 1800s marks the uppermost trailhead. To reach the upper trailhead, from the US 20–OR 126 junction, go south on OR 126 for about 2 miles and turn left for the Old Santiam Wagon Road. The lowest trailhead is reached 1.5 miles east of the community of McKenzie Bridge.

From the uppermost trailhead, a downstream hike heads south along the often-dry Fish Creek drainage to cross the footbridge at the head of Clear Lake. It then rounds the lake's east shore to Great Spring (1.5 miles). Announced by its mesmerizing pool with exacting reflections, this cold-water spring gives birth to the 43-degree F waters of Clear Lake and ultimately the McKenzie River.

The lake tour resumes rolling across a crusty lava flow dotted with vine maple and juniper before passing beneath stout, old-growth Douglas firs and rounding below Coldwater Cove Campground. Past the campground, the NRT traverses an older flow through fuller forest, bearing left at the junction to cross OR 126 at 4 miles.

From the McKenzie River footbridge, the NRT travels downstream along the west shore passing black pools and ice-blue cascades. At 4.5 miles, it overlooks the 100-foot Sahalie Falls as it plunges over a lava dam. Downstream is Koosah Falls, a 63-foot, thundering split falls. The trail then reaches Carmen Reservoir at 6 miles. For a spell beyond the reservoir, the river runs dry.

At 9.2 miles, Tamolitch Falls Viewpoint overlooks a 60-foot cliff and a site where the ground burps up the river. Upstream, the porous lava deposited some 1,600 years ago by Belknap Crater sucked the stream underground. At rare times, heavy runoffs create Tamolitch Falls.

An older, overgrown lava flow with mosses and lichens, collapsed lava tubes, and tree casts next claims the trail; the tree casts are hollowed lava molds depicting the bases of trees that stood at the time of eruption. By 10 miles, the trail enters a magnificent old-growth forest with an overflowing low-elevation Cascade flora.

At 11.5 miles, the NRT crosses FR 2672.655, and in another mile, it finds Trail Bridge Campground. Here, the NRT descends toward the boat launch, crosses Smith Reservoir Road and the Smith River footbridge to resume travel along the west slope above Trail Bridge Reservoir, another small reservoir.

A long forested stretch follows, and the McKenzie River is now much larger. At times, noise from OR 126 intrudes. At 16.6 miles, the trail crosses Deer Creek Road, briefly touring a logged-over slope, before reentering the rich ancient forest. In another mile, the NRT crosses alder-lined Frissell Creek.

Young firs and alders precede the arrival at FR 2650.610, where the NRT follows the road left for 0.2 mile. Foot trail returns for an ancient forest tour back to the river at 18.6 miles. At the river, OR 126 intrudes when a guard rail and road cut replace the natural bank, but the river remains engaging.

At 19.9 miles, the NRT heads left across the McKenzie River on the FR 2650 bridge to tour the southeast bank downstream. This relaxing, forested stretch is mostly within striking distance of the river, until the NRT gets pinched up to the highway. There, it passes a turnout and travels an abandoned paved road for a short distance before returning to ancient forest. At 21.6 miles, the trail crosses Belknap Springs Road, and at the 22.4-mile junction, the river trail proceeds straight.

As the NRT nears Lost Creek, it enters one of the finest segments of the entire tour. Here, a rich, multitextured deciduous-evergreen forest encloses the trail, while a thick spongy moss cloaks the floor. Ahead, a log footbridge spans fast-rushing Lost Creek to reach a picnic site on the opposite shore.

At 24 miles, the trail crosses over the entrance road to Paradise Campground; Paradise is a scenic, forested riverside campground. From there, the trail vacillates between OR 126 and the river, remaining in forest and crossing residential access roads to arrive at trail's end at 26.5 miles.

41 | BLACK CRATER TRAIL

Distance: 7.6 miles round trip *(wilderness permit required)*
Elevation change: 2,300 feet
Difficulty: Moderate to strenuous
Season: Late spring through fall
Map: USFS Three Sisters Wilderness
For information: Sisters Ranger District

This rugged-climbing route claims the summit of Black Crater (elevation 7,251 feet) at the site of a former lookout for a striking, up close vista of snowy-faced volcanoes and stark lava flows. North Sister and Mount Washington rise up as imposing next-door neighbors. Westward views applaud the Mount Washington Wilderness Area; eastward views overlook much of Central Oregon. Clear days find Washington's Mount Adams visible to the far north.

This is a dry trail, so carry plenty of water. The upper mountain reaches are exposed, and the demands of the trail offer a good workout.

From the US 20–OR 242 junction at Sisters, go west on OR 242 for 11 miles to reach the marked trailhead and parking area on the left-hand side of the road. Be alert on this winding route. If you pass Windy Point, you've gone too far.

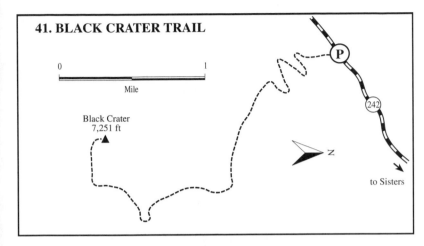

41. BLACK CRATER TRAIL

0   1

Mile

Black Crater
7,251 ft

242

to Sisters

With a straight uphill charge, the hike enters the Three Sisters Wilderness Area, touring a mixed forest of fir, mountain hemlock, and white and lodgepole pines. Although the initial incline eases, a persistent, climbing grade remains throughout the journey.

While the trees of this elevation are characteristically small in diameter and stature, the forest is full. Roots riddle the trail, but most are adequately embedded so as not to be obstacles. Tree-filtered views feature Mounts Washington and Jefferson and Three Fingered Jack.

After 1 mile, the trail passes through an open forest of lodgepole pines and fir, a meadowy area, and a fuller stand of mountain hemlock. Then, at 1.7 miles comes a brief climbing burst, before the trail settles into a switchbacking mode. In another 0.5 mile, the trail offers the first open views of the hike presenting the nearby volcanic peaks.

Ahead, the trail crosses over to the northeast-facing slope, making a brief descent above a bowl-like depression. A lupine meadow spills into the bowl, while forest shapes its rim.

An ashy floor and open forest now characterize the tour. At 2.3 miles, the trail offers a look at the summit destination. Afterward, the trail briefly rolls with easy dips and rises. When it again climbs, hikers gain looks at Black Butte.

The tour then undergoes a character change at 2.8 miles, passing from a forest hike to a mountain hike. As the trail crosses the open, high-meadow slopes, it offers eastern views of Black Butte, Smith Rock, and the high desert north of Bend. Red and black cinders blanket the upper crater.

At 3.3 miles, the trail switchbacks through a patch of small mountain hemlock and whitebark pine. Where it tops the summit ridge, east-west views greet the hiker. Here, too, comes the first bold look at North Sister, featuring the snowy volcano, the craters at its foot, and the extensive lava flow spilling from its flank.

In another 0.5 mile, the trail tops Black Crater at the site of a former lookout. This lofty post overlooks the peak's blown-out bowl, which often cradles snow well into summer.

Rising up at the heart of this Central Cascade volcanic country, Black Crater offers a prized 360-degree view. The Three Sisters, Black Butte and the Metolius River drainage, Dee Wright Observatory and the expansive flow atop which it sits, and Belknap and Little Belknap Craters along with the peaks of the Cascade Crest amply reward the climb and suggest a lingering stay. Return as you came.

42 | SCOTT MOUNTAIN LOOP

Distance: 10.4-mile loop *(wilderness permit required)*
Elevation change: 1,300 feet
Difficulty: Moderate
Season: Summer through fall
Map: USFS Mount Washington Wilderness
For information: McKenzie Ranger District

This popular trail journeys away from broad, shallow Scott Lake to top cinder-crowned Scott Mountain (elevation 6,116 feet) for a lofty panorama. It then loops back through forest and along lava flow. Views of the Mount Washington, Mount Jefferson, and Three Sisters Wildernesses contribute to the outing.

To reach the trailhead, from the OR 126–OR 242 junction east of the community of McKenzie Bridge, drive northeast on OR 242 for 15.8 miles and turn west for Scott Lake, proceeding straight for the Benson Trailhead at road's end in 1 mile. An alternate route is OR 242 southeast out of Sisters to the Scott Lake turnoff.

Follow the wide Benson Trail as it climbs away from the Scott Lake area, passing through an open-cathedral forest. Where the trail begins to contour a slope, find fuller forest and a comfortable, graduated ascent.

At 1.1 miles, spurs branch to shoreline campsites at Benson Lake, an attractive, good-sized mountain lake that makes an ideal first backpack for youngsters. Beyond Benson Lake, the trail climbs, tracing a drunken course through forest. A few auxiliary ponds and vernal pools are passed before the trail swings up a bouldery slope. More vernal pools, meadows, and small ponds dot the plateau at 2 miles; seasonally, mosquitoes can annoy.

At 2.2 miles, a rustic signpost shows the left fork to Tenas Lakes; the Benson Trail proceeds forward. With the main water body of Tenas Lakes just a 0.1 mile away, spur left for a lake visit before continuing on to the summit. Tenas Lake is a captivating, mostly outcrop-rimmed lake with a

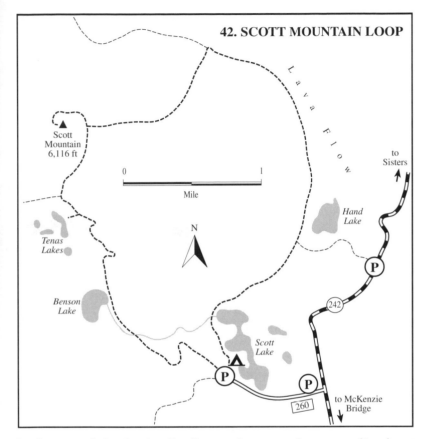

42. SCOTT MOUNTAIN LOOP

Lava Flow

Scott
Mountain
6,116 ft

to
Sisters

0   1

Mile

N

Hand
Lake

*Tenas
Lakes*

P

*Benson
Lake*

242

*Scott
Lake*

P

P

260

to McKenzie
Bridge

log jam completing its rim. Smaller ponds pepper the surrounding forest
but require cross-country exploration.

Back on the summit chase at 2.4 miles, hikers skirt a reflection pond
before arriving at the next junction in 0.2 mile. Here, hikers depart the
Benson Trail, which heads left for The Knobs. Continue forward for Scott
Mountain, soon snaring views of the mostly bald, reddish summit with
islands of trees and exposed rock.

At the mountain's base (3.2 miles), the summit trail arcs left at a large
boulder; ignore the side trail that extends beyond the boulder to the right.
In another 0.1 mile, the secondary trail seen to the right is the Hand Lake
Cutoff Trail (the loop junction). Although no sign points it out from this
direction, small trail signs guide hikers arriving via the cutoff. Make a note
of this junction and push on to the summit before taking the loop.

Just to the right at 3.6 miles, a forest gap offers looks at Three Fingered
Jack, Mount Jefferson, and just the tip of Mount Hood with Hayrick and
Hoodoo Buttes in the foreground. Now on the north flank, a brief beltway

of big-diameter trees precedes the steep climb into a congested, runty forest. The next views are of Mount Washington and Belknap Crater.

The trail then swings up through the summit meadow, expanding the view west, south, east, and north. Views span three wildernesses—Mount Washington, Mount Jefferson, and the Three Sisters—and encompass forest, flow, high peaks, and wilderness-dotting lakes. The trail tops out at 4 miles.

When the summit discovery is complete, backtrack to the loop junction at 4.7 miles and turn left on the Hand Lake Cutoff Trail, which receives irregular maintenance. Its meandering descent passes through hemlock-fir forest interspersed by small meadow clearings of berry bushes and heather. Grouse are abundant.

Tenas Lake

Generally, the path receives enough traffic to be easily followed, but a few low cairns aid hikers. At 5.4 miles, the trail skirts a low, rocky ridge, after which the tour loses most of the meadow breaks and is shaded by taller forest. In another mile, skirt a small pond, and at 6.9 miles, meet the Hand Lake Trail and go right for the loop. To the left is Bunchgrass Ridge.

By 7.2 miles, the grade eases, and the forest grows sunnier as the trail passes at the western edge of a bumpy, crusty lava flow dotted by mature trees and snags. Views are of Mount Washington, Belknap and Black Craters, and Three Sisters.

At 8.4 miles, the trail veers away from the flow to travel a gentle forested slope, and at 8.6 miles, a spur descends to the lake plain of Hand Lake. By late summer, the lake waters recede, leaving only a trace pond at the base of the flow, but the site is adequate to support osprey. The Hand Lake valley rolls out a fine, textured view: open water, wet meadow, grassy plain, forest, and peak.

Next on the loop, bypass a spur to OR 242 at 8.8 miles, continuing forward for Scott Lake. This junction also marks the return to lodgepole pines and semisunny forest travel. Next comes a pair of prairie meadow crossings as the trail traverses the gentle terrain between Hand and Scott Lakes.

At 9.8 miles, approach the first lobe of Scott Lake, which also recedes in summer, leaving a muddy ring and broadening meadow shore. The trail then rolls up the base of the forest slope before returning to shore at some primitive campsites at 10.2 miles.

To complete the tour, beyond the first of the encountered walk-in sites, bear right into the woods to locate and follow a broad trail. Keep right, bypassing spurs to sites and shore to emerge at the trailhead (10.4 miles).

43 | TAM McARTHUR RIM TRAIL

Distance: 8 miles round trip *(wilderness permit required)*
Elevation change: 1,300 feet
Difficulty: Moderate
Season: Summer through fall
Map: USFS Three Sisters Wilderness
For information: Sisters Ranger District

This hike travels the forested slope above Three Creek Lake to tag Tam McArthur Rim, a prominent ridge spanning east from Broken Top. Views building along the way string together an impressive line up of Cascade volcano peaks. From the rim, hikers gain an incredible up close look at Broken Top and South Sister in their chiseled wildness of snow, ice, and

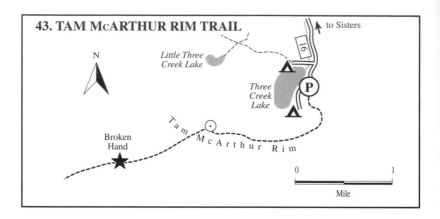

lava. The vertical cliff of the rim itself provides a dizzying spectacle with Three Creek and Little Three Creek Lakes dotting the forested basin below.

From US 20 at Sisters, turn south on Elm Street/FR 16 heading toward Three Creek Lake. In 13.7 miles, the pavement ends. In another 0.8 mile, bear right, staying on FR 16 to reach Three Creek Lake in 1 mile. The trailhead is on the left-hand side of FR 16 across from the dam.

From the basin floor, Tam McArthur Rim rises steeply. As the trail climbs, the enclosing forest quickly swallows views. Soon the trail tops a saddle and begins mounting the rim proper. At 0.5 mile, openings reveal the crowns of Middle and North Sister. A few feet beyond, the view broadens to include the Cascade volcano chain stretching north to Washington's Mount Adams. Belknap and Black Craters and Black Butte add to the view.

Where the trail takes a turn at 0.7 mile, the emphasis of the view changes to the abrupt cliff of Tam McArthur Rim. Atop the rim (0.8 mile), the trail enters an open pumice flat where hikers are first treated to views of Broken Top and South Sister. Both the forest and trail are generally open.

By 1.4 miles, detours to the rim's edge deliver sweeping views of the Tam McArthur–Three Creek Lake area, North Sister and the volcanoes to the north, and the desert plain to the northeast. Just ahead, reddish-hued Broken Top commands the view, joined by Mount Bachelor. The route grows rockier with some loose sand.

At 2 miles, the trail crosses the end of a pumice bowl that sweeps to the edge of the rim. Where the trail tops a slight rise, the view southeast is of Newberry Crater. Beginning at 2.4 miles, side trails lead to an exciting bluff vista (2.6 miles). From this jut, the view applauds most of the Oregon landmarks named earlier, while adding a dramatic look at and down Tam McArthur's own rugged, fast-dropping cliff. Below sparkle Three Creek and Little Three Creek Lakes.

Although some may choose to end the tour at the bluff viewpoint, the trail continues along the rim. At 2.75 miles, it veers south passing across a

Tam McArthur Rim

pumice flat strewn with volcanic rock and ringed by whitebark pines. The view features Mount Bachelor, Tumalo Mountain, and Cayuse Crater.

At 2.9 miles, the trail tours a cinder flat, followed by a boulder field. In another 0.5 mile, the hike skirts the base of a snowfield that often swallows the trailbed early in the hiking season. The route then climbs to the saddle of Broken Hand, a cinder ridge affording grand looks at the dominating beauty of Broken Top and the Three Sisters.

Lava bombs—football-shaped molten rocks cooled while in flight—dot Broken Hand. At 4 miles, the trail reaches the end of the cinder ridge, marking a good ending and turnaround place for the hike.

Beyond this point, the trail grows rockier and more rugged. Where the path fades, stay along the rim. To the southwest, the Cascade Lakes area soon comes into view. By 4.25 miles, all hikers lacking the climbing skill and equipment to travel this mountain terrain of rock and ice should turn back. The return is as you came.

44 | GRASSHOPPER–CHUCKSNEY MOUNTAIN LOOP

Distance: 10.9 miles round trip
Elevation change: 2,000 feet
Difficulty: Moderate
Season: Late spring through fall
Map: USFS Willamette, Three Sisters Wilderness
For information: Blue River Ranger District

Chucksney Mountain (elevation 5,760 feet) rises at the center of a peninsula of land tucked between the Waldo Lake and Three Sisters Wilderness Areas. The circuit tours wonderful low-elevation and midelevation old-growth forests and open meadows before tagging the summit for views of the Three Sisters, their wilderness, the South Fork McKenzie and Roaring River drainages, and Hiyu Ridge. The return follows Box Canyon Creek.

From OR 126 about 5 miles east of the Blue River Junction, turn south onto FR 19 toward Cougar Reservoir. Stay on FR 19 for 25.6 miles and turn right, entering Box Canyon Horse Camp. Follow the road spur to the right to reach the trailhead and parking area for the loop tour.

The hike begins on the Grasshopper Trail touring a rich, full, ancient fir-hemlock forest with vine maple, bracken fern, bunchberry, and Oregon grape. Above the horse camp, go right, bypassing the Box Canyon Trail (which branches left) to reach the Chucksney Mountain Loop Junction at 0.3 mile.

A right begins a counterclockwise mountain tour with a steady uphill

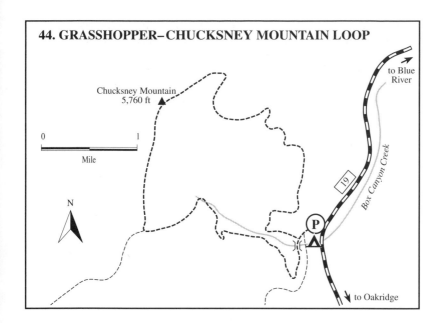

44. GRASSHOPPER–CHUCKSNEY MOUNTAIN LOOP

climb from Box Canyon. At 0.6 mile, dogwoods claim the midstory. After switchbacks, the trail contours the slope.

At 1.25 miles, a dry opening offers limited views to the east overlooking the Roaring River. Changes begin to occur in the forest mix, with enormous trees lining the intermittent drainages.

The trail next rounds above a tributary drainage emptying into the Roaring River. At 2.75 miles, it reaches a rock outcrop with limited views to the northeast and South Sister. Beyond it, a wealth of vanilla leaf fans the trail.

At 3.2 miles, a couple of switchbacks lead to the top of the ridge, but the trail again dips for an easy forest stroll. The transition between low-elevation and midelevation forest is now complete, with true fir, hemlock, and white pine forming the canopy. Small meadow patches (one with a vernal pool) interrupt the forest stands.

By 4.1 miles, the trail eases into a climb of Chucksney Mountain Ridge. Seasonally dry meadow spills beneath and between the forest stands. The trail then offers a look back over the area traveled and with a switchback tops the ridge (5.1 miles).

The summit ahead is little distinguished from the remainder of the ridge, except that its open top overlooks the rock-outcrop rim. The primary view is to the east; views west overlook the tops of small trees.

Neighboring rises on Chucksney Mountain, the forest-meadow-shrub drainage at its eastern base, the Three Sisters, and the Roaring River drainage shape the vista. To the east, one clearcut at the wilderness boundary contrasts the otherwise protected, forested expanse.

Western views improve as the trail dips from the summit to traverse the broad meadows of the mountain's west flank. Views are of the Augusta Creek drainage and the forest-and-cut patchwork on Hiyu Ridge, which houses Grasshopper and Lowell Mountains.

The trail continues at about the same height as it rounds the slope, passing through meadows and forest stands. At 6.1 miles, a tight stand of mountain hemlock steals views. At 6.6 miles is the junction with the Grasshopper Trail; go left for the loop traversing the steep slope to return to a habitat of old-growth fir.

The trail wraps and descends the slope passing through a meadow-shrub drainage at 7.4 miles, where lodgepole pines are again present. Wild strawberry abounds. Then, in full forest, the trail travels above the Box Canyon Creek drainage for 0.25 mile before crossing the often-dry upper drainage via a footbridge.

At 9.9 miles, the trail takes a switchback working its way to Box Canyon Horse Camp. In another 0.6 mile, it crosses Box Canyon Creek. By September, the creek is quite small as it slips over rocks. Ahead the loop closes. Continue along the trail above the horse camp to return to the trailhead.

45 | MINK LAKE BASIN HIKE

Distance: 23.8 miles round trip *(wilderness permit required)*
Elevation change: 600 feet
Difficulty: Strenuous
Season: Summer through fall
Map: USFS Three Sisters Wilderness
For information: Bend Ranger District

This hike swings north through Three Sisters Wilderness, stitching together an engaging series of backcountry lakes, passing meadow clearings, and crossing over the Cascade Crest before tossing a loop around Mink Lake. The route is favored by horseback riders and hikers; the setting is one for relaxation. Vistas are restricted to the lakes, and travel can be dusty.

From Bend, take Cascade Lakes Highway southwest for 46 miles and turn right on FR 4635 for Cultus Lake Campground. Go 1.7 miles, and continue right for 1 mile on FR 4635.100 to where it dead ends; it becomes a jeep trail past the campground. Dirt turnouts tucked amid the fir and pines serve hikers; turnaround space is limited. The signed trail departs the left side of the jeep trail. If camped, start the hike near site 35, joining the tour at the initial trail junction (0.1 mile).

From the primary trailhead, follow the foot trail through woods, bypassing the campground spur to skirt the north shore of Cultus Lake. The mixed pine–grand fir forest offers only tree-filtered lake views, but there are chances to spur away for closer looks. Watched over by Cultus Butte, Cultus Lake is a huge, noisy, bustling recreational water with swimming, boating, sailing, and waterskiing.

Because of a number of dead or infested lodgepole and ponderosa pines along the lake, hikers are urged to avoid smoking or building fires in this area. At 0.8 mile, side trails branch to shore and the nearby boat-to camp-sites or uphill to a compost toilet.

The hike continues straight past the Corral Lakes Trail Junction (2.5 miles) to turn right at 2.7 miles, coming to the wilderness register. The Winopee Trail now makes a gradual climb through open lodgepole pine forest or mixed forest.

A detour right at the 3.3-mile junction leads to Teddy Lakes, soon reaching the first lake, with a scenic grass-and-rush shore and thick forest rim. Rounding the lake's forested slope leads to the second mountain lake. When visiting both lakes, add 0.8 mile to the total round-trip distance.

Without the Teddy Lakes detour, the Winopee Trail keeps to its narrow,

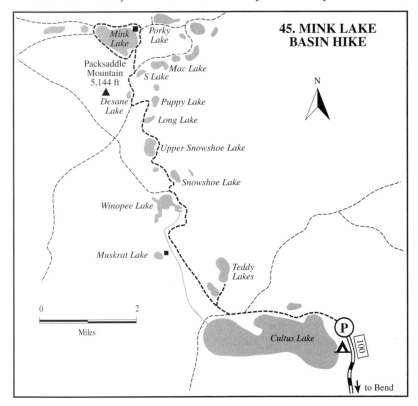

45. MINK LAKE BASIN HIKE

Mink Lake
Porky Lake
Packsaddle Mountain 5,144 ft
S Lake
Mac Lake
Desane Lake
Puppy Lake
Long Lake
Upper Snowshoe Lake
Snowshoe Lake
Winopee Lake
Muskrat Lake
Teddy Lakes
Cultus Lake
N
0   2
Miles
P
100
to Bend

Muskrat Lake cabin

forested aisle for a comfortable, modest climb. On the left at 4.4 miles is the altogether pleasant stop created by the sparkling outlet creek of Winopee Lake; shallow Muskrat Lake isolated by meadow; and a rustic, patched cabin, not considered safe for use.

The creek now guides the way upstream to its source, passing between meadow banks, open meadows, and the long sweep of Winopee Marsh. Small footbridges span tributaries.

On arrival at a larger footbridge at 6.7 miles, a trail sign tacked to a fir on the right signals the hike's turn for Upper Snowshoe Lake. The path straight ahead leads to the Pacific Crest Trail (PCT), and a side trail to the left leads to horseshoe-shaped Winopee Lake, which is mostly masked at the junction. The Winopee Lake side trail contours the basin slope, arriving at outcrops along the northeast shore of this vast, marshy lake.

The trail to Snowshoe Lake is narrower, with a moderate climb. By 7 miles, it traverses the lake bluff for unobstructed viewing of the big, deep lake. Boulder rubble claims the slope below the trail. Across the lake, outcrops and talus slopes complete the site's rugged image.

The trail next strings past ponds and meadow, and downed logs crisscross the forest floor. Upper Snowshoe Lake is at 7.75 miles. The lake is large and round with a single peninsula and a forested west ridge.

As the trail pulls away from the lake and shows a modest incline, pale green lichens adorn the tree branches. Despite the full forest, there is only partial shade. At 8.5 miles, the glare of Long Lake may be detected beyond the trees to the right, but hikers must forge their own way to it.

The main trail next reaches Puppy Lake (9.1 miles). A meadow-shrub rim distances the forest from shore. The trail then skirts meadow and lily pond before meeting the PCT at 9.5 miles. To the left is Irish Lake; turn right on the PCT toward Cliff Lake to continue the tour to Mink Lake.

A treed and talus butte overlooks Desane Lake in 0.1 mile. Beyond

Desane, the PCT makes a modest descent, bypassing a vernal pool ringed by blueberry shrubs to reach the Mink Lake Trail (9.9 miles). The hike follows the Mink Lake Trail left, but a 100-yard detour straight on the PCT adds S Lake to the bounty.

The Mink Lake Trail crosses the Cascade Crest and carries the hiker from Deschutes National Forest to Willamette National Forest. At 10 miles, switchbacks descend from the crest through forest and along meadow. The trail then tops an open ridge before its final descent to Mink Lake Basin and the loop (10.7 miles).

Turn right toward Porky Lake for a counterclockwise lake loop and to reach Mink Lake Shelter in the shortest distance. The loop contours the forested lake slope, serving up limited views and bypassing the spur to Porky Lake. Where it dips closer to the lake, find the shelter at 11 miles. Despite a few holes in the roof, the integrity of the three-sided shelter seems just fine. Do not build campfires in or within 100 feet of the shelter.

This rustic shelter looks out on Mink Lake—a lovely, big open water with a treed and rock shore, peninsulas, and quiet coves. Alder, rhododendron, mountain ash, and chinquapin are among the shoreline vegetation. Low, forested humps shape the lake bowl.

From the shelter, the loop hugs a fairly close line to shore. At 11.9 miles, pass between Mink Lake and a shallow lily pond and proceed past the right-branching trails to Junction Lake and Elk Creek Trailhead.

The basin slope steepens as the trail approaches the peninsula at 12.4 miles. Afterward, the trail climbs away from shore to shortcut across the next broad peninsula. The outcrop at 13 miles delivers a fine farewell lake view before hikers complete the loop at 13.1 miles. Backtrack the Mink Lake, Pacific Crest, Upper Snowshoe, and Winopee Trails south and east to return to the trailhead at 23.8 miles. Or, plot a course to some of the many other wilderness lakes.

46 | ERMA BELL LAKES LOOP

Distance: 8.6 miles round trip *(with all formal lake spurs)*
Elevation change: 600 feet
Difficulty: Moderate
Season: Summer through fall
Map: USFS Willamette, Three Sisters Wilderness
For information: Middle Fork Ranger District, Oakridge

This family hike rounds up the lakes tucked away in the southwest corner of Three Sisters Wilderness on the west side of the Cascade Crest in Willamette National Forest. A counterclockwise circuit passes through

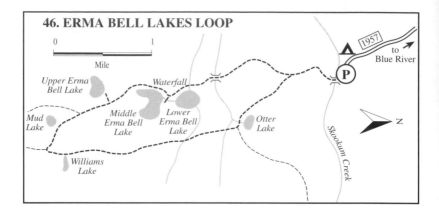

46. ERMA BELL LAKES LOOP

changing forest and meadow settings to string together all three Erma Bell Lakes plus Mud, Williams, and Otter Lakes. The loop also brushes past the northern boundary of Waldo Lake Wilderness, with its set of trails bidding for side trips. The lakes may suggest the porting of a fly rod.

From OR 126 about 5 miles east of the Blue River Junction turn south on FR 19 (Aufderheide Forest Drive) for Cougar Reservoir and go 25.7 miles. There, just past Box Canyon Horse Camp, turn left on FR 1957 and proceed 3.6 miles to Skookum Creek Campground (eight walk-in, fee sites) and the trailhead at road's end.

Descend to the footbridge over Skookum Creek at the foot of the camp and cross and register for the trail. Note that the camping at Otter Lake and the three Erma Bells is restricted to designated sites only. Pursue Skookum Creek downstream for a short spell on the slope-contouring trail. Later, the slope drops away to the drainage of the North Fork of the Middle Fork Willamette River, which feeds north out of Waldo Lake. Tall Douglas fir shade the trail.

To Lower Erma Bell Lake, the trail is wide, leveled, and groomed with an easy grade and few rocks or roots. It is intended to be a challenging barrier-free trail. At the junction in 0.6 mile, avoid the Irish Mountain Trail, which veers away left for Otter Lake. Instead, go straight for the Erma Bells and a counterclockwise loop.

At 1.1 miles, the terrain flattens as the trail enters a vibrant area of vine maple. It then descends to cross the footbridge over the Otter Lake outlet stream—a steep approach for wheelchair athletes.

A steady climb and a profusion of rhododendron precede the left spur to Lower Erma Bell Lake (1.5 miles). The trail emerges at the rocky lake ring, another difficult approach for wheelchair users. Deep and stunning blue, Lower Erma Bell claims a picturesque basin with steep forested slopes and areas of talus.

The sound of a masked inlet waterfall contributes to the lake setting.

Middle Erma Bell Lake

Stakes mark off the designated tent sites; tents must be pitched within 15 feet of the stakes.

The trail then skirts the lake, crossing the outlet and climbing the west ridge. At 2 miles, a 30-foot side path leads left to an overlook of the waterfall on the watery link between Middle and Lower Erma Bell Lakes. A forest window presents the terraced, white-icing falls spilling over a cliff of shiny black basalt. The side spur to Middle Erma Bell Lake is another 100 feet farther on the main trail.

Middle Erma is a larger, comma-shaped lake with a rolling forested basin, exposed walls of rock and shrub, and sun-gilded grassy points. Southbound, the loop skirts this lake, touring forest and traversing a low ridge showered by rhododendron.

Beyond a serene pond, at 2.8 miles, locate the 0.1-mile spur to Upper Erma Bell Lake—the smallest of the three related lakes. Its tree rim semisecludes the oval water from the main trail.

As switchbacks carry the main trail away from the upper lake, more mountain hemlock and lodgepole pines crowd the mix. At the 3.5-mile junction, proceed forward, avoiding the Judy Lake Trail to Taylor Burn Camp. The loop again contours forest slope or travels forest flats. By 3.9 miles, it serves up views of Mud Lake, a large shallow lake in the basin below. Without a formal access path, hikers must devise their own descent to this lake.

Where the trail reaches a boardwalk at 4.2 miles, take the Williams Lake Trail left (north). This trail cuts through a shrub-filled narrow meadow and open, dry forest to reach shallow Williams Lake (4.6 miles). Watch for where the main trail arcs left on arrival at the lake.

To the north stretches undulating travel with a general downhill intent. The tour is now basically a forest walk interrupted by drainage and meadow passages. The path is less traveled. After 5 miles encounter richer forest shade. Between 5.4 miles and 6.2 miles, the trail descends more sharply, sometimes wearing a channel into the terrain.

The trail again rolls for another forest-meadow mosey before descending and meeting the Irish Mountain Trail (7.1 miles). A left continues the loop to Otter Lake, soon crossing its outlet, a broadened, slow water negotiated by logs, rocks, and the occasional misstep. The trail then tours the forest of the west shore just out of reach of the lake and lake views. Near the northern end of the lake, spurs branch to shore.

Otter Lake stretches 0.25 mile, and elk frequent the surrounding area. From the northwest corner of Otter Lake at 7.5 miles, the loop pulls away, climbing and descending through forest to return to the Erma Bell Trail Junction (8 miles). A right brings this hike to an end at 8.6 miles.

WALDO LAKE TRAIL– SHORELINE TRAIL LOOP

Distance: 21-mile loop
Elevation change: 300 feet
Difficulty: Strenuous
Season: Summer through fall
Map: USFS Willamette, Waldo Lake Wilderness and
Recreation Area
For information: Middle Fork Ranger District, Oakridge

In this central Cascade region, some 12,000 years ago, a glacial cap gouged out Waldo Lake along with hundreds of potholes and other lake depressions. With no permanent inlet, the 10-square-mile Waldo Lake defies plant growth, making it one of the four clearest lakes in the world. Crater Lake, Lake Tahoe in the Sierra Nevada, and Lake Baikal in Siberia complete the list. With rocky spits, islands, and bays, Waldo Lake is a scenic destination with numerous retreats for private reflection. Cross-lake views include Charlton Butte, The Twins, Three Sisters, Waldo Mountain, Mount Fuji, and Diamond Peak.

The 21-mile Waldo Lake Trail encircles this prized water body, often traveling inland through forest. With its east-shore segment completely removed from Waldo Lake, the neighboring Shoreline Trail offers the preferred signature on the loop.

Much of the Waldo Lake Trail traces the Waldo Lake Wilderness boundary, with various side trails branching away to wilderness destinations.

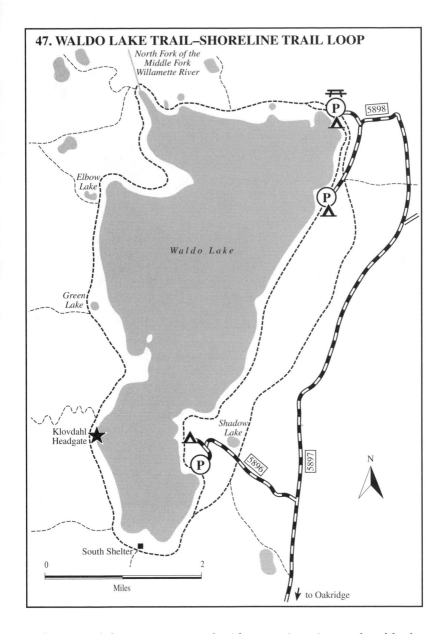

47. WALDO LAKE TRAIL–SHORELINE TRAIL LOOP

Early-season hikers must contend with mosquitos; August heralds the onset of quieter tours.

From Oakridge, travel 23 miles southeast on OR 58 and turn left onto FR 5897 toward Waldo Lake. Continue north on FRs 5897 and 5898 for

View along Waldo Lake

12.7 miles, following the signs to North Waldo Campground. Then, locate the trailhead in the upper parking lot of the North Waldo Day Use.

Rounding the lake in a counterclockwise direction, the Waldo Lake Trail travels an inland route, soon entering a massive burn. Despite the wording on an interpretive sign, this is the Charlton Fire of 1996 that scorched 10,400 acres. There is no camping here.

In its first mile, the trail bypasses a series of shallow, small ponds. At 1.6 miles is the Rigdon Lakes Trail Junction, where the lake circuit continues straight. The trail molds to the lake basin terrain, rising and dipping. Past a large pond at 2.1 miles, a Waldo Lake detour applauds the indigo lake waters over which osprey and gull soar. Soon after, the trail emerges from the fire zone.

At 3.4 miles is the North Fork Middle Willamette River. Upstream, at its lake headwaters are a gauging station, levee, beach, and primitive boat-to camp. The loop resumes through live forest with a true huckleberry–bear grass understory. The trail grows less root- and rock-bound, but narrows. The lake is close for viewing and easy access.

Approaching the peninsula at the northwest end of Waldo Lake, the trail crosses an open talus slope that plunges 30 to 50 feet to the lake. At 5.9 miles, the trail travels along and above Elbow Lake, a good-sized, shallow lake with a crook. It then bypasses a trail junction and lily pond. Moist meadow patches interrupt the rolling forest tour.

Going another 2 miles finds the junction for Green Lake, a larger shallow water located 200 yards downhill. As it continues south, the forest trail drifts from Waldo Lake and grows more rugged, with some steep rises and pitches. Small meadows and ponds lie along the way.

At 10.4 miles is the junction above Klovdahl Bay. Detouring downhill finds Klovdahl Camp and Headgate, named for the civil engineer who led a 1908 effort to divert the waters of Waldo Lake for irrigation and power projects. The legacy of the failed project is visible from this spur.

By 12 miles, the lake loop grows easier and again draws nearer to shore. In a half mile, it visits the meadow-surrounded South Shelter, an open-front overnight structure overlooking the lake.

Beyond a trailhead register at 14.1 miles is another junction: to the right stretches the long, forested route of the Waldo Lake Trail, which parallels the east shore all the way back to North Waldo Campground. To the left is the Shoreline Trail, which hugs the lake shore and ties together Shadow Bay, Islet, and North Waldo Campgrounds for the preferred return on the circuit. It visits rocky coves and points and small sandy beaches and reveals fine lake views. Either way, the loop closes at North Waldo Day Use at 21 miles.

48 | MAIDEN PEAK TRAIL

Distance: 11 miles round trip
Elevation change: 3,000 feet
Difficulty: Strenuous
Season: Summer through fall
Map: USFS Willamette, Waldo Lake Wilderness and
    Recreation Area
For information: Middle Fork Ranger District, Oakridge

This trail climbs to the summit of Maiden Peak (elevation 7,818 feet), halting at the site of a former lookout. The first 90 percent of the hike tours an undisturbed forest; the final 10 percent holds the vistas and introduces the volcanic nature of the peak.

Mountain hemlock; high-elevation firs; and lodgepole, white, and whitebark pines shade the path. Only subtle changes in the forest mix vary the tour. For the most part, it is a relaxing hike wrapped in a shroud of familiar sameness, but the steepness of the upper mountain reaches rapidly dispels this meditative quality.

The summit unfolds a grand panorama overlooking Diamond Peak to the southwest and Odell and Crescent Lakes and Mounts Thielsen and Scott to the south. Northward lie the reservoirs of the Cascade Lakes Area; the Three Sisters; Broken Top; Mounts Bachelor, Washington, and Jefferson; and Waldo, Betty, and Bobby Lakes.

From Oakridge, travel 26 miles southeast on OR 58. There, turn left at the sign for Gold Lake. Go 1.6 miles on gravel FR 500 to reach the trailhead parking turnout on the left, the trail on the right. Blue cross-country ski signs and trailhead markers indicate the Maiden Peak Trail.

The hike begins amid mountain hemlocks and lodgepole pines. For the first 0.1 mile, the trail angles up the slope above FR 500. Topping a rise, it then curves away touring a deeper forest with many firs.

Trailside mileage markers aid hikers in keeping tabs on their progress. Higher on the trees, the blue-diamond ski markers hint at the winter snow level.

The first couple of miles show a minimal grade, with the distance toppling quickly. At 1.75 miles, side-by-side logs allow a dry crossing of Skyline Creek, a year-round waterway.

Soon after, the trail reaches the primitive Wait Here Camp and a three-forked trail junction: to the left is a connector trail to the Pacific Crest Trail (PCT); to the right lies the Maiden Lake Trail, which offers a possible loop option; and straight ahead past the camp continues the Maiden Peak Trail.

The peak trail climbs steadily to the 2.3-mile trail junction. Here, it crosses over the PCT. Following the PCT to the right finds Rosary Lake; to the left is Bobby Lake.

Drawing away from the junction, the grade on the Maiden Peak Trail eases. Beyond the 3-mile marker, boulder outcrops and ridges spot the forest, which is now mostly mountain hemlock.

After 4 miles, the trail undergoes a character change, showing a steep uphill intensity, but it retains its good earthen bed free from obstruction. Ahead, tree blazes and a few cairns help indicate the path.

At 5.1 miles comes the first open view of the hike. Looks are to the south at Odell and Crescent Lakes, Redtop and Lakeview Mountains, Diamond Peak, and Mounts Thielsen and Scott. Here, too, the trail serves up its first look at the summit destination. The trail grows rockier, sandier, and more open.

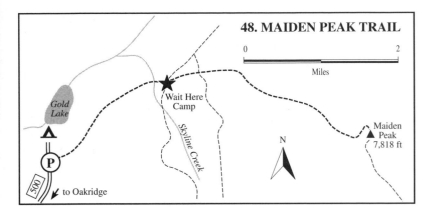

48. MAIDEN PEAK TRAIL

Gold Lake
Wait Here Camp
Skyline Creek
Maiden Peak 7,818 ft
to Oakridge
500

In another 0.2 mile, the trail is opposite a small crater bowl. While crossing to its other side finds a North Cascade vista, the trail affords similar views ahead. Spy the Three Sisters, Bachelor, Broken Top, and Mounts Washington and Jefferson, along with Davis, Wickiup, and Crane Prairie reservoirs and Waldo and Bobby Lakes.

Looking down the north face of Maiden Peak reveals some rugged, crusty red-black volcanic pillars with craggy fingers. This side of Maiden Peak is more blown out. Cinders now cap the mountain, and at 5.5 miles, the Maiden Peak summit rewards with a 360-degree panoramic view of the key Central Cascade features.

For the return trek, retrace your steps. Or add a loop, by descending the south flank of Maiden Peak to the Maiden Lake Trail and following it west and north to return to the original hike near the Wait Here Camp. Then, from there, backtrack the initial hike distance to FR 500 for a 15-mile round trip.

49 | HARDESTY MOUNTAIN LOOP HIKE

Distance: 14.5 miles round trip *(with summit detour)*
Elevation change: 3,300 feet
Difficulty: Strenuous
Season: Spring through fall
Map: USGS Mount June, Westfir West; USFS Willamette
For information: Middle Fork Ranger District, Lowell Office

Built in 1910, the Hardesty Trail is now more noted for its big trees than for its vista. Trees have nearly eclipsed the site of the former lookout. All that remains is a strained view to the north toward Lookout Point Reservoir.

This circuit ties together the Hardesty, Eula Ridge, and South Willamette Trails, often traveling through the wonder and bounty of a forest born from fire some 150 years ago. Stout Douglas firs and western hemlocks tower above the trail. Where the native rhododendron is entrenched, springtime hikers find a grand floral display. The incomparably steep Eula Ridge Trail quickly marches hikers down from the mountaintop before the South Willamette Trail carries the loop home, tracing a contour west across the base of the mountain.

From Eugene, go east on OR 58 for 20.8 miles to reach the Hardesty Trailhead on the right-hand side of the road east of Goodman Creek.

Follow the trail through a full forest with a thick vine maple midstory to the 0.2-mile junction with the Goodman Trail, and continue straight on the Hardesty Trail for a steady climb to the summit.

At the loop junction (0.7 mile), the South Willamette Trail branches left, while the Hardesty Trail heads uphill. For a counterclockwise loop, stay on the Hardesty Trail. It rounds an older cut and crosses FR 515 at 1 mile.

At 1.5 miles, the trail enters a set of short switchbacks and travels the ridge to meet FR 5835 at 2 miles. Follow the forest road to the right for 0.2 mile before resuming on foot trail and returning to the full forest of the ridge.

At 3 miles, the trail leaves the ridge and rounds the slope, encountering an abrupt transition between the full forest and a dense stand of smaller-diameter cedar and hemlock. A few rock outcrops and mossy green cliffs mark the next trail stretch. Before long, the trail returns to the ridge, taking a couple of switchbacks to reach the Eula Ridge Trail Junction at 4.7 miles.

The circuit follows Eula Ridge downhill to the left, but first stay on the Hardesty Trail to reach the summit (elevation 4,266 feet). At 4.9 miles, the Hardesty Trail bears left to claim the mountaintop, where low support columns from the former lookout remain. The deciduous bushes and evergreens allow only a limited view to the north, but the site proves a pleasant picnic stop.

To continue the loop, return to the Eula Ridge Trail (5.3 miles) and follow it downhill. This less-traveled route lacks a formal tread and mirrors the steepness of its slope for a no-nonsense descent. A wonderful hemlock forest enfolds the trail, encouraging "breathers."

By 6.3 miles, the trail is descending the backbone of Eula Ridge. In the drier, madrone-punctuated forest, openings reveal Hardesty Mountain.

At 7 miles, a more formalized trail with a cut tread and switchbacks slows the downhill pace. After the trail crosses over a couple of old forest roads, the switchbacks resume. Noise from OR 58 grows louder.

At the South Willamette Trail Junction at 8.8 miles, go left to close the loop. The South Willamette Trail (open to multiple use) rolls west, touring a forest corridor parallel to OR 58, its presence variously noted depending on the width of corridor and the forestation. Often, the tour is lush and surprisingly pleasant.

49. HARDESTY MOUNTAIN LOOP HIKE

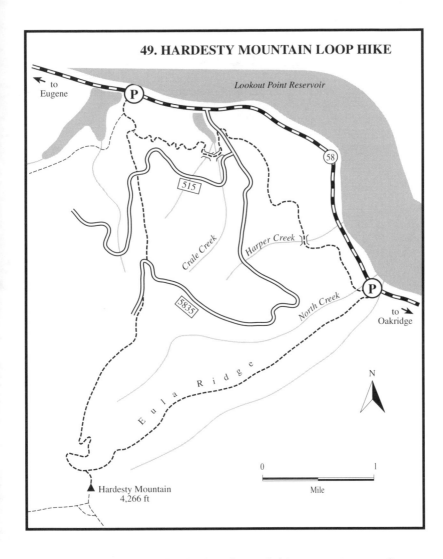

Past the Harper Creek footbridge, the trail skirts a cut site, traveling at its thick shrubby border. Then, at 11.7 miles, the route crosses over an old two-track for a comfortable forest tour to Crale Creek Road (FR 5835), at 12.4 miles.

Across the road, the trail resumes with the Crale Creek log-bridge crossing. Afterwards, it rounds the small inlet arm of Lookout Point Reservoir, wanders lush forest, crosses small drainages, and skirts a replanted private cut with vanishing views to reach the Hardesty Trail at 13.8 miles. Go right to end the hike in another 0.7 mile.

50 | TIMPANOGAS AREA LAKE TRAILS

Distance: 9.5 miles round trip *(combined distance)*
Elevation change: 700 feet (maximum)
Difficulty: Moderate
Season: Summer through fall
Map: USFS Willamette, Rogue-Umpqua Divide/Boulder
  Creek/Mount Thielsen Wildernesses
For information: Middle Fork Ranger District, Oakridge

Meadow, forest, and rugged slope border mile-high Timpanogas Lake, the hub to a system of fine, short, lake hikes. The smaller Lower Timpanogas Lake rests next door.

During an area stay, hikers can easily explore all three lake trails, beginning with the Timpanogas Lake Trail, which encircles the host lake. The other two trails venture away to June Lake, cradled in a peaceful, forested basin, and to Indigo Lake, with its incredible turquoise waters sparkling at the base of rugged Sawtooth Mountain. Longer hikes can also be crafted from the Indigo Lake area; consult the USFS map. Beware from early to midsummer, hoards of mosquitos can repel visitors; come prepared with spray and netting.

From Oregon 58, 2 miles east of Oakridge, turn south on Kitson Springs Road for Hills Creek Reservoir, go 0.5 mile, and turn right on FR 21. Follow FR 21 for 32 miles and turn left on FR 2154 for about 12 miles to enter this camp on the left. Find the trailheads in camp; it is a paved and good gravel route.

Timpanogas Lake Trail: This 1-mile loop starts from camp and tours the lakeshore. It offers views of Sawtooth Mountain and the forested ridges above Timpanogas Lake.

The overhead canopy parades Pacific silver fir, pine, and spruce; the forest mat consists of dwarf and true huckleberry, vanilla leaf, bunchberry, and prince's pine. Rockier areas sport purple penstemon, while the marshy areas sport false hellebore and shooting stars. Unfortunately, the peak wildflower season coincides with the peak mosquito season.

On the east and southeast shores, hikers encounter inlets and marshy reaches, but usually fallen logs and patches of high ground are adequate to negotiate a dry loop.

June Lake Trail: Under escort of mosquitos, we logged this trail in at 2 miles, the USFS lists it at 3 miles, and likely the truth falls somewhere in between. The trail has an elevation change of 400 feet.

From the end of the trailhead turnout above Lower Timpanogas Lake, this hike follows a closed road above the lake. The footpath begins at 0.1 mile with an uphill spurt. Initially, a midelevation fir forest frames the route.

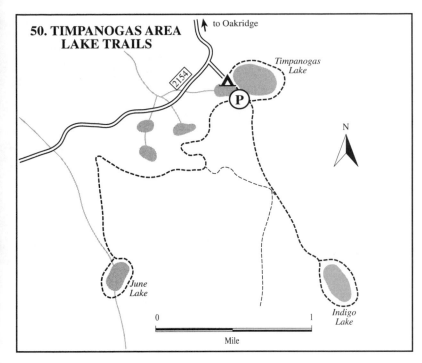

50. TIMPANOGAS AREA LAKE TRAILS

to Oakridge

2154

Timpanogas Lake

P

N

June Lake

Indigo Lake

0   1

Mile

Past a pond, the path climbs and contours a slope where lodgepole and white pines dominate a more open forest.

A small, wet-meadow drainage precedes the 0.7-mile junction for the June Lake–Indigo Lake Tie, which branches left for an opportunity to link the two lake hikes. For the June Lake Trail, continue straight.

Meadow patches intersperse stands of trees, while openings in the tree cover afford brief, limited looks at Hills Peak and Mount Thielsen. At 2 miles, the trail reaches medium-sized June Lake, nestled below the forested west and northwest ridges of Sawtooth Mountain. The return is as you came.

Indigo Lake Trail: This 1.9-mile trail has an elevation change of 700 feet. It, too, leaves from the trailhead turnout above Lower Timpanogas Lake or may be reached via the 0.8-mile June Lake–Indigo Lake Tie.

The trail travels through a forest of Pacific silver fir and Engelmann spruce with an understory of huckleberry and heather. At 0.75 mile, the trail arrives at a junction: the path ahead continues to Indigo Lake; the middle fork leads to Sawtooth Mountain in 3.5 miles; and the right fork is the tie to the June Lake Trail.

From the junction, the Indigo Lake Trail follows a sparkling tributary upstream and then laces through forest, stringing together small meadows and views of Sawtooth Mountain.

A rockier Sawtooth Mountain (elevation 7,302 feet) looms above Indigo

Timpanogas Lake and Sawtooth Mountain

Lake. A 0.7-mile trail rings the blue brilliance, touring a mixed conifer forest and crossing a scree slope. The lake is deepest below the scree slope, offering a hole for swimming or fishing; a couple of primitive campsites dot the forested shore. The return is as you came.

51 BRICE CREEK– UPPER TRESTLE CREEK HIKE

Distance: 13.5 miles round trip *(can be broken into shorter segments)*
Elevation change: 1,200 feet
Difficulty: Moderate
Season: Year round, except during low-elevation snows
Map: USFS Umpqua
For information: Cottage Grove Ranger District

At the foot of the Calapooya Mountains, this hike explores the forested slope along broad, clear-flowing Brice Creek, with a loop trip up the Trestle Creek side drainage. Brice Creek engages with cascades, pools, and picturesque swirls. Trestle Creek wins over visitors with a couple of exciting waterfalls in box-canyon settings. The rolling trail has a good bed with a few areas of loose rock and the occasional drainage crossing on stepping stones.

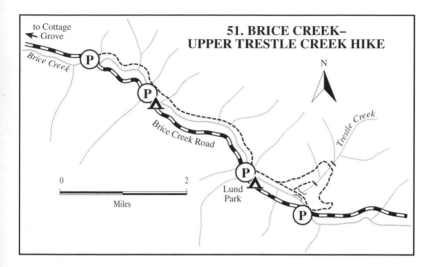

Mountain bikes may share the way on the Brice Creek Trail, but are not allowed on the Upper Trestle Creek Trail or on the spur to Lower Trestle Creek Falls because of the sensitive terrain and soft, unsuitable trailbeds.

The 5.5-mile Brice Creek Trail traces part of the Frank Bryce Trail, which provided access to the Bohemia Mining District in the early 1900s, when gold fever populated these mountain reaches. Along the trail, Lund Park was a bustling mining and freight warehouse site and an overnight wayside on the two-day journey from Cottage Grove to Bohemia Saddle.

The upstream mile of the Brice Creek Trail parallels a section of the ditch that brought water to the hydropower station at Lund Park. Trestle Creek owes its name to the flume that spanned its course.

From I-5 at Cottage Grove, take Exit 174 and go east on Row River Road for 19 miles to the Layng Junction and then continue straight on Brice Creek Road/FR 22 for another 3.2 miles to West Trailhead (the lowest trailhead), 4.5 miles to Cedar Creek Campground, 6.8 miles to Lund Park, and 8.1 miles to East Trailhead. (Find it on FR 22 as you take the turn and cross the bridge over Brice Creek.)

On a west-to-east, upstream tour, start at West Trailhead; off-road parking at the road bridge can accommodate up to 10 vehicles. The trail briefly affords Brice Creek overlooks, but after 0.25 mile, pleasing forest enfolds the tour, distancing the trail from the water.

The slope-contouring trail offers a gentle, rolling journey. Views of the charismatic waterway are mostly filtered by the tree branches. At 1.5 miles, proceed upstream. The spur to the right leads to the pedestrian bridge over Brice Creek to Cedar Creek Campground, which has vault toilets but no drinking water.

The next 2.5 miles to Lund Park present a split-character tour, first spotlighting scenic Brice Creek, then the rich forest canyon. The trail now hugs the creek course, revealing a pair of 5- to 6-foot falls (at 1.75 miles). Gravel-bar beaches and bedrock shores entice sunbather, swimmer, and angler to the water's edge. Only glimpses of the campground and Brice Creek Road deter from the natural setting.

On the second leg to Lund Park, the rich mixed forest commands attention. The trail occasionally pulls out of forest, rounding rocky slopes well above the creek. At 4 miles, a spur heads right to a second footbridge and the historic site of Lund Park, now a shady picnic ground/small dispersed campground with tables and vault toilets.

Again, keep on the upstream journey toward East Trailhead and the Trestle Creek waterfalls. The trail traces a contour some 25 feet above alder-lined Brice Creek and combines the relaxation of the forest with opportunities to admire the creek's clarity, colorful rock-and-boulder bed, and sections of white riffles.

At 4.4 miles, uphill switchbacks place the trail on a contouring course through mixed-age forest some 100 feet above the creek. At the 4.8 mile marker, cross a thin tributary and come to a junction and the first viewing of the ditch. For Brice Creek Trail, the spur to Lower Trestle Creek Falls, and a counterclockwise tour of the Upper Trestle Creek Trail, keep right. To tour the Upper Trestle Creek Trail now, head left.

For this tour, keep right, tracing the levee bank of the ditch that brought water to Lund Park for powering the machinery at the mines. Before reaching the Trestle Creek footbridge (5.2 miles), take the 0.3-mile spur left up the Trestle Creek drainage to the lower falls. Sections of this short path can be steep and uneven. Cliffs precede the box canyon, where the 50- to 60-foot Lower Trestle Creek Falls pours over a ledge to skip down the jagged rock of the cliff to a log-jammed pool.

Return to the Brice Creek Trail at 5.8 miles and cross the Trestle Creek Bridge. The confluence here may call you aside with its union of bedrock outcrops, a small gorge on Brice Creek, and the cascading arrival of Trestle Creek. The trail continues upstream to emerge at FR 22 (6.1 miles); hikers may notice claim markers showing that gold continues to play a role in area history.

To add the Upper Trestle Creek Trail and visit the upper falls, turn left and walk 50 feet along FR 22 to the trailhead on the left. This trail makes a steady ascent of Brice Creek Canyon's northern slope, taking a couple of switchbacks before the climb eases along the upper slope. The trail then passes below a massive outcrop, offers views of some magnificent old-growth trees and showings of rhododendron, and crosses a nose of the ridge (7.1 miles) to begin the slow descent wrapping into the Trestle Creek drainage.

By 7.8 miles, gain glimpses of Trestle Creek deep in the drainage below. Soon weeping cliffs replace the even-age mature Douglas fir forest, and Upper Trestle Creek Falls greets hikers. This split-level falls plummets some 80 feet from a sidewall of the box canyon. The upper falls shows a

Upper Trestle Creek Falls

droplet veil; the lower falls broadens and skips over ledges of the jet black cliff.

Follow the trail beneath the upper falls for a look through the droplet veil before drawing away from the main drainage and descending and rounding the folds of the forested slope. Side drainages reveal their own charming waterfalls/cascades. Return to the Brice Creek Trail at 8.7 miles and backtrack the first 4.8 miles downstream to West Trailhead (13.5 miles).

52 | North Umpqua Trail

Distance: 77.5 miles one way
Elevation change: 5,400 feet
Difficulty: Strenuous
Season: Spring through fall (lower parts, year round)
Map: USFS Umpqua; USFS/BLM North Umpqua Trail
brochure
For information: Diamond Lake and North Umpqua
Ranger Districts, Roseburg District BLM

This long-distance river-companion trail has its start below the Cascade
Crest at Maidu Lake. Its roller-coaster route then travels forested slope and
rocky shore, pursuing the North Umpqua River downstream to Swiftwater
Douglas County Park and the Swiftwater BLM Trailhead. En route, the trail
journeys into side canyons, visits ancient and second-growth forests, bypasses scenic cliffs and falls, and overlooks the hypnotic, blue-green host
waters.

While most hikers do not attempt the full tour, the given reason is one
of time, not offering. The trail's many access points allow for day hikes and
shorter backpacks. The USFS and BLM have divided the trail into eleven
named segments; side trails invite further exploration, and camp areas
mark the route.

Hikers will find convenient access to the trail at points off OR 138. The
easternmost drive-to trailhead is Bradley Creek Trailhead: east of the Lemolo
Lake area, proceed north off OR 138 on FR 60 and then go east on FR
6000.958 to the trail's start. The westernmost access is at the Swiftwater
BLM Trailhead: east of the community of Idleyld Park at the BLM
Swiftwater Day-Use Area, turn south off OR 138 onto BLM Road 26-3-1.1,
cross the river, and park at the trailhead on the left.

East of the Cascade Crest, hikers may access the river's headwater,
Maidu Lake, via the Miller Lake Trail (see Hike 53) to hike the full trail
distance.

From Maidu Lake, a remote trail segment journeys downstream through
the Mount Thielsen Wilderness Area, bypassing Lake Lucille in the early
miles. The trail tours a semiopen lodgepole pine forest and crosses meadows as it travels along the headwater.

At 10.1 miles, the route passes the spur to Bradley Creek Trailhead and
continues downstream. On arrival at FR 60, the North Umpqua Trail heads
north to the junction of FRs 60 and 999, where it turns west to parallel the
road on the north side of Lemolo Lake.

At 16.4 miles, the trail crosses a canal en route to Lemolo Falls, and the
next 15 miles roll out some of the trail's finest offerings. While contouring

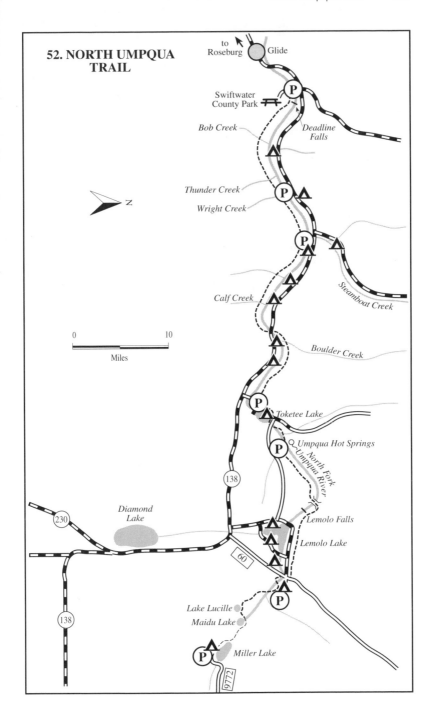

52. NORTH UMPQUA TRAIL

North Umpqua River

the wildflower-dotted open forest of the north slope, the trail overlooks a tumbling, reduced river segment marked by swirling pools, canyon bowls with 5- to 10-foot cascades, and the impressive 169-foot chute of Lemolo Falls—the most popular single attraction along the route—framed by sheer cliffs (18.2 miles).

Beyond the falls, the trail continues a high-road tour along the old-growth-forested slope bypassing rock outcrops and cliffs. It then switchbacks downhill to a bridge crossing at 19 miles. A newer trail leg now leads the way, staying closer to the river. At 19.3 miles, cross-river views find the landslide that broadened and slowed the upstream waters.

By 25 miles, scenic side creeks slice to the river. Weeping Rocks and a line-up of falls—Coffeepot, Cedar Creek, Teardrop, and Surprise—engage hikers. From the flat below Teardrop Falls, cross-river views feature the mineral-streaked cliff beneath Umpqua Hot Springs.

Upon reaching FR 3401, go right. Then, from the hot springs parking area, descend and cross the bridge. The river trail continues left (downstream), while the hot springs trail climbs steeply to the right for 0.3 mile, reaching the open-air but lean-to-covered small, steamy pool.

The steep canyon slope striped by the river trail features the classic Douglas fir–western hemlock forest common to the 2,500-foot elevation. The trail is now well above the river. Downstream from Toketee Lake (33 miles), more cut areas and utility corridors intrude on the route.

Where the trail briefly tours the south boundary of Boulder Creek Wilderness (38 miles), locate the Jessie Wright Trail and follow it across the Boulder Creek footbridge for an old-growth shoreline tour close to the river and to OR 138. At an unnamed creek west of Eagle Creek, the trail climbs and offers peeks at Eagle Rock.

At the upcoming junction, the river trail descends steeply to the left, traveling a path and old road to reach OR 138 opposite Wilson Creek (44 miles). A plaque notes the early-day homesteaders—the Wrights.

To resume the trail, cross Marsters Bridge to the south shore and follow the gravel road downstream for 600 feet; be careful of traffic on the bridge. For the next 33.5 miles, the trail rolls along the forested south canyon wall, often opposite OR 138, sometimes rounding riverside cliff. River access is limited, but the side tributaries are attractive.

At Calf Creek, the North Umpqua Trail makes use of the road bridge over the creek before rolling up and over a slight ridge to again contour above the river. The river closely companions the next leg of travel, and for a spell, the thinner forest hints at the Apple Creek Fire.

At 56.3 miles, a 5.5-mile national recreation trail segment leaves near Mott Bridge, traveling a low-level route along the river bank with nearly continuous views of the river. The trail passes moss-etched cliffs, white-bubbling side creeks, and the site of one of Zane Grey's fishing camps.

From Wright Creek at 61.8 miles, the trail again travels a "high road" through midsized forest to arrive at a side canyon housing the spectacular, quick-dropping Thunder Creek (64.1 miles). The rolling canyonside tour then continues with occasional river overlooks. The deeper forest filters out the presence of OR 138.

Nearing Bob Creek, the trail climbs to round the north shoulder of Bob Butte. It then returns to character, crossing scenic side streams and passing closer to the river. After hiking past the left-branching spur to Swiftwater County Park, come to Deadline Falls (77.25 miles). This breadth-of-the-river cascade is a watchable wildlife site where salmon and steelhead can be seen jumping the falls, June through October. It puts a final flourish on the trip before the hike ends at the Swiftwater BLM Trailhead.

53 | MILLER LAKE TRAIL

Distance: 4.25-mile loop
Elevation change: Minimal
Difficulty: Easy
Season: Summer through fall
Map: USFS Winema
For information: Chemult Ranger District

This circuit hugs the shore of Miller Lake (elevation 5,600 feet), situated in a forest pocket on the east flank below the Cascade Crest. The rolling tour passes through mixed and lodgepole pine forests and crosses moist meadow drainages, for splendid lake views with cross-lake views of Mount Thielsen, Red Cone, and Sawtooth Ridge. The lake tour also holds convenient access to the neighboring Mount Thielsen Wilderness Area.

Digit Point Campground offers hikers a comfortable base for their exploration; the facility is open from mid-June through September.

On US 97, go 1 mile north of Chemult and turn west onto improved FR 9772. Trailheads are found at the Digit Point boat launch and day-use swimming area in about 12 miles.

A counterclockwise lake tour heads southeast from the boat launch loop. The wide pumice trail normally travels just above the lake through a semiopen forest of fir, mountain hemlock, spruce, and mixed pine.

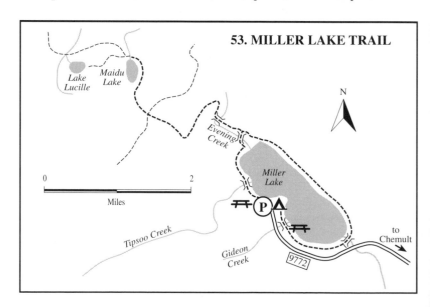

Miller Lake

Along the early part of the loop, the forest road sometimes crowds the trail. Beyond Gideon Creek, picnic tables dot an open bench where one finds easy lake access to an anchored floating dock. The view from shore features Digit Point and the blue expanse.

At 0.9 mile, the trail travels atop the 20-foot-high sandy cliffs that drop steeply to the lake. Trees cling tenuously to the eroding edge. Bald eagles may roost in the snags overhead.

Soon, the trail passes through a meadow parted by the meandering lake outlet, Miller Creek. Trails branching to the right lead to FR 9772; stay left for the circuit.

By 1.5 miles, the lake trail offers tree-filtered views of Sawtooth Ridge, Red Cone, and Mount Thielsen. Along the north shore, the forest features a few larger trees and a richer understory with prince's pine, sticky laurel, fern, and chinquapin. A few areas along shore are adequately open to allow angling, but the lake is better suited for boat fishing.

At 3.6 miles, the Skyline Trail (Maidu Lake Trail) heads northwest along Evening Creek to reach Maidu Lake in 3.25 miles. This detour proves a nice extension for hikers seeking an all-day or backpack outing. Upon entering Mount Thielsen Wilderness, the route climbs the forested slope above Miller Lake; it provides a lake overlook before crossing the Cascade Crest. The Skyline Trail then descends to midsized Maidu Lake, rimmed by low forested slopes and circled by a 0.75-mile trail.

Forgoing the trip to Maidu Lake, the Miller Lake circuit edges a grassy flat, touring close to the lapping lake waters. It then resumes its slope-wrapping, forested course tagging more inlet drainages to arrive at the day-use picnic and swim area (4.1 miles). Where the trail splits, either path leads to the day-use.

From the day-use, continue rounding shore, passing below the campground to return to the boat launch.

54 | WOLF CREEK TRAIL

Distance: 2.4 miles round trip
Elevation change: 200 feet
Difficulty: Easy
Season: Year round
Map: USFS Umpqua
For information: Roseburg BLM District

A good first hike for young family members, this short trail has fine natural appeal and concludes at a picturesque split-level waterfall. It begins at the Little River and crosses Wolf Creek to wander through a classic low-elevation Cascade old-growth forest. It halts atop a sloping outcrop for unobstructed views of the upper 80-foot falls and an overlook of the lower falls chute secluded in a rocky confine below the viewpoint.

From Oregon 138 at Glide (east of Roseburg), turn south on Little River Road (County Road 17/FR 27) and go 10.5 miles to find the paved trailhead parking lot on the right and a picnic turnout on the left, which offers additional parking and a toilet.

A crescent-shaped footbridge over the Little River launches this trail, but the south-shore cliff and the hypnotic movement of the water can delay the crossing. Where the trail branches on the opposite shore, the upstream path follows Little River for 0.2 mile to a playing field across from the Wolf Creek Civilian Conservation Center. The main trail veers away into the forest.

As the trail approaches the footbridge over Wolf Creek (0.1 mile), look left for an out-of-place 30-foot monolith amid the thick forest. Wolf Creek pulses clear over a gravelly bed, with bigleaf maples overhanging the water and vine maples crowding its shore.

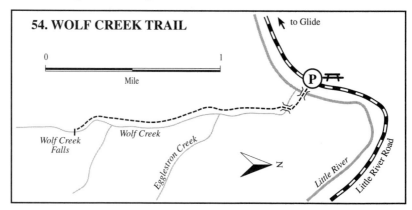

54. WOLF CREEK TRAIL

to Glide

0   1
Mile

Wolf Creek
Falls

Wolf Creek

Egglestron Creek

Little River

Little River Road

N

At 0.3 mile, a spur leads to a picnic table alongside Wolf Creek and opposite a meadowy cliff. The main foot trail continues its upstream pursuit of the creek with a few short stretches of more pronounced grade. Overall, though, the hike shows a steady, comfortable progress.

At 1.2 miles, the trail concludes along the slope opposite the upper (primary) falls—an 80-foot vertical slide, streaking the smooth face of the cliff. The lower falls segment consists of thin, racing chutes spilling over a ledge in a rocky narrow. The return is as you came.

Forest understory

55 | MOUNT BAILEY NATIONAL RECREATION TRAIL

Distance: 10 miles round trip
Elevation change: 3,200 feet
Difficulty: Strenuous
Season: Summer through fall
Map: USGS Diamond Lake; USFS Umpqua
For information: Diamond Lake Ranger District

This trail climbs to the bald summit of Mount Bailey (elevation 8,363 feet) for a wonderful Diamond Lake–Crater Lake country vista. The Cascade lineup features Mounts McLoughlin, Scott, and Thielsen, Diamond Peak, and the Three Sisters.

To access Diamond Lake's south shore, from the OR 138–OR 230 junction north of Crater Lake, turn west onto OR 230, followed by a quick right onto East Shore Road. Go 0.7 mile on East Shore Road and turn left on FR 4795, heading west along the lake's south shore. In 1.6 miles, turn left onto Bailey Road, FR 4795.300, a dirt road. The Bailey Mountain Trailhead is on the right in 0.4 mile, opposite the Silent Creek Trailhead.

The trail crosses a small drainage to ascend through an open lodgepole

Diamond Lake

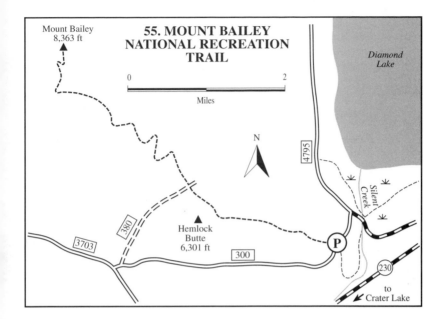

pine forest. A few climbing bursts mark the otherwise rolling ascent. Blue-diamond markers indicate the route's winter use as a Nordic ski trail.

At 0.75 mile, a break in the tree cover extends a brief view to the south. As the trail rounds Hemlock Butte, the forest becomes more mixed with a taller, fuller canopy for more shade.

From the bend at 1.5 miles, the trail travels a forested flat for 0.5 mile to reach FR 380, a high-clearance-vehicle road. (For a shorter hike option, go south from the Diamond Lake area on OR 230 and follow FRs 3703, 300, and 380 northwest to this trailhead.)

From FR 380, the trail climbs advancing in a similar manner, sometimes dusty from summer foot traffic. Wonderful big trees claim the slope.

By 2.9 miles, the forest floor becomes rockier, the trees are notably shorter, and whitebark pines enter the mix. Ahead, the climb intensifies. Gaps in the tree cover afford early looks at Diamond Lake, its meadowy south shore, Sawtooth Ridge, and Mount Thielsen.

Where the trail tops a ridge at 3.4 miles, a detour to the right finds an open view of the Diamond Lake area along with a look at the rounded summit of Bailey, its avalanche bowl, red-streaked scree, and volcanic cliffs.

The trail then wraps around the slope, tags a Mount McLoughlin vista, and again swings back toward the ridge. The route grows more exposed with an open scatter of small mountain hemlocks and firs.

By 4.1 miles, the trail tours the open lava-rock slope with views to the south and east featuring the rim skyline and Desert Ridge of Crater Lake National Park along with Mount McLoughlin.

In another 0.25 mile, the trail rounds a small crater bowl, which often cradles snow well into summer. Here, black cinders form the trail, and the view remains open.

The trail arrives atop a secondary summit knob at 4.7 miles. This post offers a nearly full 360-degree view save for an area to the north blocked by the primary summit. Among the best views are those of the avalanche chute and the summit's craggy ridge and saddle. For many, this site marks the tour's end.

For the more experienced hikers, though, the primary summit awaits. The route heads down the saddle to the bottom of a ragged cliff ridge. It then climbs along the base of the cliff for a difficult, boot-sliding tour. After contouring the steep west flank via a narrow, secondary footpath, the trail again tops the ridge at 4.9 miles. Be careful when steadying yourself with any of the sharp volcanic rock.

Once atop the ridge, a good path leads to the main summit and the former lookout site, completing the 360-degree panoramic view with Diamond Peak and the Three Sisters. The return is as you came.

56 | FISH LAKE LOOP

Distance: 10 miles round trip
Elevation change: 1,100 feet
Difficulty: Moderate
Season: Spring through fall
Map: USFS Rogue-Umpqua Divide/Boulder Creek/Mount
   Thielsen Wildernesses
For information: Tiller Ranger District

This hike explores a rich and varied old-growth forest and strings together three lakes of the Rogue-Umpqua Divide: Fish, Cliff, and Buckeye. Multiple trails access Fish Lake and its circuitous route, located on the west side of this 33,000-acre wilderness. Beaver Swamp Trail is one of the shorter routes of modest ease. Each of the lakes has a unique character. Highrock Mountain, Grasshopper Mountain, and Rocky Ridge are skyline features spotlighted along the way.

From I-5, take the Canyonville exit and head east on County Road 1 to Tiller (22.3 miles). In Tiller, go left on South Umpqua Road/FR 28. In 23.1 miles, bear right onto FR 2823. Now go 2.3 miles and again bear right, this time on FR 2830; pavement ends. In 1.6 miles at the junction of FRs 2830 and 2840, go left on FR 2840 to reach the Beaver Swamp Trailhead in another 4.9 miles. The Beaver Swamp Trail to Fish Lake heads right.

Upon entering the wilderness, the hike descends through a forest of big-diameter old-growth trees. In just shy of a mile, a burn area affords an interesting glimpse at plant succession. While the fire destroyed the smaller trees, the ancients survived little touched, and the ground cover is vital and new.

At the T-junction at 1.4 miles, a right finds Beaver Swamp; to the left lies Fish Lake and the loop. The upstream trail to the lake contours the canyon slope above Fish Lake Creek.

On arrival at Fish Lake at 1.7 miles, hikers come upon the loop junction. Here, the Indian Trail crosses the outlet waters via the log jumble to the right, while the clockwise loop (the selected tour) contours the lake slope ahead. It travels some 10 feet above the water. Fish Lake is a large, rounded, forest-rimmed lake with an inlet meadow. Highrock Mountain rises to the south; Rocky Ridge rises to the east.

At 1.9 miles, the slope eases to create a flat along shore, but keep moving

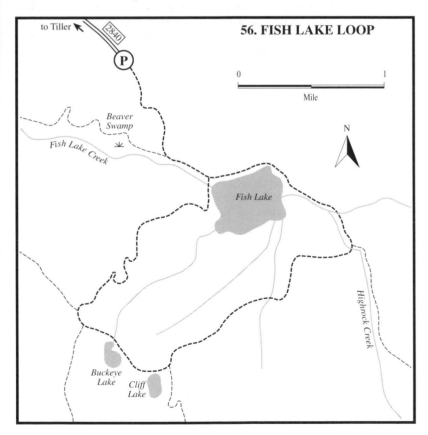

because the area's vegetation is being restored. Appropriate campsites dot the next 0.5 mile; pitch all camps at least 200 feet from water. At 2.1 miles, the trail tours an ancient forest grove of enormous firs and cedars. Horsetail reeds abound. Beyond the grove, the trail skirts the inlet meadow to leave Fish Lake.

At 2.5 miles, the primary route bears left at a marker simply reading "trail" to travel the Highrock Creek Canyon—a shadowy, old-growth haven. A low-elevation Cascade flora showers the mossy floor. Then, at the 3-mile junction, the loop heads right toward Buckeye Lake, ascending from the canyon and rounding the slope well above Fish Lake. Drainages slice through the fir-hemlock forest, and more light penetrates. The climb is steady.

From the 5.1-mile junction, the Grasshopper Mountain Trail continues uphill, while the loop trail bears right for Cliff and Buckeye Lakes. Big trees precede the trail's arrival at scenic Cliff Lake (5.3 miles). As the trail rounds the lake, it squeezes through a waist-high jungle of reeds to reach the spur leading to a primitive lakeshore campsite.

The loop continues straight ahead touring a similar mixed forest with mossy rock outcrops. The rolling trail then arrives at Buckeye Lake at 5.7 miles. Rimmed by a rock-outcrop-punctuated forest, Buckeye is larger and deeper than Cliff Lake. Beaver dams punctuate its outlet arm.

Past the outlet bridge, a spur heads left to a campsite along Buckeye Lake. The loop proceeds forward. The tour again heads straight at the 6.25-mile junction.

At the 6.4-mile junction, the loop swings right to follow the Indian Trail back to Fish Lake. This route is for hikers only; it is narrower and more rugged. Where the trail takes a sharp turn at a drainage in 0.5 mile, its grade temporarily becomes knee-taxing and steep. At 8.3 miles, close the loop by crossing the log jumble at the outlet of Fish Lake. Then, after a short, steep uphill scramble, head left on the trail, retracing the initial part of the hike to return to Beaver Swamp Trailhead.

57 COW CREEK NATIONAL RECREATION TRAIL

Distance: 12.4 miles round trip
Elevation change: 2,000 feet
Difficulty: Moderate
Season: Spring through fall
Map: USGS Richter Mountain, Cleveland Ridge; USFS Umpqua
For information: Tiller Ranger District

An ancient forest setting of magnificent sky-scratching evergreens, thick trunks, rushing ground cover, jagged snags, and the rippling South Fork Cow Creek won this route national recreation trail distinction in 1981. According to the National Trails System Act of 1968, such trails possess outstanding recreational merit and offer convenient access to this country's open-air, outdoor treasury. The trail is open to foot, horse, and mountain bike traffic and receives annual maintenance.

After taking exit 88 off I-5 at Azalea, travel east 19 miles on Cow Creek Road (County 36) to the junction of FRs 32 and 3232. There, turn right onto FR 3232. The trailhead is on the right just past the East Fork Cow Creek Bridge, in less than a mile.

Passing through an open, alder-riparian corridor, the trail briefly parallels the East Fork Cow Creek downstream before entering the South Fork drainage.

At 0.6 mile, the trail crosses the South Fork Cow Creek for the most difficult crossing of the trek. During high water, a fording is necessary. In autumn, a stone-hop crossing is possible, but beware: the stones are slippery.

The gently graded trail now travels the canyon bottom, never straying far from the murmuring creek. In spring and fall, vine maples and dogwoods add a flourish of color to the forest of fir, hemlock, yew, and cedar.

At 1.1 mile and again at 1.2 mile, the trail crosses the creek. Here, as elsewhere along the route, fallen trees may provide a dry alternative to fording, but the bare-bark areas on these natural "bridges" can be slippery.

Before long, the trail makes a modest climb away from the waterway. The bigger-diameter trees are left behind, but old-growth habitat still hosts travel. Past a swampy flat, the trail wraps around the west slope, now well above the creek. By 2.7 miles, the path returns creekside, traversing a marshy area, pungent with skunk cabbage.

Before crossing the creek at 3.2 miles, the trail bypasses a small camp or

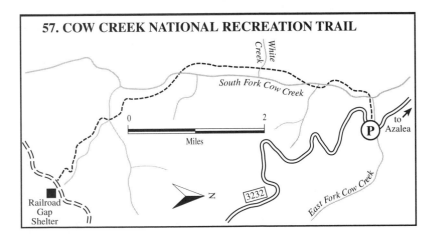

57. COW CREEK NATIONAL RECREATION TRAIL

White Creek

South Fork Cow Creek

0　　　　　　　　2

Miles

to Azalea

P

3232

East Fork Cow Creek

Railroad Gap Shelter

N

picnic site, with stump-carved stools and a rock-and-brick firepit. For a shorter hike, this site serves as a fine turnaround point.

After crossing the creek, the trail traces the slope just below an old cut, brushed by the 1987 Angel Fire, which jumped Cow Creek. Fire-scorched trees still stand trailside. From the recovering burn, the trail climbs more steeply through an open forest with rhododendron, madrone, chinquapin, and small fir.

With one more creek crossing, the trail bids farewell to the South Fork Cow Creek and then streaks up slope to Railroad Gap (elevation 4,567 feet). At Railroad Gap (6.2 miles), one discovers a rebuilt shelter with picnic table and firepit. The return is as you came.

Ancient forest

58 | Upper Rogue National Recreation Trail

**Distance: 40.5 miles one way from Crater Rim
Viewpoint to River Bridge
Elevation change:** 2,500 feet
Difficulty: Strenuous
Season: Summer through fall
Map: USFS Rogue River
For information: Prospect Ranger District

This national recreation trail (NRT) explores the early miles of the majestic Rogue Wild and Scenic River as it emerges from Crater Lake National Park. The hike can be extended south another 6.5 miles into Prospect, but the final distance along private land and a reservoir diversion breaks the romance of the spell. The trail travels past exciting volcanic ash cliffs, pristine meadows, elk wilds, sparkling river straightaways and river waterfalls, gorges, potholes, and the phenomenon of a disappearing river. Forest solitude bridges the many spectacles.

Reach the upper trailhead, Crater Rim Viewpoint, east off OR 230, 5.1 miles south of the OR 138–OR 230 junction south of Diamond Lake. For the River Bridge Campground and Trailhead, from OR 62, 8.5 miles south of the OR 62–OR 230 junction, 4 miles north of Prospect, go west on gravel FR 6210 for 0.9 mile.

Start the downstream tour of the NRT at Crater Rim Viewpoint, descending from the northeast corner of the parking area to tour an open lodgepole pine–true fir forest along the rim of a steep-sided headwater ravine. At the Boundary Springs Trail Junction (0.7 mile), proceed forward.

The NRT traces the piney rim or a deeper woods of the west canyon wall of the Rogue River. The river below beckons, but access is kept to a brief tag until Rough Rider Falls at about 6 miles. The starring features of this stretch are the pumice cliffs and bowls that push the trail higher up the slope. A striking contrast to the forest mantle, these fluted, eroded, plant-defying compressed-ash slopes plunge some 200 feet to the river.

The fury of Ruth Falls rumbles up the canyon at 2.7 miles, and richer shade graces travel past Cascade Creek. On the approach to Rough Rider Falls (6 miles), cascades build excitement, but the primary plummet is hidden. The river now remains closely paired with the canyon-bottom tour.

At 7.8 miles, bypass a third river falls—a 25-foot curvature of white water. Afterward the trail grades back to the rim, before descending via rim terraces to an alder-lined, racing river stretch and soon after, FR 6530 at 9.3 miles. Angle right across the road, still touring forest along the west side of the river. At 10 miles, come to the closed road bridge over the Rogue, which carries the NRT to the east shore. To reach Hamaker Campground, avoid the crossing and instead hike FR 900 downstream to the campground.

The NRT passes a shrub-lined river segment, entering deeper forest for the next couple of miles. A descent returns it to the river bank at 12 miles, where the OR 230 road bridge over Muir Creek is visible. The trail then hugs a close line to the river as far as the footbridge over Hurryon Creek. From there, it climbs to a brink-of-the-cliff river view for a roller-coaster journey along the dimpled canyon slope and more bluff travel.

On the next descent, the trail skirts a peaceful wetland forest and river meadow, but the calm is soon shattered by the rumble of Highway Falls (14.5 miles). Here, a broken 10-foot ledge creates a split-personality falls, with the eastern half showing a straight plummet, the western half a chaos of churning cascades.

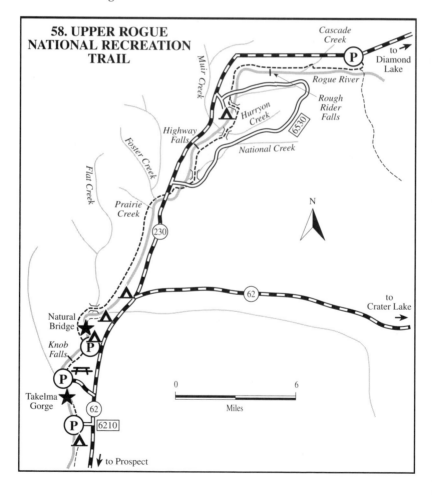

58. UPPER ROGUE NATIONAL RECREATION TRAIL

Takelma Gorge

The trail again vacillates from river to bluff. When next along the Rogue River, a fording near a log jam and a log footbridge stitch together trail fragments. After a rustic log bridge spans the crystalline waters of National Creek, a rumpled forest flat and meadow-edge tour lead to a second meeting with FR 6530 (18 miles).

Cross the road bridge, returning to the west bank to reenter forest and cross OR 230. Next, follow the trail up over the OR 230 road cut and back down to Foster Creek to ford the creek not far from the river confluence (20 miles).

The wading is usually easy at a broad, even-flowing stretch. From Foster Creek, traverse the meadow-forest bench south. Ribbons or the cut ends of logs may help clue the way; otherwise it is trial and error. By the Prairie Creek crossing (20.4 miles), the NRT is within strides of the river.

Upon crossing Marsh Outlet, the hike pursues a side drainage around the backside of a narrow ridge carved out by the channel and river. A forest meander follows. Where the trailbed is not apparent, keep the general downstream line and watch for log cuts or charred blazes.

Along the broad valley floor, the trail and what is now a sleepy Rogue River remain closely paired. A sandy beach may call at 25 miles.

From the primitive access of Big Bend (26.5 miles), the NRT crosses FR 6510, climbing the embankment. More demanding travel through furrowed canyon terrain removed from the river characterizes the next few miles. The trail only briefly emerges at the river across from Farewell Bend Campground for an exciting look at the Rogue as it churns through a collapsed lava tube.

Multistory, mixed forest again enfolds the tour. A log bridge spans Flat Creek (31.5 miles), and for a 0.25 mile, a meadow shore allows easy river access.

At 32.5 miles, pass the first of two pedestrian river bridges at Natural Bridge Campground and Viewpoint. Another mile downstream, platforms overlook the historic crossing point of Natural Bridge, a lava tube that swallows the river whole only to release it 200 feet downstream.

Cross the lower pedestrian bridge to pick up the downstream trek to Woodruff Bridge on the east shore. The NRT tours a forest bench above and apart from the river with spurs branching away to overlooks. Mossy volcanic rock can create rolling footing. Where the trail rounds the point of a ridge (35 miles), overlook the gorge and thundering spill of Knob Falls— site of another collapsed lava tube.

The trail then returns to a brushier forest bench with chances for river views before crossing FR 68 to Woodruff Bridge Picnic Area (36.5 miles), where the trail resumes south.

At 38 miles reach the upper end of 0.7-mile-long Takelma Gorge. The trail travels the gorge rim for overlooks of the surging channel. Areas of rocky footing and small sandy beaches then count down forest travel to River Bridge at 40.5 miles.

59 | UNION CREEK RECREATION TRAIL

Distance: 4.5 miles one way
Elevation change: 400 feet
Difficulty: Moderate
Season: Spring through fall
Map: USGS Union Creek; USFS Rogue River
For information: Prospect Ranger District

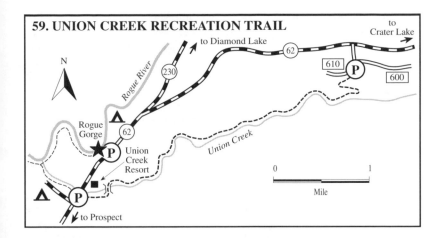

59. UNION CREEK RECREATION TRAIL

Within the prized Upper Rogue–Crater Lake–Diamond Lake recreation complex, this trail showcases crystalline waters and old-growth galleries. The trail's comfortable grade recommends it for the entire family. Unlike many creek trails that travel the canyon wall putting forest and distance between hiker and water, this trail tours the forested valley bottom right alongside clear-bubbling Union Creek.

Find the lower trailhead on the creek's south bank at the tiny community of Union Creek, east off OR 62. Union Creek Resort, on the National Register of Historic Places, claims the northeast bank. Trailhead parking is on the west side of OR 62, just south of the trailhead.

For the upstream trailhead, from the OR 62–OR 230 junction, go a couple of miles east on OR 62 and turn south (right) on single-lane FR 6200.600; a trail sign marks the turn. Another sign then points the way onto FR 610, where the trailhead is located on the right soon after taking the turn; parking is just beyond. With this trailhead less than a mile from the main highway, Union Creek Trail lends itself to shuttle hiking.

From the community of Union Creek, an upstream journey quickly crosses a log footbridge to the north bank, where it will remain for the rest of the tour. Middle-aged forest and an alder-dogwood woodland alternately frame the path as it leaves the rustic resort.

At 0.5 mile, past a small disturbed area, the trail crosses an old dirt road. The creek here holds a fine deep pool ideal for soaking your feet, especially on the return leg of a round-trip journey.

Beyond the road, the trail enters the enchantment of an ancient forest with a rich understory collage. At 1.5 miles a hiker gate allows the trail to continue. Along the way, there are many places to sit creekside or plop a fishing line in the water. As the blue-diamond markers would suggest, this trail doubles as a winter cross-country ski trail.

Where the trail briefly drifts away from the creek, more white pines and some huge Pacific yews join the ranks of ancient Douglas and grand fir and western hemlock. The tree trunks of some giants reveal the scorching of bygone fires. At 3.25 miles, view a scenic multiangled, multitiered cascade on a bend of Union Creek.

At 4.2 miles, the trail presents a closing look at Union Creek before climbing to the upper trailhead. Upstream, a cascade sends forth a tumbling, churning stream that gets squeezed by a narrow, moss-decked gorge alongside the trail. Round-trip hikers may wish to turn around here versus climbing the forest slope to FR 610.

To extend the area tour, back at the community of Union Creek, hikers can cross to the west side of OR 62 and follow Union Creek downstream through Union Creek Campground to the confluence with the Rogue River.

There, they will find two hiking options along the Rogue Gorge Trail: South leads to Natural Bridge in 2.5 miles—a geologic oddity where a lava tube swallows the river whole only to release it 200 feet downstream. North leads to Rogue Gorge Viewpoint in 1 mile, another geologic eye-teaser featuring the powerful matchup of steep, rugged basalt and bubble-churning water. Both vista sites have roadside access off OR 62, for hikers with limited time.

Union Creek

60 | MOUNT SCOTT TRAIL

Distance: 5 miles round trip
Elevation change: 1,300 feet
Difficulty: Moderate
Season: Late July through early fall
Map: USGS Crater Lake National Park; Crater Lake National
    Park map and guide brochure
For information: Crater Lake National Park

This trail climbs to a fire lookout perched on Mount Scott, the highest peak
in Crater Lake National Park (elevation 8,926 feet). Mount Scott is the
earliest-formed of the overlapping volcanic cones that constituted Mount
Mazama—the ancient volcano that collapsed some 7,700 years ago and
created the basin in which Crater Lake, the deepest lake in the United
States, formed.

Views encompass the large caldera lake; its immediate neighborhood; the
Klamath Basin; and a volcano lineup that includes Three Sisters, Diamond
Peak, Mounts Thielsen and McLoughlin, and California's Mount Shasta.
As the trail wraps around and switchbacks up the peak, it travels through
open forest and across rocky terrain. Alpine flora dot the upper mountain
reaches.

Along the Pacific Flyway, Mount Scott also offers a post for viewing

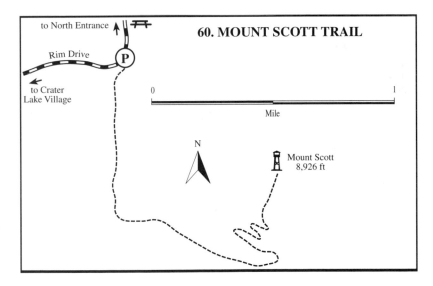

to North Entrance

Rim Drive   P

to Crater
Lake Village

60. MOUNT SCOTT TRAIL

0   1

Mile

N

Mount Scott
8,926 ft

the fall migration of raptors and waterfowl to the wildlife areas of the Klamath-Tule Basin at the Oregon-California border.

Crater Lake National Park has entrances on OR 62 and OR 138; the south entrance on OR 62 lies 54 miles northwest of Klamath Falls. The gate entry fee gives visitors seven-day park access. Find the Mount Scott Trailhead on the east side of Crater Lake, east off the Rim Drive. It is well marked and has pull-in parking. Park trail rules apply: foot traffic only; no pets.

On an old two-track, the trail travels amid whitebark pine and mountain hemlock, skirting a glacier-chiseled bowl at the base of Mount Scott. As the trail slips into the open forest to travel at the foot of the steep, rocky western slope, the two-track narrows to a wide hiker path. With much of the trail sunny and exposed, carry plenty of water.

By 0.6 mile, hikers gain early western views of Crater Lake's south end with Wizard Island, The Watchman, and Hillman and Garfield Peaks. Cloudcap (elevation 8,065 feet), which rises on the caldera rim in front of Scott, succeeds in blocking the remainder of the lake from view.

In another 0.1 mile, the view broadens to include the Klamath Basin and Mount McLoughlin. The trail steadily climbs via a well-groomed bed, which can be dusty.

Crater Lake

After 1 mile, the trail swings onto the south face of Scott, unfolding a 120-degree view encompassing much of Winema National Forest, the Sand Creek drainage, more of the Klamath Basin, and Mount McLoughlin. A look back to the west at 1.3 miles captures a fine view of Crater Lake, its rim, and Wizard Island. Soon, Mount Shasta's showy crown rises to the south.

Off a switchback in another 0.5 mile, a ridge outcrop overlooks the bowl where the trail began. This northern view pans across the caldera rim toward Mounts Bailey and Thielsen and the Diamond Lake Area, with Three Sisters to the northeast. The next switchback holds an encore view.

By 2.25 miles, the trail reaches the summit ridge of Mount Scott and tours just below the rocky spine. Here, chill winds often suggest the need for layering-on of clothes. Ahead lies the lookout tower, where all of the views come together in a grand 360-degree spectacle. The park's Pumice Desert offers a striking contrast to the surrounding forest expanse. Crater Lake is fully visible in its indescribable blue; its looking-glass face reflects the caldera rim. Return as you came.

61 | GARFIELD PEAK TRAIL

Distance: 3.4 miles round trip
Elevation change: 1,000 feet
Difficulty: Moderate
Season: Mid-July through early fall
Map: USGS Crater Lake National Park; Crater Lake National
Park map and guide brochure
For information: Crater Lake National Park

This trail switchbacks up the western flank of Garfield Peak (summit elevation 8,060 feet), ascending through a rim forest of mountain hemlock and Shasta red fir, a dry meadow-wildflower grassland, open rocky terrain, and alpine forest–meadow habitat. It begins with overlooks of the historic lodge and Crater Lake and continuously broadens its view to include the entire lake caldera, surrounding countryside, and Garfield's own impressive, steep-dropping cliff wall. Southern views span into California.

Crater Lake National Park has entrances on OR 62 and OR 138; the south entrance on OR 62 lies 54 miles northwest of Klamath Falls. The gate entry fee gives visitors seven-day park access. Find the trailhead at Rim Village at the southern end of the lake, east of the historic lodge.

A low stone wall borders the path as it strings east along the southern caldera rim for overlooks of the 2,000-foot-deep lake. The vibrant blue lake,

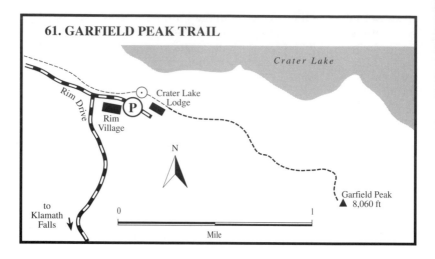

61. GARFIELD PEAK TRAIL

Crater Lake

Crater Lake Lodge

Rim Drive

Rim Village

N

to Klamath Falls

Garfield Peak ▲ 8,060 ft

0   1

Mile

forested cinder cone of Wizard Island, steep caldera cliffs, and rim and cliff reflections captivate onlookers. To the north rises Mount Thielsen.

Aster and lupine dot the dry meadow patches preceding the rim-edge bench at 0.25 mile. Afterward the tour strikes up the western flank of Garfield.

Locate a second vista bench at the 0.4-mile switchback, where western views include the meadow and forest of the south rim and the restored historic lodge. The trail now progresses via uphill-angling passages and short switchbacks, adding views south of the Klamath Basin with Union Peak to the west and Mount McLoughlin to the southwest. The rockiness of the terrain is sometimes apparent along the trail.

At 0.5 mile, the trail skirts below a water-gravity station, and at 0.75 mile, it extends another Crater Lake vista with Mount Scott viewed across a ragged shoulder of Garfield. Soon after, another bench invites a breather.

Where the trail claims the ridge at 1.1 miles, views span Crater Lake to The Watchman, Llao Rock, Red Cone, and Mount Thielsen. The picturesque rock island of Phantom Ship is then seen from the side spur at 1.2 miles.

The final push for the summit expands views south past Crater Peak and across the Klamath Basin to California's Mount Shasta. The panorama also incorporates the dry grass–patchy forest flank of next-door neighbor Applegate Peak to the southeast and showy Mount McLoughlin to the southwest.

The open, rocky-soiled summit supports low, gnarled pines and runty mountain hemlock with ground-hugging wildflowers. Views sweep a 360-degree expanse with the lookout towers atop Mount Scott and The Watchman both seen. Located directly above the lake, in many ways, Garfield Peak's summit vantage exceeds that found on Mount Scott. The return is as you came.

62 | CHERRY CREEK–SKY LAKES BASIN LOOP HIKE

Distance: 25 miles round trip
Elevation change: 2,200 feet
Difficulty: Strenuous
Season: Summer through fall
Map: USFS Sky Lakes Wilderness
For information: Klamath Ranger District

Volcanic and glacial forces shaped the terrain of Sky Lakes Wilderness. This hike incorporates a national recreation trail, a good length of the Pacific Crest Trail (PCT), and a fine lakes-wilderness tour. The region features elevation-diverse forests, multiple lakes, an impressive cliff ridge above Margurette Lake, and some small wildflower meadows. Mostly forested, the trail allows but a few prized vistas. They include lake overlooks and views of Luther Mountain, Cherry Peak, Pelican Butte, Brown Mountain, and Mounts McLoughlin and Shasta.

The many meltwater ponds of the wilderness give rise to a vital mosquito population that lingers through late summer. Hikers should carry netting and repellent. Keep the party size to eight people, twelve pack animals, and follow all wilderness rules, pitching camps at least 100 feet from water sources.

From Klamath Falls, go 25 miles northwest on OR 140 to Westside Road and follow it north for 10.6 miles. There, turn left onto FR 3450 at the sign for Cherry Creek Trail and go another 1.7 miles to reach the trailhead parking area.

Paralleling above the Cherry Creek drainage, this well-designed trail passes through a forest of grand fir and shrubs to enter the wilderness at 0.75 mile. Another mile farther finds the wet crossing of Cherry Creek (which may prove impassable in spring) and a second crossing of a side water where a beaver dam is downstream.

The trail next passes through mature, mixed forest and traverses raised walkways over wet meadow strips to arrive at a rock-and-log crossing of Cherry Creek (3.25 miles). After a side-creek crossing begins the forested uphill haul. By 5 miles, Shasta red fir and mountain hemlock command the skyline; true and dwarf huckleberry patch the floor.

Past a pond, the trail tops out at the Sky Lakes Basin Loop near Trapper Lake—a big, forest-rimmed, high lake below rocky-topped Luther Mountain. A right begins a counterclockwise tour of the basin rounding the shore of Trapper Lake. Small campsites dot the forest away from the water.

At the 6.1-mile junction, a side loop travels to Donna Lake, while the primary circuit proceeds straight, still rounding and climbing above Trapper

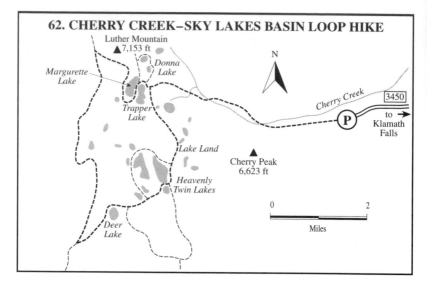

62. CHERRY CREEK–SKY LAKES BASIN LOOP HIKE

Luther Mountain
▲7,153 ft

Donna Lake

Margurette Lake

N

Cherry Creek

3450

Trapper Lake

P

to →
Klamath Falls

Lake Land

▲
Cherry Peak
6,623 ft

Heavenly Twin Lakes

0   2

Deer Lake

Miles

Lake. In a short while, the trail approaches prized Margurette Lake at the foot of Luther Mountain Ridge.

Pursuing the Divide Trail, the loop rounds a rise to the next lake bowl at 6.7 miles. After skirting this shallow unnamed body of water, the trail reaches the foot of Luther Ridge. A slow, comfortable climb follows, with long contours and switchbacks.

By 7.8 miles, the ridge trail enters rockier reaches and attains overlooks of the Cherry Creek drainage and Upper Klamath Lakes Area with Pelican Butte. The rim also extends a grand lakes basin panorama. A small, deep pond beside the trail at 8.5 miles is the last good chance to top the water jugs for a spell; as always, be sure to treat trail water sources.

Talus crossings now typify the route. Views expand to include Mount McLoughlin, Brown Mountain, and California's Mount Shasta. Ahead, the trail contours a mostly open slope to reach the 9.3-mile trail junction where the loop follows the PCT left (south) toward Island Lake.

Southbound, the trail rounds the rocky east slope below the ridge skyline, building upon the Upper Klamath vista; small hemlocks and firs offer shady breaks. Look for the talus encounters to end at 10 miles, where the ridgeline dips to meet the trail. The tour now follows the open-forested ridge, crisscrossing the crest before descending the west side. Some dry meadow patches interrupt the otherwise full forest. At 12.2 miles, a 300-foot side path branches right to overlook the forested expanse of the South Fork Rogue River drainage.

The trail again climbs to cross over the crest at 12.5 miles. An open rocky slope affords vistas before the trail descends a forest-shaded slope to arrive at a small meadow.

Trapper Lake

At 14.6 miles is the PCT–Sky Lakes Trail junction. The loop proceeds left, reaching Deer Lake at 15.2 miles.

Beyond the lake, Cold Spring Trail enters from the right as the loop bears left to travel a boulder-studded terrain rolling toward the Isherwood Trail junction (16 miles). Here, the primary basin loop continues straight; the Isherwood Trail heads left, adding 0.5 mile to the distance and four more lakes to the trip.

The Sky Lakes Trail takes the primary basin loop across the narrow strip of land separating the Heavenly Twin Lakes—two large pools with attractive, irregular shorelines and grass-invaded shallows; Luther Mountain overlooks the northern lake. At 16.7 miles, the Isherwood Trail rejoins the tour.

Ahead stretches an open passage through lodgepole pines. Off the trail at 17.6 miles is the oval water body of Lake Land. Afterward, the trail rolls and skirts a couple of mirror ponds to round the east shore of Trapper Lake. Upon crossing the outlet, the loop closes at 19 miles. A right on Cherry Creek Trail then ends the hike at 25 miles.

63 | MOUNT McLOUGHLIN TRAIL

Distance: 11.5 miles round trip
Elevation change: 3,900 feet
Difficulty: Strenuous
Season: Summer through fall
Map: USFS Sky Lakes Wilderness
For information: Klamath Ranger District

This popular hike climbs to the summit of southern Oregon's premier peak, Mount McLoughlin (elevation 9,495 feet), for a top-of-the-world panorama spanning parts of Oregon and California. Of all the Oregon volcano peaks, this one is the easiest to conquer. The route passes through old-growth forest and a boulder-studded open forest before breaking out above timberline to scale the rugged, rocky, exposed upper slope.

Mount McLoughlin, a composite volcano, sports a crown of cinders and volcanic rock and debris from its most recent eruptions some 12,000 years ago. Ice Age glaciers excavated great amounts of rock from the northeast face. An overlook of this glacier-chiseled face paired with a grand view of the mountaintop at 4.5 miles marks an alternative ending site.

To tackle the mountain, wear sturdy boots and carry a good supply of water. Morning hikes tend to offer more comfortable temperatures, crisper views, and an escape from afternoon thunderstorms.

Because of the hike's popularity, hikers must be responsible for the care and protection of this mountain and its wilderness integrity: schedule

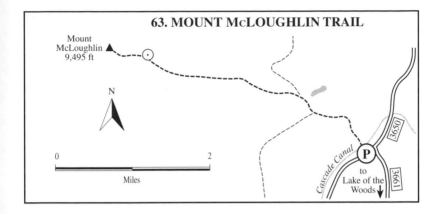

63. MOUNT McLOUGHLIN TRAIL

Mount McLoughlin 9,495 ft

N

0   2

Miles

Cascade Canal

P

to Lake of the Woods

3650

3661

fewer visits and keep your party size small. Do not use paint blazes or other markers along the rocky upper-mountain reaches. If you feel uneasy without the security of a trail, select another hike.

From OR 140 near Lake of the Woods, turn north onto gravel FR 3661, heading toward Fourmile Lake. Go 2.8 miles and turn left onto FR 3650 to reach the large trailhead parking area on the right in another 0.2 mile.

A wide trail launches the hike and crosses the Cascade Canal footbridge to enter a forest with interruptions of wildflower meadows. At 1 mile is the Mount McLoughlin–Pacific Crest Trail (PCT) junction. For the summit route, go right. The hike now follows the PCT north for 0.4 mile before branching away to the left.

The draw at 2.4 miles signals a change from the comfortable forest tour to a progressively rugged, steep climb. In another mile, the intensity of the climb again steps up as the trail tours a boulder-studded, semiopen forest. Variously, the trail is dusty or gravelly or sports large boulders to negotiate. Any faint red-dot paint blazes are unwelcome and unofficial trail markings.

Although forest gaps afford snapshot views, better views await above tree line. At 4.5 miles, the trail tops a ridge for a bold look at the glacier-planed northeast face of the volcano with its jagged crags, snowfields, and moraines (mounds of moved earth) recording the bottoms of ancient glaciers. The ridge greeting also includes an impressive first view of the summit crown, along with a 180-degree panorama of California's Mount Shasta, the Cascade Crest stretching north, the nearby lakes, and Upper Klamath Lake.

Although the summit builds upon the view, this bold confrontation with the mountaintop is truly the most striking view of the tour and suggests the turnaround point for many.

A much rougher, make-your-way rock scramble to the top follows. As you leave the regular footpath, climb staying along the east ridge to avoid the more difficult slope ahead. The occasional cairn or footprints left by earlier travelers may assist in the route selection, but hugging the ridgeline remains key.

At 5.25 miles, the summit route offers a second look at the glacier-gouged bowl and volcanic palisades of the northeast face. After tracing the bowl's rim comes the final, steep 0.25-mile assault on the summit. Loose gravel and rocks sometimes foul footing.

The top has two vista posts separated by the former lookout. Together they build a 360-degree panorama. Views stretch south to Mount Shasta and the Klamath-Tule Basin and north to the far-distant Three Sisters. Views west overlook the Rogue River drainage; views east span the Upper Klamath-Agency Lakes area.

Backtrack as you came, again hugging the east ridge to avoid losing or complicating your way. Every summer hikers get lost on their descent, so keep frequent visual tabs on the ridge.

64 VARNEY CREEK–MOUNTAIN LAKES LOOP HIKE

Distance: 17 miles round trip
Elevation change: 2,000 feet
Difficulty: Strenuous
Season: Summer through fall
Map: USFS Mountain Lakes Wilderness
For information: Klamath Ranger District

This hike travels up a gentle creek drainage to string through broad basins and along ridges tagging the shores of several small lakes and the wilderness's star lake attraction—Lake Harriette. Varied forests; dry, wildflower meadows; and peak vistas mark the route.

A collapsed ancient composite volcano houses this wilderness tour. Over time, glaciation, running water, wind, and weathering have smoothed its caldera rim. Numerous small tarns and ponds speckle the crater bowl, but the glacial rupturing of the rim defied the creation of a single great caldera lake, such as Crater Lake to the north. The snowmelt pools support a thriving mosquito population that can turn back early-season hikers. Carry repellent, keep the total party size to ten, and follow wilderness rules, pitching camps away from water sources.

From Klamath Falls, go 21 miles northwest on OR 140. When arriving from the north, from the OR 140–Westside Road Junction, go east on OR 140

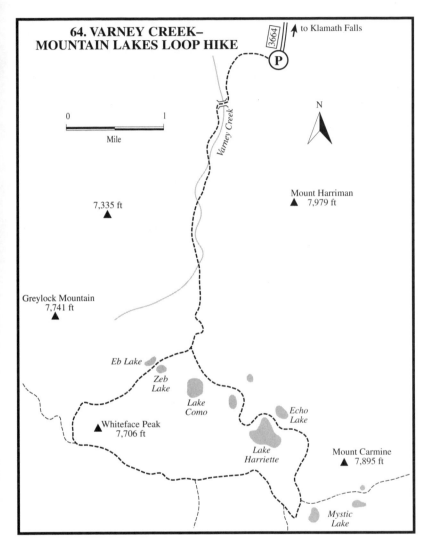

for 4 miles. At the sign for Varney Creek Trailhead, turn west on gravel FR 3637, go 1.7 miles, and turn left onto FR 3664. The trailhead is on the right in another 1.9 miles, with parking just beyond at road's end.

Varney Creek echoes up from its drainage as this comfortably graded trail explores a fir and ponderosa pine forest. At 1 mile, the trail enters wilderness.

After a log boardwalk spans Varney Creek, the trail alternates between the open stands of lodgepole pine and fir and the dry meadow slopes of wild rose, lily, currant, lupine, and fireweed. Mount Harriman commands the early view.

By 3 miles, the trail affords up-canyon looks at the semibald ridge of Greylock Mountain. A high-elevation forest now houses the tour, while dwarf huckleberry spots the floor. At 3.75 miles, the trail tops out, and at 4 miles, it meets the Mountain Lakes Loop Trail.

A right begins a counterclockwise tour, quickly introducing the shallow twins, Eb and Zeb Lakes. Whiteface Peak overlooks Zeb Lake, while an unnamed, counterpart of equal height rises above Eb.

The trail then mounts the forest-talus saddle between Whiteface Peak and its counterpart. Atop the saddle at 5.2 miles, northeastern views feature the Varney Creek drainage, the Klamath Lakes area, and the nearby wilderness peaks.

Across the saddle, the opposite slope shows a more mixed forest; gaps in the tree cover reveal Mount McLoughlin, Brown Mountain, and the Lake of the Woods. At 5.6 miles is an open saddle and trail junction; go downhill to the left for the loop. The spare slope soon gives way to a mountain hemlock–white pine forest.

A leveling of the trail precedes the 6.6-mile junction, where the loop again heads left; straight is Clover Basin. The loop then rolls through forest and crosses tongues of talus. At 7.3 miles, it swings left to climb along a tree-blazed route. Remain alert, because in places, the path grows faint.

Where the Mountain Lakes Loop tops the ridge overlooking Lake Harriette and Mount Carmine, it heads right and dips just below the ridge only to again top it in another 0.5 mile. As the lakes loop crosses over the ridge at 8.7 miles, a look to the right finds Aspen Butte (elevation 8,208 feet). Descend and round the steep forested slope above Mystic Lake, gathering views of Paragon and Mystic Lakes and Aspen Butte's cliff and talus face.

Where the trail comes to the 9.3-mile junction, a right leads to large and remote South Pass Lake; a left continues the loop tour to Lake Harriette with a long, forest-shaded descent. At 10.7 miles, the trail flattens to edge a couple of green ponds.

Next up is Lake Harriette, the pride of the wilderness, shining beautiful, deep, and blue. Although Lake Harriette is the most popular day and overnight destination in the Mountain Lakes Wilderness, its shore remains wild and its water pristine. Crisp reflections duplicate the forest rim, which is interrupted by tongues of white talus. The forested shore adequately isolates the visiting parties, ensuring private enjoyment.

The 11.1-mile junction is encountered as the trail rounds Lake Harriette. Here, the loop bears left; to the right lies Hemlock Basin. The loop then climbs away from Lake Harriette and crosses a saddle for a rocky, dusty descent through mixed forest to the Lake Como basin at 12.6 miles. Where the loop closes at 13 miles, retrace the Varney Creek Trail to end the hike.

65 | PACIFIC CREST NATIONAL SCENIC TRAIL

Distance: 424 miles one way
Elevation change: 7,200 feet, with an average elevation of 5,120 feet
Difficulty: Strenuous, with short samplings of all difficulty levels
Season: Summer through fall (for entire route)
Map: USFS Pacific Crest Trail: Oregon portion (3 maps)
For information: Nature of the Northwest, USFS

First proposed in the 1930s, the Pacific Crest Trail (PCT) is one of two national scenic trails named under the National Trails System Act of 1968; the other is the Appalachian Trail. By description, these trails possess outstanding scenic, historic, natural, or cultural value and are long distance. The year 1987 marked the completion of the Oregon portion of this 2,600-mile hiker filament that lies across the Sierra Nevada, Siskiyou, and Cascade crestlines from Mexico to Canada.

In Oregon, the trail passes through bureau lands, national forests, wilderness areas, scenic areas, and Oregon's only national park, with brief stretches across private lands. The Oregon portion also incorporates segments of the 1920s-built Oregon Skyline Trail, which links Mount Hood and Crater Lake.

The premier trail boasts a well-designed, -constructed, and -maintained bed suitable for foot or horse traffic, with some sensitive areas exclusively for foot traffic. Management and construction considerations have placed the PCT to avoid steepness, generally rounding versus mounting ridges. It also bypasses wet areas where passage is difficult and the damage potential is great. Likewise, it skirts areas of heavy use (lakes, vistas, and other drawing-card destinations) to minimize hiker influence on crestline treasures.

Despite its responsible routing, the trail still reveals many of the state's wild and natural offerings. For times when the call to "come see" is too great, a vast network of interconnecting trails invites side trips.

At the Cascade mountain passes, large, formal, marked trailhead parking areas on the east-west highways provide convenient access to the PCT. Trailheads for the PCT tie trails also serve this long-distance route.

From California, the trail enters Oregon east of the Applegate River and southwest of Mount Ashland, passing over Observation Gap. The trail leaves the state for Washington via the Bridge of the Gods, crossing the Columbia River near Cascade Locks.

The southern Cascades hold the PCT's highest Oregon point—the pass between Devils and Lee Peaks in the Seven Lakes Basin of Sky Lakes Wilderness. The Columbia Gorge houses the low point, where the PCT approaches sea level at the Bridge of the Gods crossing.

As the PCT travels Oregon's rolling ridges, the typical forest setting features some combination of mountain hemlock, true fir, and lodgepole and

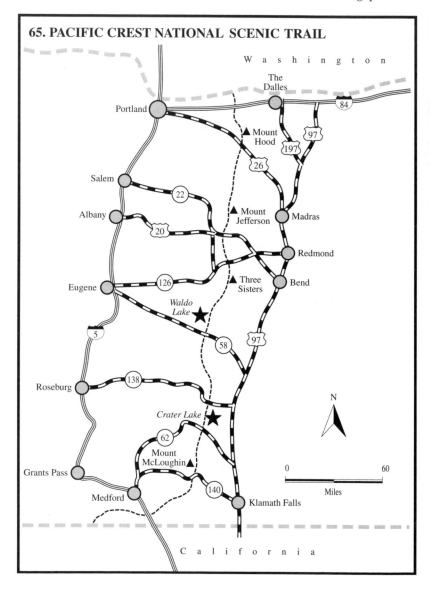

65. PACIFIC CREST NATIONAL SCENIC TRAIL

whitebark pines—barely brushing the state's forest diversity. Lake-bound basins; wet, prairie, and alpine meadows; lava lands; and a few harvest and clearcut sites interrupt the forest legs. Along the way, hikers find grand wildflower displays, with peak blooms in late summer. Bear grass and huckleberry bushes often reclaim the cut areas.

Volcano vistas punctuate the journey and mark northbound (or southbound) progress through the state. Vistas along the Oregon segment of the PCT span from California's Mount Shasta to Washington's Mount Rainier, with Oregon's all-star volcano lineup sandwiched in between. Where the PCT overlaps the Timberline Trail (see Hike 25), hikers are treated to up close looks at Oregon's own Mount Hood (elevation 11,235 feet), with its glaciers, deep-chiseled canyons, and lahar (a ridge of rock and debris deposited by a mud flow).

The PCT brushes Oregon history where it follows or parallels segments of Indian trails and pioneer and military wagon routes. Navigational landmarks used by early settlers similarly serve contemporary travelers. The countryside holds tales of early-day prospecting and logging.

For many users, the PCT's primary appeal is that of a gateway for day hikes and short backpacks. The PCT easily facilitates loops with neighboring trails. For PCT samplings, see Hikes 21, 22, 25, 32, 33, 45, 48, 62, and 63, or contact the appropriate managing agency or agencies for information about PCT tours of your choosing. Entire books have been devoted to this premier trail; consult your local library or bookstore.

Gray jay

66 | McCall Point Trail

Distance: 3 miles round trip
Elevation change: 1,000 feet
Difficulty: Moderate
Season: May 1 to October 30
Map: None
For information: State Parks, Portland/Columbia
    Gorge Area

A springtime bonanza awaits at this Columbia River Gorge site. The bloom calendar runs from mid-March to early June, making the first month of the trail's opening a favorite time to tour, but nature discoveries are found throughout the hiking calendar.

The native grasslands, mounds, swales, rocky rims, and Oregon oak woodlands along the trail and across the road at the main part of Tom McCall Preserve introduce uncommon floral variety with rare and endangered plant species.

The trail begins from Rowena Crest nearly 750 feet above the Columbia River and climbs to McCall Point (elevation 1,722 feet). En route to the summit, the narrow path wriggles up and across the multilevel benches of the steppe plateau, passing through grassland and Oregon oak woodland, while offering river overviews. From the grassy summit, the snowy crowns of Mounts Adams and Hood vie for attention. Because the trail is dry and can be hot, carry plenty of water. With much of the area having preserve status, stay on the trail and do not disturb the vegetation or wildlife.

The trailhead lies about 10 miles west of The Dalles. From I-84 westbound, take Exit 76 for the scenic loop, Rowena, and Mayer State Park. After crossing to the south side of the freeway, continue west 2.8 miles to the Rowena Crest Viewpoint. From I-84 eastbound, take the Mosier-Rowena Exit 69, and follow US 30, the Rowena Loop Scenic Drive, east for 6.4 miles to the crest viewpoint.

On the native grass bench above the entrance road, a wooden sign marks the start of the trail. Its grassy footpath leaves the viewpoint circle to travel along the abrupt edge of the plateau. Overlooks are of the winding Rowena Loop Scenic Drive and the upstream Columbia River; cross-gorge views find Lyle, Washington. On the rim rises McCall Point.

Before long, the footpath merges with an old two-track slowly arcing to the base of the next plateau level, where the McCall Point Trail bears left (0.25 mile). In a short distance, the footpath resumes, passing through a grove of small oaks. Ahead, a sign reminds hikers of the crest's preserve status and warns of the presence of ticks, snakes, and poison oak.

The grade steepens where the trail again climbs along the plateau edge.

66. McCALL POINT TRAIL

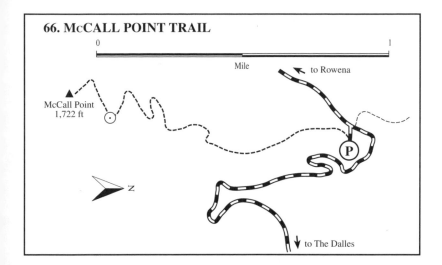

The growth-stunting impact of the wind on the trees is readily apparent.

As the trail ascends, a full-volcano view of Mount Adams slowly emerges. Downstream views across the plateau find a few clustered oaks, single ponderosa pines, and an occasional vernal pool dotting the open, semiarid grassland. The river is hidden from view.

At 0.7 mile, the trail passes beneath a utility pole. From there, the route briefly hugs the edge of the plateau before entering a series of short switchbacks advancing up the slope through another grove of low-growing white oaks.

After a fine western view at 1.25 miles, the trail makes one last climb through oaks, drawing out onto an open grassland slope for the final assault on the summit. Grass-topped McCall Point offers views to the north and west that include Mounts Adams and Hood and scenic downstream images of the Columbia River. Footpaths travel the summit point for different vantages. The return is as you came.

67 | VIC ATIYEH LOOP

Distance: 4.5-mile loop
Elevation change: 500 feet
Difficulty: Moderate
Season: Year round
Map: Park brochure
For information: State Parks, Portland/Columbia Gorge Area

Named for a former Oregon governor, this hike explores upstream along the eastern bank of the Deschutes Wild and Scenic River and then climbs the canyon slope for a loftier river perspective and a downstream return. Sage-grassland and basalt outcroppings characterize the canyon. The river is a prized fly-fishing water.

This canyon was the site for the historic railroad race to first serve Central Oregon, with competitor tracks laid along both banks. The abandoned grade on this side is now a bicycle trail that runs 25 miles upstream to Macks Canyon.

Ticks and rattlesnakes are to be expected in this wild river canyon. Keep alert.

The trail begins at Deschutes River State Recreation Area. From I-84, about 17 miles east of The Dalles, take Exit 97 and go east for 3 miles on OR 206 to reach the park campground on the east side of the river. The trail leaves from the parking area at the south end of the campground.

From the parking lot, strike out upstream across the open lawn to the south to reach the trail's signboard in 0.1 mile. This loop unites the Atiyeh Deschutes River Trail and Ferry Springs/Upper River Trails. The Middle Trail and Bike Trail offer parallel routes by which to vary the loop.

Keep right following the cinder path of the shoreline trail, which is well tracked by hikers, anglers, and birdwatchers. Near the start, look for the abandoned fruit trees from an old homestead and an alder-entangled weathered frame with rusting gears. At 0.4 mile, a bench seat extends views of the river and canyon rim.

Proceed forward past the spur to the Middle Trail at 0.6 mile. A few larger white alders offer a shady reprieve on this otherwise sunny journey. Past the next bench, a boardwalk spans a spring-drained area of vibrant greenery.

At 1.1 miles, locate a small sandy beach and an outhouse serving river

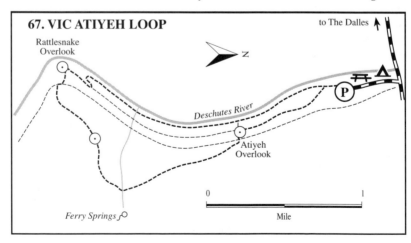

67. VIC ATIYEH LOOP

to The Dalles

Rattlesnake Overlook

N

Deschutes River

Atiyeh Overlook

Ferry Springs

0   1

Mile

Deschutes River

users. Looks downstream out the Deschutes River Canyon find the Washington shore of the Columbia River. Just upstream is another bench in a grove of cooling alders.

Beyond it, the trail crosses the flat stones bridging the trickling flows of Ferry Springs, and at 1.4 miles is a junction. Turn left for the loop. The river path still continues upstream; it is initially well trampled but afterwards unmaintained.

A fairly steep, switchbacked ascent leads to a T-junction with the Middle Trail at 1.5 miles. Go right for the Upper River Trail and chosen 4.5-mile loop; a left makes a 3-mile loop via the Middle Trail. To the right, meander atop a wildflower-adorned sagebrush plateau about 150 feet above the river; basalt cliffs plunge toward the river.

Where the trail swings left toward the Bike and Upper River Trails at 1.8 miles, reach Rattlesnake Overlook, which extends a view from atop the river cliffs. Below is Rattlesnake Rapids, a class III white water. Upstream view the patchwork of the Columbia Plateau agricultural lands and the glistening river as it threads between rugged, black canyon walls.

From the overlook, the trail dips to the Bike Trail; go right for 20 strides to pick up the Upper River Trail for the 4.5-mile loop. A left on the Bike Trail shaves off distance and elevation for an easier return.

The hillside tour ascends the sage-grassland of the canyon's east slope, soon crossing a step stile over a fence. At 2.4 miles, a bench seat welcomes a breather and offers an overlook of the Deschutes River mouth, Columbia River, and Washington shore.

After crossing the drainage at Ferry Springs Canyon, a canyon descent follows. Rock outcrops and boulders accent the upper grassy slope, and views are continuous. With a step-stile crossing, the Upper River Trail ends at the Bike Trail (3.6 miles).

Angle left across the grade, descending 100 feet along a side drainage to reach the outcrop point and a pair of benches at Atiyeh Overlook. From here, hikers can scan a good amount of the lower river, which Governor Atiyeh helped save.

From the overlook, follow the Middle Trail north downstream, crossing the side drainage to creep down the lower canyon slope, passing amid hackberry trees and sagebrush 10 feet high. Bypass a bench and a short spur to the River Trail, staying on the Middle Trail for a rolling return.

At 4.2 miles, reach a jeep trail and follow it left downhill to close the loop at 4.4 miles; return to the trailhead at 4.5 miles.

68 | TROUT CREEK TRAIL

Distance: 7.75 miles one way
Elevation change: 100 feet
Difficulty: Moderate
Season: Year round
Map: USGS Gateway, Eagle Butte
For information: Prineville District BLM

The Deschutes Wild and Scenic River is the focal point for this arid river-canyon tour. The trail follows a former railroad grade, with sections of foot-path dipping to shore for more intimate river views. Steep golden-colored sage and grassland slopes pair with the dark basalt or red rock rims. Eagles, ospreys, ducks, herons, geese, magpies, red-winged blackbirds, deer, and beavers grow the roster of wildlife sightings.

The grassy flats along shore suggest a camp or prolonged visit. Several flats have vault toilets. Mecca Flat, the upstream terminus, occupies a historic river crossing site where the Deschutes River Canyon opens up.

To reach the Trout Creek Trailhead, from the US 97–US 26 junction at

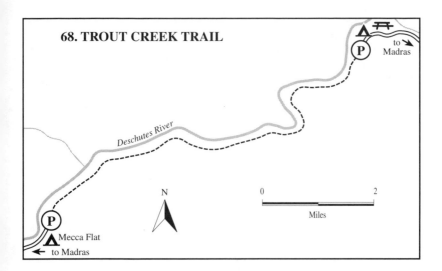

68. TROUT CREEK TRAIL

Deschutes River

to Madras

P

Mecca Flat

to Madras

N

0   2

Miles

Madras, go north on US 97 for 2.4 miles and turn left toward Gateway on Cora Lane/Clark Drive. In 3.9 miles, as the main road bears right, veer left for Trout Creek Recreation Site; there is a small sign at the junction.

At Gateway in 4 miles, go right on gravel Clemens Drive toward the Deschutes River–Trout Creek. Where the road dips toward the river in another 4.2 miles, go left (upstream) to reach the campground in 0.3 mile, the trailhead in 0.7 mile.

To reach the Mecca Flat Trailhead, from the US 97–US 26 junction in Madras, go west on US 26 for 11.9 miles and turn right just before the Deschutes River Bridge to find a four-way dirt-road junction. Take the upper-middle fork along a public easement and the former railroad grade to reach the trailhead in 1.6 miles. The road has been improved to accommodate passenger vehicles.

Start the upstream tour from Trout Creek Recreation Site by crossing a cattleguard and rounding a gate to follow the former railroad grade. A low abutting ridge semiblocks the early river view, but over-the-shoulder looks find a couple of large, red buttes and the downstream canyon.

Beyond the low ridge stretch open river views. At 0.75 mile, a wooden bench overlooks the river before the next high bank. Beware of ticks while in this arid terrain.

The first of many side paths branches to the river at 1.2 miles. Although the old rail line travels within 100 feet of the Deschutes River, in places its steep embankment discourages river access.

In another mile, the trail again passes through a sunken, narrow corridor enclosed by towering, dark basalt cliffs. Just upstream, a picturesque side canyon angles to the southeast; yellow lichens etch its rim.

At 2.5 miles is the first of a pair of gates, where the trail crosses a broad river bench. Along the river are small islands with hummocky yellow-gold grasses. Up-canyon views unfold with each bend.

At 3.4 miles, a juniper-shaded wooden bench invites a stop, particularly on hot summer days. After the foot-horse gate at 5.2 miles, side trails again dip to the river.

Where the weeds begin to push up through the railroad grade at 5.8 miles, the hiker route leaves the grade on a footpath descending the bank to the river. A Bureau of Land Management (BLM) "Trail Boundary" sign marks the site.

The path briefly rolls along the rocky slope of the grade and beneath some head-brushing branches to reach a hiker gate at 6 miles. Here, the route travels a public right-of-way across private property. Stay along the river's edge, bypassing the residence. Pass quickly and quietly, respecting owner privacy, and obey posted signs. There is no horse access across this private stretch of land.

The trail next travels along a windbreak of trees to round a fence and leave the easement via a pedestrian cattleguard at 6.8 miles. Soon, deep canyons punctuate the canyon wall of the Warm Springs Indian Reservation across the river.

Where the trail emerges from a willow thicket, it strays from the base of the old rail line to follow a two-track along the grassy, sometimes brushy river flat to reach the Mecca Flat Trailhead and its improved camping area—the end of the one-way tour.

69 | BLUE BASIN HIKE

Distance: 4 miles round trip
Elevation change: 700 feet
Difficulty: Easy to moderate
Season: Year round (when trails are dry)
Map: John Day Fossil Beds National Monument brochure
For information: John Day Fossil Beds National Monument

John Day Fossil Beds National Monument consists of three geographically separated units featuring rainbow-colored hillsides, dramatic cliffs, and fossils dating back 50 million years. This particular tour visits the eroded, blue-green amphitheater dubbed "Blue Basin," located in the Sheep Rock Unit.

Nearby flows the main stem of the John Day River. Irrigated grassy fields intersperse the sage-juniper-bunchgrass expanse, and badlands spread beneath the desert sky.

Two interlocking trails explore this geologic gallery: The 3-mile Overlook (Loop) Trail skirts the outer bowl of Blue Basin and mounts a ridge for prized looks into the basin and across the John Day country. The shorter Island in Time Trail probes the basin interior, visiting sites with replica fossils and storyboard explanations.

The Overlook Trail is steep in places and slippery when wet. While touring this sensitive landscape, keep to the trails; off-trail hiking is prohibited. As these trails are exposed, save for a few juniper-shaded benches, carry ample water.

From US 26, 6.7 miles west of Dayville, turn north onto OR 19 to reach the visitor center in 2 miles, the Blue Basin Trailhead in 5 miles. The visitor center is open daily, March through October; closed weekends and holidays in winter.

Passing through the turnstile, hikers immediately come to a display and a junction: a right enters the basin; a left finds the Overlook loop. First, go left for a clockwise rounding of the basin.

The initially wide, gravel trail travels at the foot of a sage slope and above a field, offering looks at the John Day Valley and the eroded, arid hillsides to the north and west. At 0.2 mile, the trail curves, serving up the first view of the volcanic-ash outcrop known as Blue Basin. Soon, an earthen path continues the journey as the trail passes a more extensive ridge of the eroded formation that is isolated by a juniper-dotted drainage.

At 0.7 mile, the trail crosses over the drainage and climbs to travel a similar shrub complex below a wall of light-colored ash. Nearing the end of

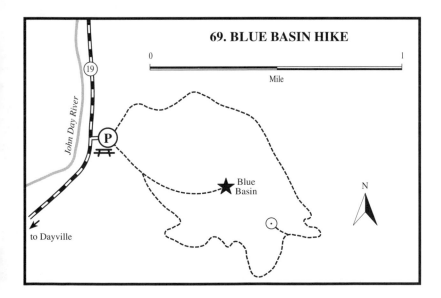

69. BLUE BASIN HIKE

the exposed cliffs, the trail climbs more quickly, advancing via boardwalks. At 1.2 miles is a juniper-shaded bench where the trail leaves the drainage.

Ahead, the serial red ash beds to the northeast draw attention. Then, atop the ridge, the trail arrives at a viewpoint junction (1.5 miles). Here, a short detour from the loop finds a grand overlook of the fluted walls of Blue Basin, the main stem of the John Day River, and the surrounding multicolored badlands and terraced ridges.

From the junction, the loop quickly descends to a stairstep crossing of a fence signaling the start of a right-of-way across private property. Stay on the trail and use your best hiker manners to ensure the privilege continues. With a second stairstep crossing at 2 miles, the trail leaves private land.

The trail next contours the slope. Where it approaches the red rock rim, the route switchbacks downhill to meet the Island in Time Trail.

By turning right at the foot of the hill (3 miles), the tour proceeds upstream, crisscrossing the basin drainage of bluish water and mud. Trailside exhibits describe the badlands, which measure between 500 and 700 feet thick here, their geology, and the fossils dating back 29 million years.

The nature trail then halts at the heart of the basin at 3.4 miles to present an impressive view. When ready to leave, backtrack along the nature trail and keep right to return to the trailhead in 0.6 mile, completing the basin tour.

Blue Basin overlook

70 | SMITH ROCK–GRAY BUTTE HIKE

Distance: 14 miles round trip
Elevation change: 2,500 feet
Difficulty: Strenuous
Season: Year round
Map: Smith Rock State Park flier
For information: State Parks, Central Oregon Area;
  Crooked River National Grassland

This hike begins at the 640-acre high desert park of Smith Rock, where the scenic waters of the Crooked River sleepily curl around a stunning group of rhyolite-ash spires. It then enters the Crooked River National Grassland for a rare native grassland tour to reach Austin Creson Viewpoint, an exciting outcrop vantage along the west flank of Gray Butte. The hike strings together the state park's Perimeter Trail, Burma Road, and the BLM/National Grassland's Gray Butte Trail. Come prepared for wind and sun, and carry plenty of water. Beware of ticks and rattlesnakes.

At Smith Rock, a world-renowned climbing park, Smith Summit rises 800 feet above the Crooked River, and eagles nest on the high rock ledges.

From US 97 at Terrebonne (north of Redmond), turn east on Smith Rock Way. Then follow the park signs that mark the road junctions as the route travels county roads north and east to enter the park in about 3.1 miles.

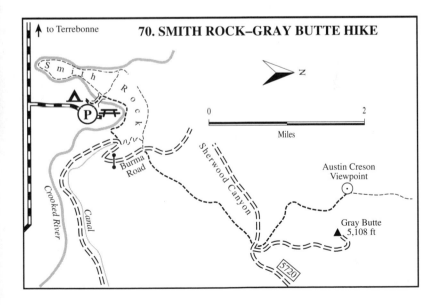

From the park picnic area, the trail descends 200 yards to a canyon vista and another 0.25 mile (or 0.4 mile via the closed road) to the river footbridge; the old road offers the easier grade and footing. Cross over the Crooked River and head right upstream on the Perimeter Trail toward Student Wall and Staender Ridge. Other trails climb straight uphill to Red Wall and left to Asterisk Pass and the Dihedrals. All along the canyon bottom, spurs branch to climber routes.

To the right, the narrow, dirt shoreline path skirts the base of the rock and passes amid the sagebrush, rabbitbrush, fire-rejuvenated grasses, and fire-culled junipers. Spurs branch to the bouldery riverbed. In another 0.2 mile, depart the burn.

Where the trail wraps around a river bend, views are of Staender Ridge with its sheer cliffs, rugged skyline, and nearly vertical drainage fissures. At 1.1 miles is a BLM trail register and a rescue litter, with the trail forking just beyond. Either fork will eventually get to Burma Road. For this hike, go right along the base of the slope.

Before long, the trail climbs beside a green side drainage and again forks. By going right, the trail adds a view of the Crooked River, the basalt rim, and downstream rocks. Continue the ascent, meeting Burma Road (the canal road) at 1.4 miles and turning left.

Keep to Burma Road for the next 1.1 miles for a steady climb to the ridgetop and the trailhead for the Gray Butte Trail. Views sweep from Newberry Crater to Olallie Butte with the immediate Smith Rock–Crooked River area. The grade is exposed and dry, with boot-skidding pebbles.

Where Burma Road arcs to the other side of the ridge, locate on the right the unlabeled northbound foot trail to Gray Butte; a yellow-green lichen-etched outcrop is near the junction. A few strides up the trail, a BLM trail stake shows the path is open year-round to foot, horse, and mountain bike. In another 0.2 mile, another trail stake points hikers left away from a hillside-streaking trail.

The trail contours a bunchgrass-juniper slope, with western views applauding the Cascade volcano chain from Mount Bachelor to Black Butte beyond the vast juniper desert plain of Sherwood Canyon. To the north rises Gray Butte.

Where the trail crosses over a sag in the ridge at 3.3 miles, it again crosses the old trail that rolls over the hill to the right. Views to the east–southeast add an area of desert plains, ranchland, ridges, and picturesque rock outcroppings.

As the trail angles down the eastern flank, it still travels juniper-grassland. Soon after, the trail crosses back to the west flank. Proceed forward across an old road at the next ridge sag.

At the gate at 4 miles, pass from BLM lands into the Crooked River National Grassland. The hillside now reveals a sage-rabbitbrush-grassland with fewer juniper until the trail rounds the drainage at the head of Sherwood Canyon (4.7 miles).

Sherwood Canyon

After crossing over the dirt road that travels the belly of Sherwood Canyon, the trail parallels a seldom-used crossroad. Switchbacks advance travel.

At 5.4 miles, the trail swings away from the old road and climbs via S-bends to top a saddle for a northwest view of Mount Jefferson (5.75 miles). Pass through the next gate, securing it behind you, and keep right at the trail fork for Gray Butte (the sign may be missing). The butte and its stirring ridge skyline reclaim interest. Ahead, the trail snakes up through the drainage folds of Gray Butte.

Atop a basaltic side ridge at 7 miles, a spur to the left leads to Austin Creson Viewpoint, the selected ending for the hike. Vistas sweep from Broken Top to Washington's Mount Adams, with Haystack Butte and Reservoir seen to the northwest.

The side ridge is in the shadow of Gray Butte's summit, a cross-country scramble away, but the summit would be hard pressed to beat the wildness of the present view. The return is as you came, or you may continue north 2 miles more to Old Orchard Trailhead for more grassland discovery.

71 | RIM TRAIL–CHIMNEY ROCK

Distance: 2.8 miles round trip
Elevation change: 500 feet
Difficulty: Easy to moderate
Season: Year round
Map: USGS Stearns Butte
For information: Prineville District BLM

In the narrow canyon realm of the main stem Crooked River, the BLM's Rim Trail ascends the arid east canyon wall to the saddle of Chimney Rock for a lofty perspective. From the saddle outpost, views sweep the Central Cascades, the Crooked Wild and Scenic River, and the stunning, high-walled rock canyon. Rim features include columnar buttes and crests, bulging palisades, and vertical rib fissures. A strict no fire/no smoking ban is in effect June 1 to October 15.

From U.S. Highway 26 in Prineville, turn south on Main Street/Oregon 27—the Crooked River Highway—and proceed 16 miles to find Chimney Rock Campground on the right; the trailhead is on the left.

The earthen footpath of the Rim Trail strikes uphill from the north end of the trailhead parking lot. It contours a slope of basalt, juniper, grass, and purple sage, with a dotting of wildflowers. Switchbacks quickly elevate the trail to the top of the first basalt tier.

As the trail wraps south around the slope, it extends new perspectives on the river before entering a narrow side canyon with an impressive skyline of lichen-streaked rock. Brief pockets of scree are crossed by the trail, and more junipers frame the way where the trail departs the side canyon.

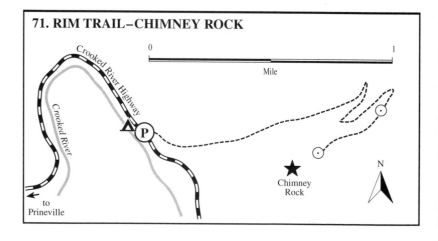

71. RIM TRAIL–CHIMNEY ROCK

Crooked River Highway

Crooked River

0　　　　　　　　　　　　　　　1
Mile

P

★
Chimney
Rock

N

to
Prineville

Rim Trail view

Early morning and evening tours present the canyon at its best and also promise more comfortable temperatures for summer hiking. In the next small side drainage, walls shoot up on either side of the trail. Watch for lizards, snakes, deer, and chukar.

After dipping through the canyon folds, the trail again settles into a contouring line of travel with cross-canyon views of pillars, promontories, and the caps of three Cascade volcanoes. A switchback and steady climb then puts hikers atop the rim at 1 mile, with a full view revealing the Three Sisters and the world beyond the canyon.

At 1.1 miles, a bench seat overlooks the multidimensional landscape uniting the interior of the corkscrew canyon, the arid plateau, and distant Cascades. The trail then cuts across the western front of the rim to tag the saddle of Chimney Rock and arrive at a second viewpoint bench (1.4 miles).

Chimney Rock—an aptly named boxy pillar—commands the immediate view, rising 30 feet above the saddle and 500 feet above the Crooked River. The twisting Crooked River stars below. Although short and easily accessible, this trail comes up a winner for its vistas and wild canyon aspect. The return is as you came.

72 LAVA LANDS VISITOR CENTER TRAILS–LAVA CAST FOREST TRAIL

Distance: 1.25 miles total *(Lava Lands)*; **1-mile loop**
(Lava Cast Forest)
Elevation change: Minimal (Lava Lands); 100 feet (Lava
Cast Forest**)**
Difficulty: Easy (both)
Season: Spring through fall (both)
Map: USFS Deschutes
For information: Bend/Fort Rock Ranger District

The three trails that explore the volcanic backdrop of Lava Lands Visitor Center along with the interpretive loop at Lava Cast Forest help introduce the explosive past of Newberry National Volcanic Monument. Inside the visitor center, displays and programs further help in unfolding the tale. The center is open April to October, with daily hours of 9:30 A.M. to 5:00 P.M. from mid-June to Labor Day. Expect reduced hours before and after that.

The Trail of the Molten Land allows for an up close discovery of the lava flow, while the Whispering Pines Trail offers a look at the vegetation of the region. The nearby Lava Butte Trail, reached via the visitor center shuttle, rings the landmark butte's explosion crater and delivers views.

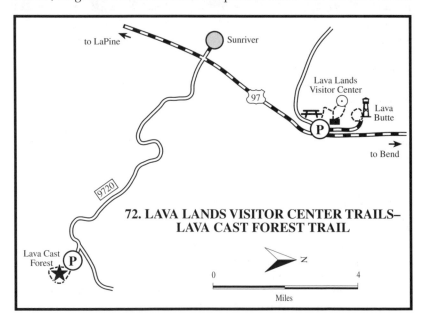

**72. LAVA LANDS VISITOR CENTER TRAILS–
LAVA CAST FOREST TRAIL**

Completing the tale is the paved loop at Lava Cast Forest. It rounds past tree casts (or molds) that record the standing forest at the time of a Newberry Volcano eruption, 6,000 years ago.

From the US 20–US 97 junction in Bend, go 11 miles south on US 97 and turn west at the signed entry to Lava Lands Visitor Center. For Lava Cast Forest, continue south on US 97 about 4 miles more and turn east on FR 9720 (opposite the turn for Sunriver). Follow the gravel road 8 miles to FR 950, which ends at the trailhead in less than a mile; there can be some rough road sections.

Starting from the center's entryway, the Trail of the Molten Land and the Whispering Pines Trail are both all-ability trails, with portions of the former being unsuitable for wheelchairs.

The 0.75-mile **Trail of the Molten Land** takes hikers through the crusty landscape of the lava flow, journeying to the breach of Lava Butte. Interpretive panels introduce the natural and geologic history of the site, while the tour allows for a close viewing of the rock. The lava averages 30 to 40 feet deep, with some sites as much as 100 feet deep.

The 0.25-mile **Whispering Pines Trail** stays along the outskirts of the lava flow, passing beneath the ponderosa pines. It offers a window to this arid, sometimes harsh climate. Interpretive panels introduce the flora and explain the history of logging and ongoing forest management practices.

The 0.25-mile **Lava Butte Trail** rims the cinder cone's explosion crater (depth 180 feet) and visits the summit lookout (elevation 5,020 feet). Lava Butte is one of hundreds of cinder cones on the flank of Newberry Volcano. On this site, an eruption 6,000 years ago spewed forth cinders that fell back to the earth, forming this 500-foot-high symmetrical butte. As the explosion event continued, it later breached the butte, releasing a flow of molten rock over a 9-square-mile area, damming and altering the Deschutes River.

Panoramic views from the crater rim encompass forest and flow and the Cascade volcanoes—Mount Bachelor, Three Sisters, Mount Jefferson, Mount Washington, and Three Fingered Jack. The rough red cinders of the crater demand the wearing of sturdy-soled shoes.

The **Lava Cast Forest Trail** begins at the picnic area and swings a 1-mile loop through a 6,000-year-old flow that originated from a side vent in Newberry Volcano (visible to the south). When Newberry erupted, the molten rock flowed over the landscape, engulfing living trees in its midst. When the rock cooled, it hardened around the trees, which died and decomposed to leave a perfect impression of their shape and often their bark. Hundreds of these tree casts riddle the 5-square-mile crusted field of the forest; the trail visits more than a dozen—all remarkable.

Lodgepole and small ponderosa pine now rim the flow, with a few larger ponderosa pines dotting the landscape. Sticky laurel and manzanita occupy the more open areas. Prince's pine, Indian paintbrush, and purple penstemon lend a delicate contrast and splashes of color to the black flow. Bring water as none is available at Lava Cast Forest.

73 | PETER SKENE OGDEN– PAULINA LAKE HIKE

Distance: 15.5 miles one way
Elevation change: 2,100 feet
Difficulty: Strenuous
Season: Late spring through fall
Map: USFS Deschutes
For information: Bend/Fort Rock Ranger District

The Peter Skene Ogden National Recreation Trail (NRT) begins this hike, pursuing Paulina Creek upstream through open pine-fir forests and past scenic cascades and waterfalls, including Paulina Falls. Capping the journey, a 7-mile hiker-only loop explores the shore of the creek's headwater— Paulina Lake. It is the larger and deeper of the two Newberry Crater lakes; East Lake is the other. The combined tour reveals the volcanic origins of the region, traveling surfaces of ash, pumice, cinder, lava, and obsidian.

The 100-foot divided-drop of Paulina Falls spills into a canyon of reddish-brown volcanic cliffs, while the cobalt-azure waters of Paulina Lake shine up from its crater bowl. The lake circuit offers looks at craggy Paulina Peak (elevation 7,985 feet), the highest remnant on the crater rim.

From Bend, go 22 miles south on US 97 and turn left (east) onto County 21/FR 21 for Newberry National Volcanic Monument. In another 3.3 miles, turn left for Ogden Group Camp and follow the marked spur to reach the trailhead alongside Paulina Creek in about 0.2 mile.

With a Paulina Creek fording or log crossing, the hike travels upstream along the gravelly shore, soon crossing over a low ridge. Horseshoe markers indicate the often dusty route. Open and tree-filtered views reveal the lower creek. At 0.4 mile, the trail crosses an old jeep road.

After squeezing through a rock barrier at 0.75 mile, the NRT bears left to follow a closed jeep road for 0.2 mile, coming to a footbridge crossing. The pine-shaded trail now shows a steady uphill progress.

At 2.5 miles, find a tree-limited view of a 20-foot falls, where a gorge-narrowed Paulina Creek spills over a brownish green cliff. The opposite shore holds the preferred vista. The trail soon rounds above McKay Crossing Campground and continues upstream. Within the next 0.75 mile, the trail enters the McKay Butte Fire of 1998 for about a mile.

Where the trail follows an old manufactured grade, the forest corridor between the trail and the creek grows both fuller and wider. Before long, the creek canyon gains more definition, featuring numerous falls and cascades. At 4.6 miles, the trail overlooks a 15-foot watery veil spilling into a circular blue pool, all enfolded in a scenic rock bowl. Then, upstream, the creek splits into three bubbling 30-foot falls spread across a 70-foot-wide terrace.

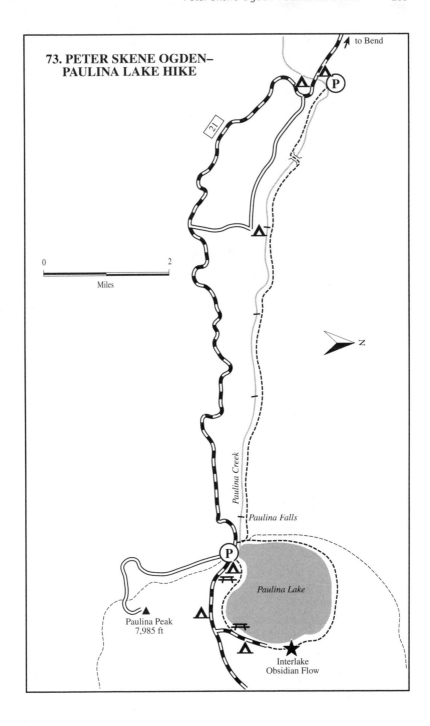

**73. PETER SKENE OGDEN–
PAULINA LAKE HIKE**

to Bend

21

0   2
Miles

N

Paulina Creek

Paulina Falls

Paulina Lake

Paulina Peak
7,985 ft

Interlake
Obsidian Flow

Paulina Falls

At 5.3 miles, the Peter Skene Ogden Trail continues straight where a horse trail descends to a bridge. Passing a funnel-shaped falls at 6 miles, the trail bears left to follow a jeep trail a few feet before the path resumes to the right.

Afterwards, the trail drifts a bit farther from the creek canyon. At 7 miles, hikers gain a quick view of the creek, its cliff and boulder confine, and the forested canyon walls. The upper canyon is more rugged and narrow.

At 8.25 miles, the trail serves up a Paulina Falls vista. While this shore delivers the best angle for viewing the southern fork of the falls, it only hints at the northern fork. A wire mesh fence keeps onlookers back from the rim.

Beyond the falls, the NRT follows the cascading creek upstream to Paulina Lake (8.5 miles). Here begins the lake circuit, which visits both natural shoreline and developed and primitive camp areas.

From the outlet, a counterclockwise lake tour skirts along the Paulina Lake Day Use and Campground to reach a mixed-forest setting and a rockier shore. Past the group camp, meadow, beach, and forest stretches follow as the route passes summer homes and the Little Crater Day Use and Campground.

On the east shore, jagged lava tongues jut into the lake, creating ideal posts for lake viewing and angling. Craggy Paulina Peak overlooks the setting. At 12.2 miles, the trail travels the base of Interlake Obsidian Flow, a ridge of shiny black volcanic glass. Beyond are tiny hot springs.

Where the trail climbs the red cinder slope (12.9 miles), views feature the lake, Paulina Peak, a lava flow, and Little Crater. Semiopen slopes of manzanita and juniper next claim the way.

At 13.75 miles, the trail arrives at a coarse gravelly beach near North Cove Campground. A mixed forest frames the remaining distance. After bypassing the small lake resort, the loop closes at 15.5 miles.

74 FREMONT NATIONAL RECREATION TRAIL, YAMSAY MOUNTAIN SEGMENT

Distance: 16 miles round trip
Elevation change: 1,800 feet
Difficulty: Strenuous
Season: Late spring through fall
Map: USFS Fremont, Winema
For information: Silver Lake Ranger District

This trail travels across a northwest portion of the Fremont National Forest to claim the summit of Yamsay Mountain (elevation 8,196 feet), located in next-door Winema National Forest. Yamsay Mountain is an exciting crater destination. From a distance, it gives little clue to its eruptive history.

En route to the summit, the trail tours a forest of mixed pines and mountain hemlock, moist and dry meadows, and the crater rim. The 360-degree summit vista sweeps the crater bowl, the Cascade volcano chain from the Three Sisters in the north to California's Mount Shasta in the south, Fort Rock, Hager Mountain, the rim country of Fremont National Forest, Newberry Crater, and the High Desert expanse.

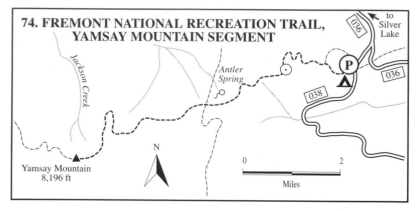

74. FREMONT NATIONAL RECREATION TRAIL, YAMSAY MOUNTAIN SEGMENT

From Silver Lake, take OR 31 northwest for 0.8 mile and turn left onto County 4-11/FR 27 at the sign for Silver Creek Marsh Campground/ Thompson Reservoir. In 8.7 miles, turn right onto FR 2804. Go another 2.5 miles and turn left onto FR 7645. Stay on FR 7645 for 5.4 miles, coming to a T-junction. Now turn left on FR 036, go 1.5 miles, and turn right on FR 038. Continue 0.6 mile more to enter Antler Campground and Trailhead on the right. Signs to Antler Trailhead mark several of the junctions.

From the campground circle, two spurs access the NRT to Yamsay summit; both are marked by trail signs. The horse trail departs near the camp corral; the foot trail leaves the camp loop below and to the left and adds slightly more distance and often a few more downfalls. Whichever access path is taken, upon meeting the NRT, turn right for Yamsay Mountain; a left journeys to Silver Creek Marsh (8 miles).

The NRT traverses a forest of lodgepole pine and grand fir with meadow sites. A steady, moderate climb leads to the first switchback at 0.6 mile. True firs now replace the lower-elevation grand firs.

Hike past the Scenic Rock Loop Trail, which is signed and on the right, still ascending the gentle slope of Yamsay Mountain. At 1.4 miles, the trail bypasses a rock outcrop that may bid pause, but a log bench awaits at 1.6 miles. It offers views east across the treetops to Hager Mountain and Thompson Reservoir.

The climb next flattens for a comfortable stroll. There are ample sandy flats for pitching tents, but avoid building fires in the dry forest. At 2 miles, the trail enters an area of platy, fractured outcrops adorned in lichen. Afterward, a slow, gentle undulation leads to a meadow crossing. The stream here at 2.7 miles is generally reliable and spanned by a log pallet.

The trail then ascends the drainage slope shaded by large mountain hemlocks and passes springs. The forest floor is barren. Atop the drainage ridge at 3.1 miles, return to dry, pine forest.

At 3.6 miles begins a long, slow descent through sandy forest. Where runoff finds the line of the path, its traces can sometimes confuse. A few multitrunk mountain hemlocks later add visual interest and shade.

Where the NRT meets abandoned FR 024, at 4.5 miles, cross over the road for the second leg to Yamsay summit. A 0.2-mile detour right on FR 024 leads to the water, lush grass, and false hellebore meadow at Antler Spring.

The NRT resumes in an open-canopied forest of lodgepole and whitebark pines. By 5 miles, mountain hemlocks supply welcomed shade. A slow climb follows. Later, forest gaps extend looks north-northwest at the Three Sisters–Fort Rock area. The trail provides a first look at Yamsay Mountain at 5.6 miles.

In summer, elk feed on the higher mountain slopes. At the moist meadow at 6.5 miles, buttercups, Lewis monkey flowers, shooting stars, bog orchids, American globeflowers, and elephant-heads put on a spring–summer show.

The trail then crosses over a creek at the upper meadow to climb the dry, pine-forested slope. At 7 miles, it switchbacks uphill to reach the crater rim. By stepping off the trail at 7.2 miles, hikers can overlook Yamsay Crater. Sharp, ragged volcanic rock shapes the rim; the north opening indicates where the volcano blew out. Cross-crater views find the Cascade lineup of Mounts Thielson, Bailey, and Scott.

Passing through a tilted rock, the trail continues to round the crater, passing along or just below the rim. The route adds new perspectives on the crater bowl and views of the Three Sisters, Fort Rock, and High Desert.

At 8 miles, the pumiceous trail makes its final climb and extends views to the south-southeast. The trail then tags the summit at the site of a former lookout. Here, a grand 360-degree vista pulls together the celebrated landmarks and crater interior.

From the rocky summit, a closed jeep road descends into Winema National Forest; for this hike, return as you came.

75 | SUMMER LAKE'S WINDBREAK DIKE HIKE

Distance: 8.4 miles maximum round trip, if add tour of Gold Dike
Elevation change: None
Difficulty: Easy
Season: Year round, unless posted otherwise
Map: ODFW Summer Lake Wildlife Area map and rules
For information: Summer Lake Wildlife Area

This hike traces a dike into a wetland mosaic where the birdlife diversity calls for repeat tours. The wildlife area is at the north end of extensive Summer Lake. To the west rises Winter Ridge (elevation 7,100 feet). The wildlife area consists of open water, a reedy marshland, ponds, alkali-mud flats, and sagebrush expanses. Such variety creates habitat for an array of birds and mammals.

Spring and fall migrations swell the bird population. Sightings can include bald eagles, white pelicans, tundra swans, common ducks, and even great horned owls.

Wildlife Area managers say the best time to visit is in late March and early April, when temperatures are mild, the birds are still numerous, the water is high, and the grasses are low. But anytime is good. The biting insects are most bothersome from May on. Insect repellent should be a staple, and netting wouldn't hurt.

To access the dike, about 1.2 miles south of the town of Summer Lake, turn east off OR 31 for the Summer Lake Wildlife Area Headquarters. There, stop for a map and a copy of the rules and follow the gravel Wildlife Viewing Loop south and east into the refuge. Go 1.4 miles and turn right at the sign for Windbreak Dike. Then continue 0.8 miles more to the cable barricade and start of the hike.

Park at the broad, open flat at the barrier—this is the primitive Windbreak Camping Area. Bring and carry water in ample quantity because the desert basin demands it. Travel is shadeless.

Round the barricade to explore Windbreak Dike, which is generally closed to motorized travel. The dike leads south into a marsh improvement

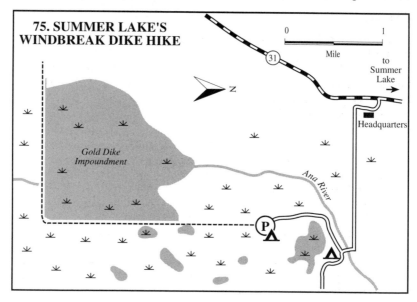

75. SUMMER LAKE'S WINDBREAK DIKE HIKE

0   1
Mile

to Summer Lake →

Headquarters

Gold Dike Impoundment

Ana River

P

Ana River

project and travels the western extent of the wildlife area in the shadow of Winter Ridge.

Marsh habitat spreads in both directions from the raised walkway. Views east span the bulrush expanse to the treeless desert mountains in the vicinity of Diablo Peak. To the north rises a perfectly symmetrical cone peak—Squaw Butte, which stands in contrast to the flatness of this basin-and-rim terrain.

Terns, egrets, and low-flying hawks can start eyes darting. Areas of open water riddle the marsh. Muskrats, ducks, coots, and cormorants can be spied, with night herons lurking at the water's edge. During breeding season, look for red-winged blackbirds; other times, lines of ibis cross the refuge sky.

At 0.3 mile, pass the first pair of several overgrown side dikes. These spurs allow short explorations into the marsh, although seeds can be a nemesis.

The landscape alters with season. Areas of open water may be replaced by hummocky algae or even cracked mud. On the right at 1 mile, cattails temporarily displace the bulrushes.

Before the trail gets too near the eastern side dike with the few willows at 1.2 miles, raise the binoculars to scan the tree branches for owls. Roosts and perches are few in this landscape, and the chance for sighting an owl or raptor is high. The owls are most commonly here in fall and winter, but sightings are possible anytime.

After 1.2 miles, the refuge mosaic becomes more mottled and textured. Snags on the eastern side dike at 1.8 miles signal the next chance for spying marsh hunters. Past the spur dike, sweet clover frames and encroaches on the levee path, but the lane again opens up where the levee bends west and becomes Gold Dike (2.4 miles).

Along this remote stretch of marsh, hikers may detect the chortling call, long swooped neck, and red crown of the sandhill crane, and, for the first time, glimpse the shimmer of the northern extent of Summer Lake, a vast desert platter. Travel now narrows to a two-track. At 2.8 miles, Gold Dike crosses the Ana River channel.

Where Gold Dike traverses an artificial impoundment, impressions and sightings again change. Hawks often send a flurry of small birds into flight. Life is seldom silent on the sweeping flat. At 4.2 miles, Gold Dike halts at a fence and private property, signaling the end of the line. Backtrack to the vehicle.

76 | BLUE LAKE TRAIL–THE NOTCH HIKE

Distance: 14.5 miles round trip
Elevation change: 1,800 feet
Difficulty: Moderate
Season: Late spring through fall
Map: USFS The Gearhart Mountain Wilderness, Fremont
For information: Bly Ranger District

This hike journeys to the heart of this 22,800-acre south-central Oregon wilderness and visits the key features of Gearhart Mountain and Blue Lake. Gearhart Mountain, a remnant shield volcano (elevation 8,364 feet), towers above a neighborhood of Ice Age–carved valleys and cirques. Mixed pine-fir forests and aspen-wildflower meadows spill outward from the mountain. Blue Lake, a deep, circular lake situated below a side ridge of Gearhart Mountain, extends an invitation to serenity.

The Notch is the portal to panoramic views. The standout image is that of the rugged, vertical north wall of Gearhart's summit rock, rising some 250 feet above The Notch. The ridge, the cliff bowl of the volcano, the Dairy Creek drainage, and distant Abert Rim complete the scene. Identifiable

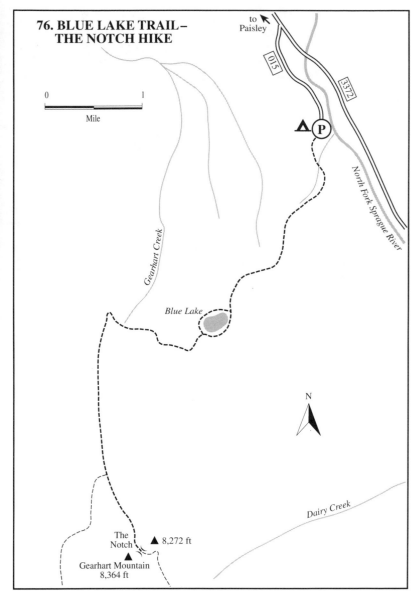

76. BLUE LAKE TRAIL–
THE NOTCH HIKE

from afar, The Notch is what sets Gearhart Mountain apart from the other rim features of Fremont National Forest.

From OR 140 1.4 miles southeast of Bly, turn north at the sign for Gearhart Mountain Wilderness. Go 5.2 miles on the county road. Where it enters a 90-degree turn west, leave the pavement, going straight on the red dirt road. This is FR 3411; it has no sign. Stay on FR 3411, following it northeast for 17.4 miles. There turn right onto FR 3372. In 1.9 miles, at the sign for Blue Lake Trail, Gearhart Wilderness, turn right onto FR 3372.015. A large trailhead parking area, primitive camp, and pit toilet are in 1.2 miles. All forest roads are passable for conventional vehicles.

Entering the wilderness from the northeast, this hike begins above the meadow of the Upper North Fork Sprague River. The lodgepole pine forest boasts an uncommon meadow floor and some huge trees.

Sunrise hikers often spy deer or elk in the meadow. One of the largest elk herds within Fremont National Forest ranges the Gearhart Mountain Wilderness; it numbers some thirty to forty animals.

After the trail crosses over a small creek at 0.6 mile, it progresses with a slow rise interrupted by a few brief, steeply climbing spurts. Firs enter the mix, and the forest floor shows the traditional spare cover of a high-elevation forest.

At 1.4 miles, the trail crosses over a usually dry meadow drainage bordered by aspen. Beyond lies a thick stand of lodgepole pines punctuated by a few grand old ponderosa pines. A scenic lupine–false hellebore meadow next claims travel.

The trail then makes a sharp climb at 2.4 miles only to resume its meandering. A tight stand of lodgepole pines precedes Blue Lake at 3 miles, where a 0.9-mile trail encircles the lake and forested campsites sit back from shore.

A left on the lake loop travels the south shore to the 3.4-mile junction with the Gearhart Trail. A north-shore tour awaits for the return trek.

Follow the Gearhart Trail to the left to continue the hike to The Notch. The trail alternates between pine forest and meadow patches, crossing the drainage of Gearhart Creek at 4.25 miles. Soon after, the trail begins to climb, tracing the gentle, uphill curvature of the Gearhart Mountain ridge. The trail enjoys patchy shade much of the way.

At 6.1 miles, where the trail bypasses a rock outcrop, the intensity of the climb increases. The lone star of the forest is now the lodgepole pine. By 6.6 miles, the trail travels close to the ridge drop-off. Gaps in the forest offer limited views northeast of Winter Ridge, Lee Thomas Meadow, Gearhart Marsh, and the extension of Gearhart Mountain.

Going another 0.8 mile finds the junction for the Boulder Spring Trail, which descends to the right. Just before the junction, the forest opens up. Beyond it, the Gearhart Trail levels out as it tours the west slope just below the ridge.

At 7.25 miles, reach The Notch and a bold view of Gearhart Mountain's rugged, inaccessible rock summit. A 0.1-mile off-trail scramble up the small rise north of The Notch finds a better vantage on Gearhart's vertical rock, the cliff bowl, the dips and saddles in Gearhart Ridge, the Dairy Creek drainage, and Abert Rim in the eastern distance.

The Gearhart Trail continues from The Notch, descending and working its way south through the wilderness for another 5 miles to reach the trail system's southern terminus, Lookout Rock Trailhead. Extend your tour, or return as you came.

77 | ROCK CREEK HIKE

Distance: 4 miles round trip
Elevation change: 400 feet
Difficulty: Easy
Season: Late spring through fall
Map: USGS Warner Peak
For information: Hart Mountain National Antelope Refuge

Established in 1936, Hart Mountain National Antelope Refuge serves as the fair-weather range for the antelope herds that winter in Catlow Valley, east of here, or some 35 miles away on the Charles Sheldon National Wildlife Refuge in northwest Nevada.

No formal trails explore this 275,000-acre high desert sanctuary, but the old cattle trails along Rock Creek help shape an informal canyon tour. Rock Creek's headwater springs dot the eastern flank of Hart Mountain. This upstream hike halts in a basin at the foot of Hart Mountain's highest feature, Warner Peak (elevation 8,065 feet).

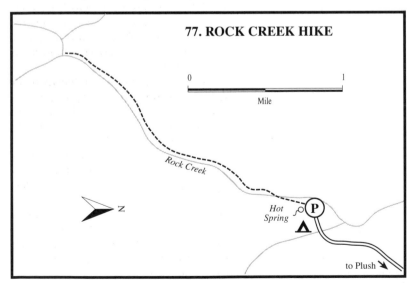

Obsidian shards and broken arrowheads and scrapers scatter much of the refuge land. The wildlife bounty of this area and neighboring Warner Lakes to the west attracted early Native American hunting parties. Look, but do not disturb the artifacts. All are protected under the Antiquities Act.

Backpackers planning to camp in the canyon will need to secure a free special-use permit from the headquarters or the Lakeview refuge office. Backcountry camping is not allowed within 0.5 mile of any open road. For other public-use regulations and area information, be sure to secure a refuge brochure at the headquarters visitor room. An added attraction at the primitive refuge campground is a hot springs bathhouse with a 5-foot-deep, steamy pool in an open-sky structure.

To reach the refuge, from OR 140 at Adel (east of Lakeview), take County 3-10 north for 17.3 miles to Plush. From there, go another 0.8 mile north and turn right onto County Road 3-12 for Hart Mountain and Frenchglen. Go 23 miles to reach the refuge headquarters. The camp area lies another 4 miles beyond; follow signs. The route to the refuge is part of the Lakeview to Steens National Back Country Byway; the road to camp requires high clearance.

This upstream hike leaves the end of the camp road following a well-tracked footpath along the east bank of Rock Creek. Juniper, aspen, and willow shade the route.

In 0.1 mile is a barbed-wire fence, but the unanchored top wire allows for an easy stepover. Up ahead, the hike requires a creek crossing to the west bank. The fording site is just below a beaver pond.

Hart Mountain rises to the west, while the arid dividing ridge between Bond and Rock Creeks rises to the east. Farther ahead, the sage foothills steal Hart Mountain from view.

Once on the west shore, hike along the base of the sage slope to avoid the downfalls, branches, and wet meadow stretches that tend to line the creek. With the absence of cows on the refuge and so few hikers, the animal paths have grown faint. Hiking is essentially cross-country.

Gooseberry, snowbrush, and chokecherry intermix with the grasses and sagebrush. It is a hot, open tour, but the aspens below offer shady escapes.

Deeper in the canyon, mountain mahogany claims the eastern ridgetop. Mule deer are often seen.

By 1.2 miles, the canyon gap reveals Warner Peak to the southwest, identifiable by the microwave tower at its summit and sometimes by the snow it retains longer than its neighbors.

Just ahead, the canyon splits. Continuing along the path that travels up the main stem finds a more pinched canyon with a rugged western flavor.

At 2 miles, the canyon opens up to a peaceful mountain basin at the foot of Warner Peak. The crooked ribbon of Rock Creek parts the basin. Sagebrush marches up the canyon sides, and high on the slope, aspens crowd the headwater springs.

Rock Creek below Warner Peak

Refuge hikers should beware the sage-grassland habitat does present a springtime tick problem, and also be alert for snakes. The return is as you came.

78 | BIG INDIAN GORGE HIKE

Distance: 15.5 miles round trip *(to headwall vista)*
Elevation change: 1,600 feet
Difficulty: Moderate
Season: Summer through fall
Map: Desert Trail Association's Desert Trail Guide: Steens
    Mountain to Page Springs; BLM Steens Mountain
    Recreation Land
For information: Burns District BLM

This hike explores a wilderness study area via an abandoned jeep track and informal trail. It travels up one of the deep-gouged canyons of Steens Mountain—a 30-mile-long fault block feature rising a vertical mile above the Alvord Desert floor. A valley glacier originating near the summit (elevation 9,773 feet) carved out the headwall cirque of Big Indian Gorge. Springs and snowmelt feed the creek drainage. Historically, Big Indian Gorge was a popular Native American summer-gathering ground for fishing, hunting, and sport.

The rugged, arid canyon enfolds the sage, juniper, and aspen vegetation belts. Lupine, geranium, columbine, monkey flower, buttercup, and paintbrush adorn the meadow tapestry of the canyon floor. Blooms peak in July and August.

From U.S. Highway 20/395 in Burns, go east on Oregon 78 for 1.7 miles, turn right (south) on OR 205, and proceed another 69 miles. There, turn left on South Steens Loop Road at the sign for Upper Blitzen. Drive 18.8 miles to South Steens Recreation Site, where the trail starts. Park outside of the recreation site at the pullout located next to a toilet between the equestrian and family campgrounds.

The trail enters the canyon at the far side of camp near a group site; it follows the jeep track of Big Indian Canyon Road. This rough, high-clearance/4-wheel-drive-vehicle road is open for motor travel for 2.2 miles, but due to its condition, it is best to park at the recreation site and hike the additional 2.2 miles to the wilderness study area.

Despite following an old jeep trail, the hike retains a rugged, wild flavor. The tour begins juniper shaded, then grows more open passing at the edge of a vast sage-grassland expanse.

The Big Indian Creek fording at 2.2 miles signals where the road becomes closed to motorized travel, including mountain bikes. Cottonwoods, alders, and junipers shade the good-sized creek. A footpath then leads to the Little Indian Creek fording, just ahead.

At 2.4 miles, the route passes through a gate in an old rail fence and becomes more a true trail. The rounded bottom of the glacier-scoured gorge offers a mostly flat tour.

In another 0.3 mile, the trail passes an old, weathered, juniper-log cabin. Be careful not to disturb this or any other cultural resources of the gorge. Knee- to waist-high grasses brush against hikers. The seeds are demons of fall; ticks are a concern in early summer. At 3 miles, an aisle of small aspens leads to a fine camp flat and the next fording.

The often open, sunny trail now travels below the north wall just away from Big Indian Creek, but within a reasonable distance for obtaining water. Yellow-green lichens etch the dark, vertically layered volcanic-rock cliffs. Springs dot the route, often lined by aspen and seasonally announced by colorful wildflowers. Where the trail enters a bend at 3.75 miles, the gaping "U" of the canyon frames a lovely view of the head basin.

By 5 miles, the open trail passes through a meadow flat where willows separate the creek from the trail. The rim becomes more rugged with free-standing pillars.

After passing through a fence opening, the trail nears the creek, and at 6 miles, the track fades before reaching a large, creekside cottonwood grove. Upstream is a well-tracked footpath several yards north of the creek.

At 7.6 miles, the trail crosses over a small drainage originating on the north canyon wall. Here, one of the Desert Trail options charges steeply uphill to the north rim. The route is faint with a few low cairns for guides, but a good hike ending lies along it. Just pick your way as best you can.

At 7.75 miles, this steep, rugged path finds a rocky viewpoint overlooking a water-slide on a side creek. It also presents an open view of the headwall and cirque basin along with an impressive look at the large, rounded jut of the south canyon wall.

Return as you came; the down-canyon hike presents new perspectives on the wilderness study area.

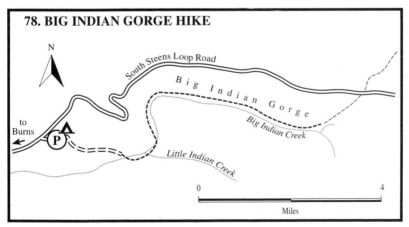

78. BIG INDIAN GORGE HIKE

79 | OC&E Woods Line State Trail

**Distance: 14.2 miles one way, Horse Glade to
    Sycan Marsh**
Elevation change: 100 feet
Difficulty: Moderate to strenuous
Season: Late spring through fall (Nordic skiing in winter)
Map: State Parks OC&E Woods Line State Trail brochure
For information: Collier Memorial State Park

This addition to the state park system is another victory for the rails-to-
trails system, which offers the country a growing network of paths for
recreation, while banking transportation ways should they become needed
in the future. This 100-mile rail-to-trail conversion represents Oregon's
longest linear park. The trail is open for nonmotorized recreational use and
is still being improved.

This northern 14-mile sampling of the Woods Line offers a good look at
things to come. It traverses the characteristic dry forests and natural
meadow openings of the Klamath Basin. The grade passes through Fremont
National Forest to halt at The Nature Conservancy holding of Sycan Marsh.

Carry ample water and come prepared for sun. Do not trespass on the
adjoining private properties, keep pets leashed, and camp only in designated areas.

From OR 140, 3 miles west of Bly (46 miles west of Lakeview; 50 miles
east of Klamath Falls), turn north on Ivory Pine Road/FR 30 and go 12.3
miles. There turn left (west) on FR 27 to reach the USFS Horse Glade
Trailhead (signed Horseglades Trailhead) on the right in 1.3 miles. It is
just before the culvert crossing at Five Mile Creek. Find a picnic table, vault
toilet, and an off-road gravel parking lot where overnight camping is

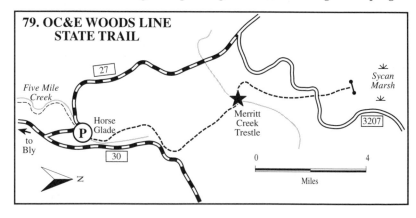

Railroad spike

allowed. The rail grade traces the east bank of Five Mile Creek. To the north is Sycan Marsh; south is Beatty in 18.7 miles.

Hike north along seasonally dry Five Mile Creek, touring the open cathedral, pine-edged grade of red-basalt cinders. Views north are of a conical butte.

Quickly, the trail enters the Horse Glade prairie, with its dotting of trees and a rustic corral. Mileposts on the Woods Line count off the distance from Beatty; look for milepost 19 at the glade.

Some mullein or other vegetation can overtake the trail in places, but mostly the railroad grade offers unhindered walking. Replanted and native lodgepole pine forests alternate with the prairie edge. Where intersections occur, the line of the primary grade is readily apparent, with the vehicle barriers mostly in place.

Along the first leg of travel, sounds from FR 30 can carry to the trail. For more than a mile, filtered views east are of far-sweeping Horse Glade. The elevated grade levels out the rumpled terrain, and the changes of direction are either subtle or handled in big, swinging arcs. Although ascending, the climb is barely perceptible.

A few tall ponderosa pines fill out the forest, but there are none of the big yellow bellies. Aspens grow next to the grade nearing milepost 23 (some 4 miles into the hike). In another mile, a long straightaway greets hikers. Next, sweeping gold-and-green meadows spread out from the tree-fringed grade as it alternates between forest and meadow. Be on the watch for wildlife.

Reach Merritt Trestle at 8.5 miles. This bridge spans 400 feet across Merritt Creek Canyon and rises some 100 feet from the drainage bottom. It provides an intriguing perspective on its immediate area and is a trail landmark. Merritt Creek is stunning in spring but typically dry by late summer.

Upon crossing the trestle bridge, the grade again vacillates between areas of trees and prairie-transition habitat, crosses over two-tracks, and skirts private properties. Keep to the grade.

At the crossing of FR 3207 (12.8 miles), the grade resumes north, traversing a basalt-studded wildflower prairie. An edge of twisted juniper and pine and a wetland pool are final images of the tour. The hikes ends at the gate to The Nature Conservancy property of Sycan Marsh (14.2 miles). Access to the marsh is strictly controlled by appointment and permission only. But before turning around, hikers can at least view the sprawling treeless expanse of Sycan Marsh.

For shuttle hikes, the northern terminus is FR 3207: from the Horse Glade Trailhead go 9.4 miles northwest on FR 27, and turn right on FR 3207, going 5 miles east to where the railroad grade crosses the road. Parking is roadside; be sure the vehicle is plainly visible.

For a shorter, alternative hike from Horse Glade Trailhead, follow the railroad grade south (downstream) for 5 miles to milepost 14. This section closely pairs with Five Mile Creek, which begins as an intermittent stream fed by snowmelt but becomes a spring-fed, year-round waterway in a couple of miles. The presence of water varies the discovery.

80 | DESERT TRAIL–PUEBLO CREST

Distance: 7 miles round trip
Elevation change: 2,000 feet
Difficulty: Strenuous
Season: Late spring through fall
Map: Desert Trail Association's Desert Trail Guide: Pueblo
  Mountains—Oregon (necessary)
For information: Burns District BLM

This hike offers a sample of the adventure, the challenge, and the rugged wildness found along the extensive Desert Trail, which traverses the southeast corner of the state. The hiking is cross-country between cairns, which stand 3 to 4 feet high and are generally spaced from 0.1 to 0.3 mile apart. The Desert Trail Association's trail guide includes a map, compass readings from point to point, and verbal descriptions to keep you on track. Binoculars can aid in the search for cairns, though many markers are readily visible to the eye when panning the skyline.

There is no single direct line between the cairns, although game trails sometimes suggest an easier, tried route. The idea behind the trail was to retain as much as possible the naturalness of the area. Much of the trail falls within the Pueblo Mountain Wilderness Study Area, so low-impact recreation techniques should be exercised to preserve the land's wilderness integrity.

With the springs often far spread, through-hikers should plan that a good amount of the carried weight will be water; always treat trail sources. For this short trail sampling, pack in the water that you will need and be generous. The desert is harsh, the terrain rugged, and the time and effort to accomplish the distance is greater than normal.

A high-clearance vehicle is required to reach the trailhead. From the junction of OR 78 and OR 205 east of Burns, go south for 112 miles on OR 205 to Fields, where services are available. From Fields, continue south on OR 205 another 2.9 miles and turn right on the dirt road marked "Domingo Pass."

Cairn along Pueblo Crest

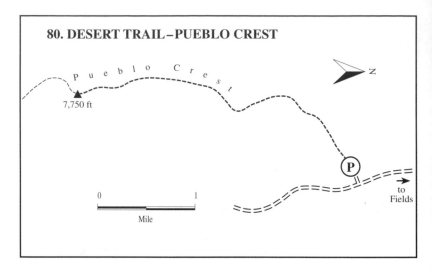

80. DESERT TRAIL–PUEBLO CREST

Pueblo Crest

7,750 ft

to Fields

0   1

Mile

In 4.7 miles, the road forks around a ditch; stay left to round the fenceline. In 1.2 miles, the route crosses over a small creek or spring. In another 0.9 mile, turn right on the overgrown two-track heading west; pay attention to the odometer and keep a sharp eye. Wide areas for parking lie ahead at 0.2 mile and again at 0.4 mile. From the 0.4-mile turnout, hike 100 feet west along the overgrown track to find cairn #1 amid the sage on the right. Consider the drive to the trailhead the first test of the journey.

From cairn #1, the hike journeys south to climb the mountain, eventually reaching cairn #5 atop the saddle just east of the yellow lichen-etched cliffs. The cairns in between suggest a line of travel that crosses the sage flat, rounds to the left of a foothill rise, travels alongside a drainage, and climbs the steep, spare upper slope, skirting rock outcrops and passing through mountain mahogany to claim the saddle at 1.3 miles. Views feature Ladycomb Peak and the desert north, east, and south. The terraced, treeless slopes of the expanse possess striking beauty.

From the saddle, the journey continues generally south to top the next saddle at 1.5 miles. Cairn #6 rises to the right; an old-time sheepherder's cairn sits atop the cliffs to the left. It was well placed; hikers will find it a familiar skyline friend.

Where the route heads up the next rise, it locates the site of a natural arch housed in a bowl-cut rock (cairn #7). From there, the trail dips to travel a ridge to a saddle on the crest.

The Desert Trail now crosses to the Pueblos' west slope, following a game trail just below the crestline. For the next half mile, such trails frequently ease the going. From the trail, the slope drops steeply away to a shadeless frontier spreading as far as the eye can see. At 2.1 miles, the route passes below a cliff wall, which sometimes shadows the trail, bringing welcomed coolness.

Western views grow to include the Rincon Valley, Catlow Rim, Lone and Square Mountains, and a distant Hart Mountain with the plateau lands to the southwest.

On a rocky ridge above the 2.5-mile saddle sits cairn #12; it is best to skirt well below this cairn to the west, avoiding most of the rocks. The route then climbs sharply toward cairn #14 atop the crest, which has been visible for a long while. A good game trail simplifies the final uphill; seek it out.

Cairn #14 marks both the end of this tour and the high elevation point for the Desert Trail in the Pueblos (elevation 7,750 feet). It holds excellent views of the rugged Pueblo front range, the jagged skyline to the southeast, Rincon Valley, and Catlow Rim. The view is nearly 360 degrees. Mounting a nearby rise completes the three-state picture of Oregon, California, and Nevada.

From the rise, hikers also can see the spring below on the east wall where the route will soon travel. Day hikers, return as you came.

81 | TWIN PILLARS TRAIL

Distance: 11 miles round trip
Elevation change: 1,500 feet
Difficulty: Strenuous
Season: Spring through fall
Map: USFS Ochoco
For information: Prineville Ranger District

This trail accesses the 17,400-acre Mill Creek Wilderness, applauding its meadows, the forest diversity, a wildflower showcase, the bubbling waters of East Fork Mill Creek, and an exciting rock destination. Multiple creek crossings left to the hiker's device advance the first half of the journey; a steady climb often amid old-growth ponderosa pines characterizes the second half. Fire has swept through the wilderness with its renewing force.

From the base of Twin Pillars, the panorama consists of the rock towers and the wilderness expanse. Clear days contribute a look at South Sister in the distant southwest.

From the junction of Main and Third in Prineville, travel 9.2 miles east on US 26. There, turn north on Mill Creek Road/FR 33 toward Wildcat Campground; a sign indicates the turn. Go another 10.4 miles to reach the campground via the paved and gravel route. The hike begins at the upstream end of the campground or at the day-use area.

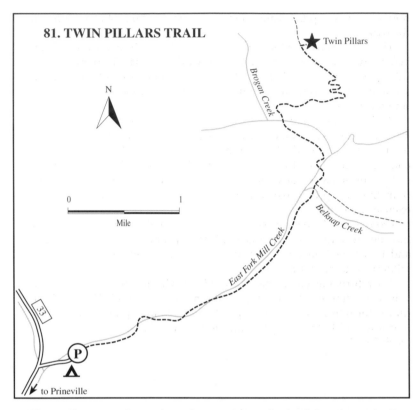

81. TWIN PILLARS TRAIL

Twin Pillars

N

Brogan Creek

Belknap Creek

East Fork Mill Creek

0   1
Mile

33

P

to Prineville

The trail tours a slope of ponderosa pine and mixed firs above the East Fork Mill Creek. As it draws deeper into the wilderness, it alternately tours forested slope and meadow floor, staying alongside the scenic 5- to 7-foot-wide waterway.

Shooting star, lupine, larkspur, buttercup, and dandelion color the meadow. Heart-leafed arnica and Jacob's ladder add spring accents to the forest. May through June, the wildflower show is at its finest.

The trail slips easily back and forth across the East Fork. Only a few gentle rises punctuate the first 1.5 miles. At 1.5 miles, the trail climbs to skirt a small gorge before it dips to the Belknap Trail Junction (2.6 miles). After the final creek crossing at 2.8 miles, the trail undergoes a character change with a fast, steep uphill charge, but the climb quickly moderates.

The first glimpse of the featured attraction comes at 3.5 miles, as the trail draws over the ridge saddle between Brogan and East Fork Mill Creeks. The branches of a nearby ponderosa pine deny clear viewing, but the vista adequately answers one's curiosity about the Pillars.

The trail then rounds the slope and descends into Brogan Creek Canyon. At 3.7 miles is the rock-hop crossing of Brogan Creek. This marks the last opportunity to top the water jugs for the final 1,000-foot elevation gain to the rocks.

The trail briefly climbs a low ridge paralleling Brogan Creek upstream before swinging a wide curve back toward the Pillars through a wonderful, open ponderosa pine forest. The trail climbs steadily. By 4.3 miles, white firs begin to fill in the midstory. After switchbacks at 4.9 miles, the trail levels off.

At 5.25 miles, a sign posted on a trailside tree indicates the steep secondary route heading uphill to Twin Pillars; the primary trail proceeds forward to an upper trailhead. Because the steep slope and loose rock and sand complicate the climb to the base of Twin Pillars, exercise care and be especially cautious when descending. Although this segment is less hospitable than the trail previously traveled, its shortness and rewarding vistas excuse any faults.

From the rocky base of Twin Pillars, hikers gain a neck-craning view of the tilted rock towers and a fine wilderness panorama featuring the Brogan and East Fork Mill Creek drainages. Wildcat Mountain rises outside the wilderness to the southwest.

The return is as you came. But for hikers who arranged to have a shuttle vehicle waiting for them at the northern trailhead on FR 27, the hike continues north from the 5.25-mile junction for about another 3 miles through meadow and lodgepole pine thicket. Consult the forest map for how to reach FR 27.

82 | LOOKOUT MOUNTAIN TRAIL

Distance: 14 miles round trip
Elevation change: 3,000 feet
Difficulty: Strenuous
Season: Spring through fall
Map: USGS Lookout Mountain; USFS Ochoco
For information: Big Summit Ranger District

This trail climbs to the top of Lookout Mountain (elevation 6,926 feet) and the site of a former lookout for a grand overlook of the Ochoco neighborhood and the distant Cascade volcanoes. The summit plateau affords 360-degree viewing and houses the largest alpine habitat in the entire Ochoco National Forest.

The trail tours the Lookout Mountain Management Area, which is a primitive-use area. Frequent habitat changes enfold the route. The trail passes through mixed and single-species forest stands, tours wet and dry meadows, rounds arid sagebrush slopes, and traverses a rocky plateau.

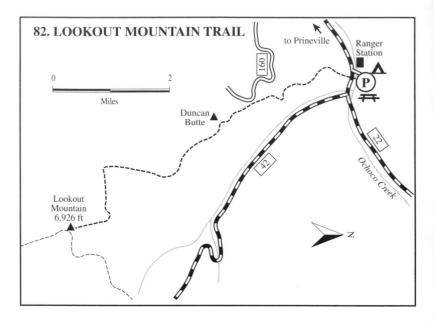

82. LOOKOUT MOUNTAIN TRAIL

With these habitat changes comes a wonderful and varied wildflower show: balsamroot, iris, larkspur, false hellebore, fritillary, and yellow bells, among others. Commonly, hikers come upon meadow-grazing deer or elk.

From Prineville, travel 17 miles east on US 26 and bear right for the Ochoco Ranger Station. Follow Ochoco Creek Road/FR 22 northeast, reaching the ranger station and Ochoco Creek Campground in 8 miles. The trail begins at the campground's picnic/day-use area.

From the Ochoco Creek footbridge, the trail passes through a meadow and crosses FR 22 to begin its uphill odyssey. The good-quality trail tours a forest of ponderosa pine and white fir above a floor of grasses, arnica, and lupine.

By 0.7 mile, the trail is touring a drier meadow floor beneath smaller pines, juniper, and mountain mahogany. Mileage markers tacked to the trees help hikers monitor their progress.

At 1.1 miles, the trail crosses a grass-overtaken skid road to top a small rise. The route then slowly descends into a select-cut ponderosa pine forest with an iris-spangled meadow floor in springtime—one of the finest Oregon iris displays east of the Willamette Valley.

The trail then rolls and dips, crossing small saddles, touring a fuller forest of Douglas and white fir, and passing through a meadow of false hellebore and small juniper. At 2 miles, a side path arrives on the right from a turnout on FR 160. Not far from the junction, the uphill grade picks up pace.

Nearing the midway point, the trail crosses over the saddle of Duncan

Snow fences

Butte, where hikers earn their first views of the summit destination. The trail next contours an eroding slope where agates may be found.

At 4 miles, a log-laced knob offers a prized view of the distant Three Sisters, Mount Washington, Three Fingered Jack, and Black and Belknap Craters. Below lies the Ochoco Creek drainage.

Rounding below a rocky ridge on a drier sagebrush–mountain mahogany slope, the trail affords fine looks at both Mount Jefferson and Duncan Butte. At 5.1 miles, it crosses over a small, unreliable spring; plan to pack in the necessary water for a round-trip tour. Ahead, a detour off-trail to a fir-shaded rock outcrop finds another Cascade-Ochoco vista.

The trail then wriggles up through rocky, high-mountain meadows. Lookout Mountain commands the view with its alternating forest and high-meadow slopes, steep cliffs, and bald summit knobs.

After serving up a grand look at the Three Sisters, the trail climbs and rounds toward the summit's North Point. It then crosses to the opposite side of the mountain, passing just below the rocky ridge. Views here feature Round Mountain and Big Summit Prairie.

At 6.3 miles, the trail tops Lookout Mountain, with open views to the west and tree-obscured looks east. Below the trail to the west lies a big talus drop. As the summit broadens, the trail tours the rock-plate mesa floor, following low cairns to an old jeep trail, which then leads to the former lookout.

Where the jeep road splits, both forks lead to the former lookout site. A low ring of stacked rocks marks the site's perimeter. Return as you came.

83 | BLACK CANYON CREEK TRAIL

Distance: 11.6 miles one way *(Boeing Field to confluence)*
Elevation change: 3,000 feet
Difficulty: Strenuous
Season: Late spring through fall
Map: USGS Aldrich Gulch, Wolf Mountain; USFS Ochoco
For information: Paulina Ranger District

This Black Canyon Wilderness tour begins alongside Owl Creek. Upon its arrival at Black Canyon, the trail follows Black Canyon Creek downstream, crisscrossing it multiple times. The trail passes through ancient forest and crosses dry meadow slopes before descending into a rugged, squeezed cliff canyon. The hike concludes at the confluence of Black Canyon Creek and the South Fork John Day River.

From Paulina, follow County 112 for 4 miles east and bear left at the Y-junction toward Beaver Creek and Rager Ranger Station. In 7 miles, turn right onto FR 58, and in another 1.4 miles, turn left onto improved FR 5810. In 8.7 miles, bear left still following FR 5810 (formerly this road segment was labeled FR 5820) northeast to the marked Boeing Field Trailhead in a couple of miles.

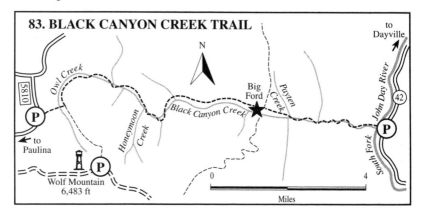

83. BLACK CANYON CREEK TRAIL

For the lower trailhead (a low-water option only), turn south off US 26 at Dayville onto County Road 42, following the South Fork John Day River upstream. The unmarked trailhead is in 11.8 miles; pavement ends after 1.4 miles. Keep an eye to the west for the canyon mouth, that signals both the confluence and the trailhead. Parking is alongside the road; the hike begins with a river fording to reach the trail's start on the north bank of Black Canyon Creek.

The hiking spur from Boeing Field follows cairns across a rocky meadow and passes through forest patches to reach Black Canyon Creek Trail in 0.5 mile. To the right finds a similar 1.5-mile forest and meadow tour with one limited view before coming out at the trailhead below Wolf Mountain (a high-clearance vehicle access). To the left is the main canyon tour.

The primary trail travels along but just away from Owl Creek, enjoying an easy downhill grade passing through open white fir–western larch forest, dry meadows, and moist false hellebore patches. At 2.6 miles, the trail crosses Owl Creek near its confluence with Black Canyon Creek.

A downstream tour of Black Canyon Creek finds a more mixed forest with twin flower, arnica, prince's pine, and dwarf huckleberry. Along the route, little-traveled secondary trails branch north and south.

Where the trail travels higher on the slope, it passes beneath old-growth ponderosa pines, larch, and some scenic snags. From the fording near Honeymoon Creek (4 miles), the trail briefly tours a riparian area—humid and shrubby. The crossing site at 4.2 miles is easily missed when hiking downstream. Look for the small trail sign on the north bank.

Near a marker for the Wheeler-Grant county line at 5.7 miles is a primitive camp flat with a fire ring and benches. The trail next travels a transition habitat between the canyon-bottom forest and the open-prairie slope.

In another mile comes the first of a double-drainage crossing as the trail wraps around the north canyon wall. Bracken fern meadows and springs precede the arrival at Big Ford, a large, pine-dotted grassland bench above the creek.

At 8.5 miles, the trail briefly parallels a fence. Where the path fades in the prairie meadow, stay along the foot of the slope until the trail again reveals itself. A series of marshy springs follows. Payten Creek (9.4 miles) signals the end of the 5-mile north-bank tour and a return to the game of creek-bank tag.

By 10.3 miles, the open canyon floor offers views of the layered cliffs above the arid grassland slopes. Pillars, hollows, and irregular, intriguing skylines accent the rock walls. The creek is wider but just as clear. Plants brush the trail, and darkened snags record a past fire.

With more creek crossings, the trail departs the wilderness via a gate at 11.4 miles. The confluence just beyond marks the turnaround site for round-trip travel or the final obstacle to a one-way shuttle tour. In spring, beware ticks in the prairie meadow.

84 | North Fork John Day Trail

Distance: 10 miles round trip to the Crane Creek confluence/Wagner Gulch or 12.6-mile loop via Crane Creek and North Crane Trails *(for experienced hikers only)*
Elevation change: 700 feet (river trail alone); 1,200 feet (loop)
Difficulty: Moderate (river trail); strenuous (loop)
Season: Spring through fall
Map: USFS Umatilla, North Fork John Day Wilderness
For information: North Fork John Day Ranger District

This hike samples a portion of the 22.9-mile-long wilderness trail that travels the north canyon wall alongside the North Fork John Day Wild and Scenic River. The wilderness area features both historic and present-day mining cabins and claims along with its natural boasts.

Open forest stands of lodgepole and ponderosa pine and western larch frame much of the area. The meadow floors and prairie slopes sport knee-high grasses spangled with spring and summer wildflowers. The legacy of a fire in the late 1980s lingers on the forest face, but the understory is vibrant with renewal. With the openness of the river trail and the infrequent river access, carry plenty of water.

Loop travel is reserved for experienced hikers only. It requires a river fording (possible during low waters only) and the navigation of a sometimes disappearing trail. Because the Crane Creek and North Crane Trails receive only light use, their paths are not well worn and meadow stretches typically require some search.

For both the river hike and the loop, start from the north end of the North Fork John Day Campground. The campground is reached west off FR 52 at its intersection with FR 73, 8.3 miles north of Granite; 39 miles southeast of Ukiah. There is no water at the camp.

A narrow path begins the hike with a log crossing of a side creek, a meadow passage, and a log-bridge crossing over the larger Trail Creek. A well-defined trail then leads the way along the north canyon wall, touring a homogeneous lodgepole pine forest with some beetle-kill and no shade.

At 0.5 mile, the trail travels along a river channel isolated from the main flow by a high ridge of tailings—the rubble of discarded rock and boulder left behind from mining. The river itself is mostly an even band of rushing water, spilling over a rocky floor. Its scenic bends add to the beauty of the tour. Special fishing regulations protect the anadromous fishery.

Gradually, the forest shows more variety and a host of wildflowers. After descending an open slope marked by cliffs and rock outcrops, the trail

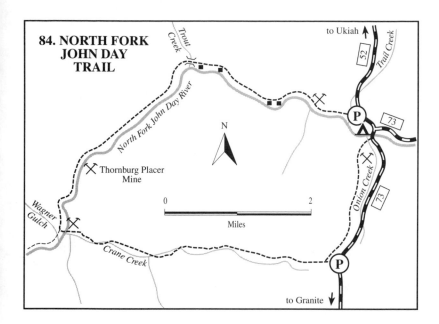

84. NORTH FORK JOHN DAY TRAIL

Trout Creek

to Ukiah ⬆

52

Trail Creek

North Fork John Day River

N

🅿

73

✕ Thornburg Placer Mine

Oriton Creek

Wagner Gulch

0 ——————— 2

Miles

73

Crane Creek

🅿

to Granite ⬇

begins passing the historic and present-day cabins and claims at 1 mile.

The cabins of various sizes and styles of construction show the common household wares of the miner. Do not disturb the sites. They are either private or otherwise protected under the Antiquities Act.

The trail gently rolls along the slope occasionally revealing the river. Huge red larch punctuate the forest near the Trout Creek bridge at 2.6 miles. The trail now bids farewell to the mining cabins.

Across the bridge, the trail briefly follows an old two-track. Before long, it enters a fire zone. Deeper into the burn, the fire's impact is more complete, leaving blackened snags and a helter-skelter array of logs.

At 3 miles, the trail comes to a campsite and the junction with old Trail #800. The river trail now bypasses more mining operations and claim markers. Much of the way, the steep slope denies easy river access.

In another mile, the trail skirts above a landslide. A few live ponderosa pines provide patchy shade. Ahead, the trail overlooks where the Thornburg Placer Mine gobbled up sections of hillside. Where the trail levels and tours along an old mining ditch, the burnt forest promises no shade for many years to come, but yarrow, mallow, paintbrush, and aster present a whimsy of color.

Nearing Wagner Gulch, the trail dips to the North Fork John Day River–Crane Creek confluence (5 miles). Here, hikers have the option of following the remainder of the 22.9-mile river trail, returning as they came, or fording the North Fork John Day River for a 12.6-mile loop.

For the loop, stage the fording upstream from the North Fork–Crane

Creek confluence, reaching the North Fork Crossing Camp on the opposite shore. From there, the route curves left to follow the 5.1-mile Crane Creek Trail upstream. This trail is more untamed, with a 1,100-foot elevation change. It crisscrosses Crane Creek, touring live and burned forest, forest-meadow transition habitat, and long serial meadows. Be alert for tree blazes or the cut ends of logs that indicate past trail maintenance and stay roughly parallel to the creek.

Where the Crane Creek Trail arrives at its developed trailhead parking area off FR 73 (1.8 miles south of North Fork John Day Campground), the loop proceeds north on the 2.5-mile North Crane Trail. It skirts the western edge of the parking lot to pass through forest and meadow areas. At the meadows where the trail grows faint, generally keep to the upper meadow edge or maintain the same north-bound line of travel.

The trail rolls across old mining ditches and rubble mounds before crossing Onion Creek via a plank or an outright fording (12.4 miles). It comes out on FR 73 just south of the North Fork John Day River bridge and North Fork John Day Campground. Hike north via the road shoulder to complete the loop back at camp.

85 | ELKHORN CREST–
ANTHONY LAKE LOOP

Distance: 9-mile loop *(13.6-mile hike adding spurs)*
Elevation change: 1,100 feet
Difficulty: Strenuous
Season: Summer through fall
Map: USFS Wallowa-Whitman, Travel Opportunity Guide:
   Baker Ranger District (topo)
For information: Baker Ranger District

This circuit develops an impressive snapshot of the spectacular scenery for which the Anthony Lakes Area is famous. The loop and its spurs travel to and overlook lush high-meadow basins, glacial cirque lakes, craggy ridges, and rugged peaks. In the summertime, alpine wildflowers color meadow, forest, and granite outcrops.

This hike samples the highest trail touring the Blues and dips into the North Fork John Day Wilderness. Celebrated vistas feature the skyline above Anthony Lake, the Grande Ronde Valley, the distant Wallowas, and the endless rolls of the Blue Mountains.

Fire zone, North Fork John Day River

Anthony Lake and Gunsight Mountain

From I-84 north of Baker City, take the North Powder/Anthony Lakes exit (Exit 285) and head west on North Powder River Lane. At the junctions, follow the signs to Anthony Lakes, traveling county roads and FR 73 to reach the Elkhorn Crest Trailhead, 19.5 miles from the exit.

A clockwise loop follows the Elkhorn Crest Trail rolling through a boulder-studded, semiopen forest of lodgepole pine, fir, and spruce. Early views spotlight Gunsight Mountain.

Stay on the Elkhorn Crest Trail; junctions are well marked. Beginning at 0.6 mile, the route travels upstream alongside the Black Lake outlet. By 1 mile, it overlooks the lake.

After a couple of quick switchbacks, the trail settles into a steady climb. Van Patten Butte fills the view, before the trail rounds the slope above the Antone Creek drainage and follows the side of a long granite outcrop.

The next set of switchbacks occur below Angell Peak as the setting grows more rugged. Overall, the trail is open and sunny, so carry ample water.

Nearing the crest's headwall, the trail overlooks the creek-laced meadow of the Antone drainage and the far-sweeping Powder River Valley. At 2.8 miles, silver snags signal the gateway to a saddle crossing and views

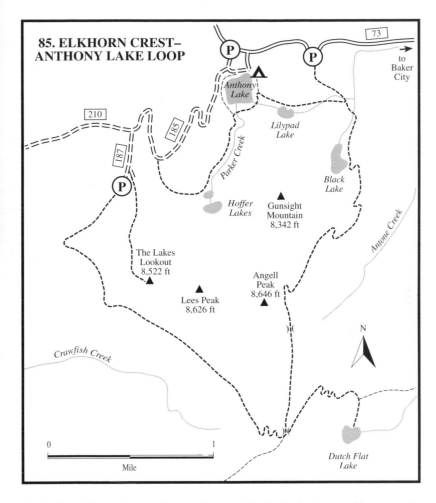

85. ELKHORN CREST–ANTHONY LAKE LOOP

73

to
Baker
City

Anthony Lake

210

185

187

Parker Creek

Lilypad Lake

Black Lake

Hoffer Lakes

Gunsight Mountain
8,342 ft

Antone Creek

The Lakes
Lookout
8,522 ft

Angell
Peak
8,646 ft

Lees Peak
8,626 ft

N

Crawfish Creek

0   1

Mile

Dutch Flat Lake

of the Blue Mountains to the southwest. The basin below cradles a scenic meadow pond. The trail next slowly descends to enter the North Fork John Day Wilderness.

An overlook of the Dutch Flat Lake basin and drainage from the small saddle at 3.2 miles prefaces the trail's arrival at Dutch Flat Saddle (3.4 miles). At the trail junction here, the Elkhorn Crest Trail continues straight for a long-distance skyline tour, the loop bears right following the Crawfish Basin Trail, and the Dutch Flat Trail beckons a detour left.

The 1.3-mile trail to Dutch Flat Lake descends 600 feet, passing through forest and prized wildflower meadows. Small trout percolate the shallow lake, which is rimmed by meadow, spruce forest, and granite outcrop.

Without the lake detour, the Crawfish Basin Trail advances the loop with downhill switchbacks through an open whitebark pine forest and generally dry meadows. Elkhorn Crest and Crawfish Meadow command the view. At 3.8 miles, the trail contours through a fuller, mixed forest.

At the small drainage crossing at 4.3 miles, hikers can usually top the water jugs. A more open lodgepole pine forest follows as the trail rolls below Lee's Peak and the Lakes Lookout. After a couple of quick switchbacks, the trail leaves the wilderness area and angles up slope to the Crawfish Basin Trailhead at 6 miles.

From that trailhead, strike up the road a short distance coming to a T-junction with FR 187: the loop continues to the left, but a 1-mile detour to the right tags the top of Lakes Lookout. The rocky, tree-skeleton-lined Lakes Lookout Trail climbs 700 feet from FR 187 to claim a 360-degree vista overlooking Crawfish and Anthony Lakes, the North Fork John Day Valley, and the Blues, the Elkhorns, and distant Wallowas.

For the loop alone, follow FR 187 left to find a Y-junction. There, go right, hooking downhill on FR 185 to travel the east-facing slope above the Anthony Lake basin. In 0.5 mile, the Hoffer Lakes Trail branches to the right. Hikers may either take the trail or continue the descent via FR 185 to Anthony Lake.

Opting for the trail, the loop descends skirting a meadow basin with views of Angell Peak and Gunsight Mountain to arrive at the two small Hoffer Lakes, situated below Lee's Peak and the Lakes Lookout. From the lakes, the trail then descends sharply, traveling alongside stair-stepped Parker Creek to Anthony Lake at 7.7 miles. Go right on the lakeshore trail, bypassing the historic camp and crossing inlet creeks to arrive at the boat launch.

From the southeast end of the boat launch parking area, continue the loop by following the Anthony Lakeshore Tie to the Elkhorn Crest Trail. This route passes through forest and meadow, skirting shallow Lilypad Lake. Gunsight Mountain looms overhead. At the 8.5 mile junction, go left, retracing the Elkhorn Crest Trail back to the trailhead to complete the 9-mile loop.

86 | STRAWBERRY BASIN– SLIDE BASIN HIKE

Distance: 11 miles round trip
Elevation change: 1,400 feet
Difficulty: Moderate to strenuous
Season: Summer through fall
Map: USFS Malheur, Strawberry Mountain Wilderness
For information: Prairie City Ranger District

This Y-shaped tour of the Strawberry Mountain Wilderness introduces the pristine features of two scenic lake basins—Strawberry and Slide. It explores a realm of snow-patched peaks, cliffs, crags, tinsel-like streams, a waterfall, and wildflower-spangled meadows and crests. The hike rounds up four mountain lakes, with brook trout found in all and rainbows sharing the water of Strawberry Lake.

From US 26 in Prairie City, turn south on Main Street, go 0.3 mile, and turn right on Bridge Street; it begins paved becoming gravel and changes name to FR 6001 upon entering national forest. Reach Strawberry Campground in 10.8 miles; trailhead parking is adjacent to the camp. Individuals with horses should enter the wilderness via the Slide Connector Trail: find its trailhead between the Slide Creek Camp and Slide Creek Horse Camp, east off FR 6001, 2 miles before Strawberry Campground.

Start on the Strawberry Basin Trail, following the wide trail as it

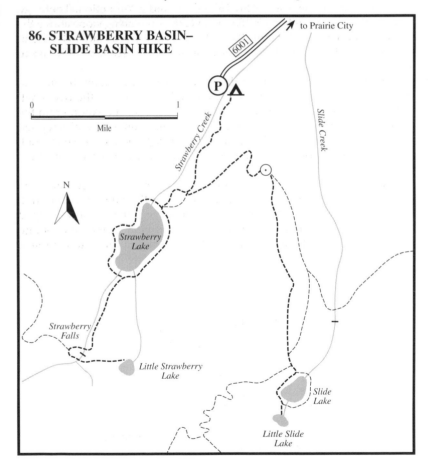

**86. STRAWBERRY BASIN–
SLIDE BASIN HIKE**

to Prairie City

6001

P

0   1

Mile

Strawberry Creek

Slide Creek

N

Strawberry
Lake

Strawberry
Falls

Little Strawberry
Lake

Slide
Lake

Little Slide
Lake

switchbacks up slope, drawing above camp and away from Strawberry Creek to enter the wilderness. The route skirts boulder fields and passes through a mixed, high-elevation forest with showings of dwarf huckleberry and prince's pine.

In shy of a mile come to the Y-split: The path straight ahead takes the Strawberry Basin Trail to Strawberry and Little Strawberry Lakes and the 70-foot Strawberry Falls. To the left is the splendid ridge tour to Slide Lake Basin (Trail 372).

First go right, bypassing the Slide Basin Cut-across to come out at the north end of Strawberry Lake at 1.4 miles. A trail encircles the stunning 31-acre lake, traveling the forested rim, skirting earthen beaches, crossing inlet-creek meadows, and traversing the rocky south-facing slope.

For this hike though, follow the Strawberry Basin Trail along the densely forested east shore, journeying south from Strawberry Lake to reach the falls and Little Strawberry Lake. The trail crosses Little Strawberry Creek above the south end of the lake and at 2.5 miles, serves up a side-angle view of Strawberry Falls, a lacy drop contained by moss-mantled cliffs.

The ascent then continues crossing Strawberry Creek above the falls to reach the next junction (2.7 miles). Here, a left takes the tour to Little Strawberry Lake; to the right leads to Onion Creek Trail and ultimately Strawberry Mountain (see Hike 87).

Go left, crossing back over Strawberry Creek. The hike passes through forest and extends a cliff view before descending to Little Strawberry Lake (3.3 miles), which shines lime green and clear at the foot of a dark cliff.

To add the Slide Basin tour, backtrack to the 1-mile junction and head right on the Slide Basin Trail. Or, take the Slide Basin Cut-across, which heads right 0.2 mile north of Strawberry Lake and shaves 0.2 mile from the total distance. The hike to Slide Basin rounds and ascends the forested slope to attain a ridge. The way can be dusty and is marked by switchbacks.

Atop the ridge, a detour from the trail onto an open knob dotted with mountain mahogany presents a view north out Strawberry Canyon to the John Day Valley. At the trail junction here, continue to follow the Slide Basin Trail as it curves right; avoid the path ahead. Junctions are generally well signed.

The narrow trail now contours along the steep western slope of Slide Canyon. A wonderful array of summer wildflowers graces travel. Patches of high-elevation firs punctuate the open slope, while crags and spires adorn the skyline. Across Slide Canyon rise Slide and Graham Mountains.

Farther along, down-canyon views again present the John Day Valley; up-canyon views salute Slide Basin. Hikers may also spy the top of a falls on Slide Creek below. Continue forward (south) on this rolling, west-canyon-wall trek for Slide Basin; then, at 7.3 miles, go left for Slide Lake where the path straight ahead leads to High Lake.

On arrival at Slide Lake (7.5 miles), hikers discover a beautiful 13-acre lake oval below a dark, layered cliff colored by lichens and mineral leaching. At the south end of the lake, a good secondary path reached near the inlet leads up over a small ridge to the cloudy, green 3-acre pool of Little Slide Lake (7.8 miles), which appropriately sits at the base of a slide.

When ready to surrender the hospitality of the lakes, backtrack to the 1-mile junction (10 miles) and turn right to retrace the way north to Strawberry Camp.

87 | STRAWBERRY MOUNTAIN HIKE

Distance: 7.5 miles round trip
Elevation change: 1,100 feet
Difficulty: Easy to moderate
Season: Summer through fall
Map: USFS Malheur, Strawberry Mountain Wilderness
For information: Prairie City Ranger District

This hike explores the wilderness skyline en route to the top of Strawberry Mountain (elevation 9,038 feet). From the bald summit, a 360-degree panoramic view sweeps the deep-gouged canyons of the surrounding wilderness, Rabbit Ears Mountain, the John Day Valley, and the Strawberry Wilderness Fire of 1996. The far-reaching eastern view contributes the Greenhorn Mountains, the Elkhorn Crest, and the distant Wallowas.

The forces of volcanic, faulting, and glacier action shaped this exciting wilderness terrain. South above Little Strawberry Lake, the descriptively named Rabbit Ears Mountain represents the neck of one of the Miocene-era volcanoes that deposited the volcanic rock that built up Strawberry Mountain.

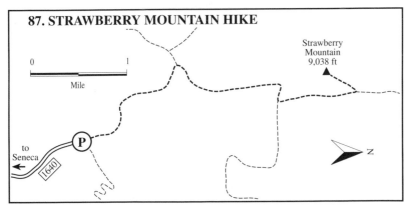

87. STRAWBERRY MOUNTAIN HIKE

Strawberry
Mountain
9,038 ft

0   1
Mile

to
Seneca

1640

N

From US 395 at Seneca, turn east onto paved FR 16. Go 14.1 miles and turn left (north) onto gravel FR 1640 for the wilderness. In 9.5 miles, the trailhead is found on the left, as the road enters a curve; look for a register and wilderness boundary sign.

The hike begins following the Pine Creek Trail along an abandoned, rocky jeep trail. As the flat-touring trail wraps around and below a ridge, it offers an open southern view of the rolling forested hills and the expansive prairie valleys. Ahead, it serves up preview looks at Strawberry Mountain and the western wilderness.

Whitebark pine and subalpine fir (living and dead) create an open forest; dry, alpine meadows spread between the stands. At 1.2 miles, small springs muddy the slope. For practicality, though, consider this a dry trail and carry water.

At the upcoming junction, a bold look at Strawberry Mountain greets hikers. Here the Pine Creek Trail descends the west-facing slope; the route to Strawberry Mountain now follows the Onion Creek Trail, which curves right, traveling just below the ridge.

A footpath replaces the jeep trail, as the route contours the steep, west-facing slope above Indian Creek drainage, which suffered a 100 percent burn. Trailside trees also fell victim to the fire.

By 1.8 miles, the trail passes or traverses tongues of talus. Openings offer looks at the rugged headwall of the Indian Creek drainage—a long, lichen-etched cliff. Ahead rises bald, conical, steep-flanked Strawberry Mountain.

Approaching the saddle at 2.25 miles, the trail tours an open slope where only a few whitebark pines remain. After taking a switchback, the trail comes to a junction at 2.7 miles: downhill to the right lies Strawberry Lake; striking uphill to the left continues the hike to Strawberry Mountain.

As the trail travels the opposite side of the saddle, views span the meadow mosaic of Onion Creek, the stark silvered forest, the Strawberry and Slide creek drainages, and the distant John Day Valley. By 2.8 miles, the trail begins rounding the talus middle of Strawberry Mountain.

Where the trail tags a side ridge at 3.25 miles, catch your breath for the final assault on the summit and find the next junction. Here, the Onion Creek Trail goes right; the hike to Strawberry Mountain continues left. By stepping some 40 feet away from the junction toward the open slope, hikers gain a John Day Country panorama and a grand look at the next ridge over, rugged and cliff tiered.

A few cairns mark the early switchbacks, and in places, the summit trail crisscrosses the telltale segments of the old direct-line trail that went up the rocky top of Strawberry. Overall, though, the route is easy to follow. At 3.75 miles, the trail claims the summit near the site of a former lookout for a top-of-the-world view pulling together all of what was seen before. Swallows circle the summit, while hikers look down upon eagles. When fully refreshed and quenched by the view, retrace your steps.

88 | LITTLE MALHEUR RIVER TRAIL

Distance: 16.2 miles round trip
Elevation change: 1,400 feet
Difficulty: Moderate
Season: Spring through fall
Map: USFS Malheur, Strawberry Mountain/Monument
    Rock Wilderness
For information: Prairie City Ranger District

This hike tours Monument Rock Wilderness, tracing the downstream courses of Elk Flat Creek and the creek-sized Little Malheur River. The trail seldom strays far from its watery hosts as it weaves from shore to shore, passing through lodgepole pine forest and across meadow. The lower portion of the tour explores a multistory, mixed forest where old-growth ponderosa pine and western larch are the star features. Monument Rock Wilderness boasts one of the finest western larch stands in the state.

Platy, volcanic rock outcrops and cliffs sometimes rise within the forest. The shallow-flowing Little Malheur River averages only about 15 feet wide, with most of the crossings easily managed atop stones or logs.

In Prairie City, turn south off US 26 onto Main Street. Go 0.3 mile and bear left on Bridge Street to follow County Road 62 southeast out of town. In 7.8 miles, turn left onto FR 13, an improved surface and paved route.

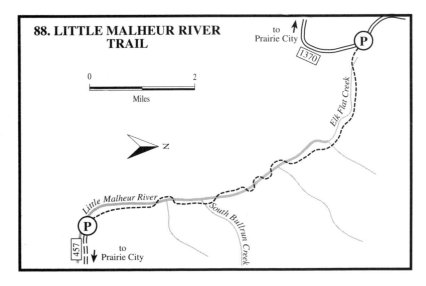

88. LITTLE MALHEUR RIVER TRAIL

After going 11.6 miles, turn left on FR 1370 for the upper (Little Malheur North) trailhead. In 4 miles, look for FR 1370 to bear left, and continue 0.6 mile farther to find the marked trailhead on the right-hand side of the road. Its parking area is just beyond.

The lower trailhead is more remote and best reached by high-clearance vehicle. From the junction of FRs 13 and 1370, continue southeast via FRs 13 and 16. Then follow FRs 1672 and 1672.457 upstream along the Little Malheur to reach the wilderness entry some 38 miles from Prairie City.

From Little Malheur North Trailhead, a downstream tour begins, passing through a thick lodgepole pine forest on the west side of Elk Flat Creek, which is frequently dry by midsummer. After entering Monument Rock Wilderness, the route crosses over Elk Flat Creek at 0.3 mile.

At 0.75 mile, the hike affords a downstream view of a flat rock atop a bald ridge—Bullrun Rock. Clusters of false hellebore and pockets of standing water now spot the drainage.

As the narrow path rolls along the slope, it wraps around the first outcrop of fractured, platy volcanics at 1.1 miles. A magnificent old-growth, fully branched western larch presides at the end of the outcrop.

Patches of 3- to 4-foot-tall yellow wildflowers provide striking interruptions to the forest stands. By 2 miles, Elk Flat Creek loses its intermittent quality becoming a reliable, running creek.

Ahead, the trail crosses a small tributary that arrives from the east, climbs an open meadow slope, and crosses the Little Malheur River above its confluence with Elk Flat Creek. The forest becomes more mixed, with fir and larch. The Little Malheur proves a clearwater, gurgling companion marked by a few deep holes.

Occasionally the steepness of the slope forces the trail uphill, but it never ventures far from the river. At 2.9 miles, the trail passes below a rock outcrop with a broad talus skirt. Soon, mammoth-sized, old-growth larch trees draw eyes skyward.

At 3.3 miles, the trail begins its crisscrossing tour of the river. Downstream, the vegetation along shore becomes thicker.

The South Bullrun Creek crossing comes at the gulch at 5.3 miles. Large ponderosa pines grow nearby and become abundant in number and size on the east slope above the trail. In 0.5 mile, a cliff outcrop abruptly replaces the piney slope.

Where the trail again crosses the Little Malheur, the river broadens in the widening valley. At 6 miles comes the final river crossing.

The hike now tours the east shore and slope to the wilderness boundary. At 6.5 miles, resecure the gate upon passing; cows have downstream range.

As the canyon slope reemerges, the trail gets pushed up onto it at 7.2 miles. Small springs can muddy the going, and the forest becomes more open. The wilderness boundary and lower trailhead on FR 1672.457 are at 8.1 miles. Round-trip hikers return as you came.

Little Malheur River

89 | MALHEUR RIVER NATIONAL RECREATION TRAIL

Distance: 7.8 miles one way
Elevation change: 600 feet
Difficulty: Moderate
Season: Late spring through fall
Map: USGS Dollar Basin; USFS Malheur
For information: Burns and Prairie City Ranger Districts

This relaxing downstream tour explores the western canyon slope and forest-meadow shore along a wild segment of the Malheur Wild and Scenic River. A multistory forest of ponderosa and lodgepole pine, western larch, and white fir mounts the slope and shades the trail. The Malheur River, wide and crystalline with a changeable face, invites frequent access. The trail is currently open to foot, horse, and mountain bike use.

From US 395 at Seneca, turn east onto FR 16 and go 16 miles. There, turn right (south) onto FR 1643, a one-lane improved surface road. In 8.4 miles, bear left onto FR 1651 for the Malheur River. Malheur Ford Camp and the upper trailhead lie 1.2 miles ahead. The improved trailhead has parking, a toilet, tables, and signing.

To reach the lower trailhead, from the junction of FRs 1643 and 1651, stay on FR 1643 for 6 miles. Turn left onto FR 1643.142 for the river trail. The good gravel two-track ends at the Hog Flat Trailhead in 1.3 miles.

Begin a downstream tour by skirting the edge of a moist meadow flat at Malheur Ford to enter a ponderosa pine and fir forest alongside the

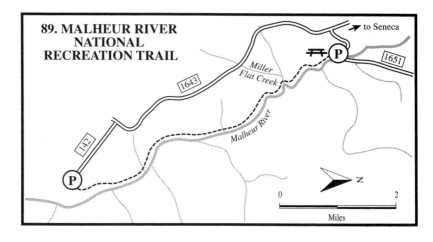

**89. MALHEUR RIVER
NATIONAL
RECREATION TRAIL**

to Seneca

1651

Miller Flat Creek

1643

Malheur River

142

0   2
Miles

Ponderosa pine

river. The trail quickly crosses a log cattleguard to string along the bank, slope, and river flat of the west shore.

At 0.7 mile, the trail climbs and rounds a grassy slope with beautiful, large ponderosa pines. It then dips to a log-and-rock crossing of Miller Flat Creek. A roller-coaster course follows.

River overlooks and up- and down-canyon views come with each rise. At 1.7 miles, where the trail climbs and drifts inland to round an open rocky slope, cross-river views find the high, rugged scree slope of the east canyon wall.

At 2.4 miles, the trail crosses an open talus slope for some nice river views. Where the trail again rises, it overlooks a picturesque stand of red-trunked ponderosa pines on the opposite shore.

Where the trail next traverses a long, narrow flat for a shady trek close to the river, venturing off-trail leads to pleasant riverside retreats. The river maintains an even flow, rarely forming deep pools.

The second portion of the tour is more gently rolling, and downstream, the wildflower bloom occurs earlier. Mid-June promises the best overall show. A burn at 5 miles displays fire's rejuvenating quality. The arnica-meadow floor is vibrant and full, the trail remains semishaded, and most of the big trees loom healthy and thriving, only slightly darkened by the fiery episode. Only the small firs and pines were culled from the forest. At 5.7 miles, the trail departs the burn.

Where the trail tours the meadow and open forest shore of the broad river flats, it becomes more rock studded. Both canyon walls now show occasional rock outcrops, slides, and rocky rims. The river is wide and fast rushing.

At 6.4 miles, the trail grows faint where it passes through a meadow flat, before climbing to the canyon plateau. To avoid the uphill climb, round-trip hikers may choose to turn around here.

The trail's switchback course, however, offers a comfortable ascent. It also unfolds the finest wildflower show of the tour, climbing from full forest to an open forest to a grassland–sage prairie slope. The upper trail reaches afford commanding down-canyon views. At 7.8 miles, the trail meets FR 1643.142 (the Hog Flat Trailhead). Antelope range the upper plateau.

90 | NINEMILE RIDGE TRAIL

Distance: 15.8 miles round trip
Elevation change: 2,700 feet
Difficulty: Strenuous
Season: Late spring through fall
Map: USFS Umatilla
For information: Walla Walla (Washington) Ranger District

A west entrance to the North Fork Umatilla Wilderness, this hike ascends the southern flank of Ninemile Ridge to reach and travel its spine. The ridge is the dividing landmark between the North Fork Umatilla River and Buck Creek drainages. The west end of the tour explores the bald grass-land of the summit ridge, where a few solitary ponderosa pines dot the stage. Farther east, the route alternately passes through mixed forest and grassland. In late spring and early summer, the tour holds exceptional beauty and discovery with a bonanza of wildflower blooms and flowering shrubs.

Vistas encompass the Umatilla River fork drainages, the forested wilderness reaches, and the westward-rolling, bald, grassland ridges with their deep-drainage furrows. The grassland slopes of Ninemile Ridge attract deer, and encounters are common.

From Mission Junction, 2 miles north of I-84, Exit 216 east of Pendleton, head east on Mission Road. At the intersections, follow the route indicated for Gibbon, continuing northeast along the Umatilla River for 27 miles to reach the Umatilla Forks Campground on FR 32. The route is mostly paved, becoming gravel. At the south end of the campground, turn left off FR 32 onto FR 3200.045, the road indicated for Buck Creek Trail in 0.25 mile. The Ninemile Ridge Trail, marked by an iron stake, is on the left-hand side of the road before Buck Creek Trailhead parking.

The Ninemile Ridge Trail heads uphill with a steep, steady incline to enter the wilderness. Ocean spray, wild rose, orange honeysuckle, thimbleberry, and alder crowd its bed. At 0.3 mile is a junction: to the left is the old trail abandoned to halt erosion; the new trail journeys right.

A long, comfortable switchback crosses the open meadow slope, and the rush of Buck Creek echoes up from the valley bottom. Where the trail dips into forested drainages, hikers find a reprieve from the sun.

Graves Butte, Bobsled Ridge, forested Buck Mountain, and the Buck Creek and South Fork Umatilla River drainages combine for the early vista. Even the casual naturalist will note dozens of wildflower varieties.

At 1.9 miles, the trail begins to trace the ridgeline. Each new rise offers deeper looks into the heart of the North Fork Umatilla Wilderness. In places, the uphill grade intensifies. Where the trail overlooks Ninemile's forested north face, views feature the North Fork Umatilla River drainage and Grouse Mountain.

Just south off the trail at 4 miles are two summit knobs that afford a 360-degree view. The panorama expands on previous views, adding the lookout

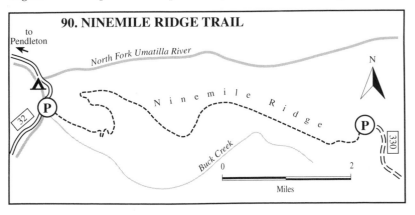

90. NINEMILE RIDGE TRAIL

tower above Spout Springs, High Ridge Lookout, and a greater extent of the Umatilla River drainage.

The eastbound journey then resumes touring the grassy ridgetop. Wildflowers interweave the grasses, which soon hide the trail. Follow the same general line across the broad top to relocate the path.

At 4.4 miles, the trail enters forest. Trees now mount the slope from both the North Fork Umatilla and Buck Creek drainages stealing views. Where the trail enters the next meadow flat, it again vanishes amid the vegetation. Keep a sharp eye as the route descends to enter another forest stand.

Often overgrown and slightly canted, the trail rolls, either tracing the ridge or traversing the grassland slope of the south flank just below it. By 5.4 miles, the trail returns to the ridge as it rounds behind a rock outcrop. From here to the trail's end, the route remains easy to follow.

At 5.8 miles, the trail switches over to the north slope, touring a transition shrub-bunchgrass habitat. The Douglas firs on the slope deny looks at the river below. After climbing through forest and grassland, the trail leaves the wilderness at 7.7 miles.

Ahead, a time-reclaimed two-track replaces the foot trail for the final journey to the trailhead on FR 3100.330, near Shamrock Spring. FR 3100.330 is a high-clearance-vehicle road reached via FR 31 off OR 204. Round-trip hikers, return as you came.

91 | WENAHA RIVER TRAIL

Distance: 19 miles round trip to Fairview Bar or 18.7-mile shuttle to Cross Canyon Trailhead (when river is low for fording)
Elevation change: 500 feet to Fairview Bar; 2,500 feet to Cross Canyon Trailhead
Difficulty: Strenuous (both)
Season: Spring through fall
Map: USFS Umatilla, Wenaha-Tucannon Wilderness
For information: Pomeroy (Washington) Ranger District

Housed in a remote deep-cut canyon near the Oregon-Washington border, this hike samples the offering of the long-distance companion trail to the Wenaha Wild and Scenic River. The tableland odyssey boasts arid grassland and rim-outcrop beauty, outstanding wildlife sightings, and minimal poison ivy. The route alternately rounds canyon wall and crosses river flats for exciting river overlooks, access, and enjoyment.

This area extends one of the best opportunities anywhere to view bighorn

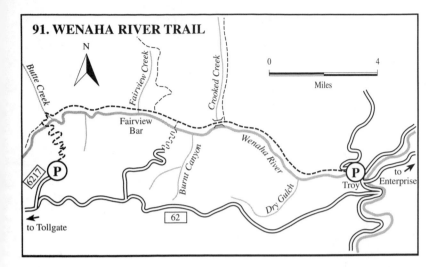

91. WENAHA RIVER TRAIL

sheep in the wild. Deer, elk, coyote, osprey, dipper, wild fish (including the threatened Snake River Basin Chinook salmon and bull trout), various snakes (including rattlesnakes), and a kaleidoscope of butterflies broaden discovery.

To reach the lower (main) trailhead out of Troy, from the OR 82–OR 3 junction at Enterprise, go north on OR 3 for 32.6 miles and turn left at the sign for Flora and Troy. Follow the well-marked, paved and good gravel route for 15.2 miles and cross the bridge into Troy. Pass through town, taking a right toward the Wenaha Game Management Area. In 0.2 mile, turn left toward Pomeroy. The marked trailhead with pull-in parking is found on the left-hand side of the road in 0.3 mile.

For the Cross Canyon Trailhead, on the south side of the Wenaha River at Troy, follow FR 62 west for 17 miles to FR 6217 and turn right (north), going 2.7 miles to road's end and the trail. Or, from OR 204 at Tollgate, go north on FR 64 for 10.2 miles and turn right on FR 63, staying on it for the next 8.7 miles. From there, follow FR 62 northeast for 19.2 miles and turn left on FR 6217 to reach the trailhead.

Starting at the trailhead just outside of Troy, pass through a gate and briefly descend a grass-overtaken road to where the footpath begins on the right. The trail then contours the sometimes steep grassland slope of the north canyon wall traveling some 60 feet above the Wenaha River.

At 0.4 mile, the trail tours an open ponderosa pine flat just removed from the river; more such flats—all ideal for camps—follow. The Wenaha River flows wide, big, and riffling and is clear even at flood stage. Down-canyon views stretch to the Grande Ronde River Canyon. Farther upstream, small islands divide the river.

Wenaha River Trail, Wenaha-Tucannon Wilderness, Umatilla National Forest

Eventually, the north canyon wall undergoes a character change with rocky rims and cliffs parting the grasslands, and the trail slips higher up the slope. At 2.6 miles, it enters Umatilla National Forest opposite Dry Gulch, a conifer-lined drainage. Around the next point stretch upstream views. Switchbacks then take the trail to the edge of the river, where water jugs can be topped (earlier creeks can be unreliable).

The trail again alternates between river flats and pine-dotted arid slopes. At 4.5 miles, resecure the gate upon passing and keep the binoculars handy because bighorn sheep travel the cliffs and rim outcrops that now rise above the trail.

In places along the river, the trail requires pushing through body-brushing shrubs. The tour now alternates between moist, shrubby corridors and the open, dry slope. Beyond the rock overhang at 5.7 miles, enter Wenaha-Tucannon Wilderness.

After a riverbank section, the trail curves right to enter the Crooked Creek Canyon. At the Wenaha River–Panjab Trail Junction (6.5 miles), the river trail bears left, crosses the Crooked Creek footbridge, and enters an open forest with arnica.

At 8.3 miles, the trail rounds a point for a great up-canyon view. It then travels along a cliff and scree slope to enter a grassy flat where the Hoodoo Trail branches left to cross the river and climb the south canyon wall.

At Fairview Bar (9.5 miles), isolated ponderosa pines spot shade to the grass and bracken fern flats that line both banks of the braided river. The bar may signal a turnaround point or just another stop on the upstream sojourn.

Upstream hikers headed for Cross Canyon or one of the other upstream trailheads will bypass the Weller Butte Trail to follow the upper edge of extensive Fairview Bar. Inconspicuous gray-weathered signs mark the junctions.

Find easy travel above the bar and along the canyon slope. The tour continues to serve up grand views of the wild river and the canyon. Bluff promontories offer lofty vantages.

After 11 miles, the trail alternates between dry slopes and the vegetated river bars where the encroaching knee- to shoulder-high vegetation sometimes requires bushwhacking. When the riverside plants are dew soaked or the humidity is high, expect soggy, tedious going. Some of these choked stretches are as much as 0.5 mile long. Trail use is light.

Ahead, more rock promontories add to or serve up views. At 12.5 miles, cross Weller Creek via logs or fording and ascend to contour higher up the slope for the next 0.5 mile. Views are of the S-bending river.

More roller-coaster travel occurs before the trail is routed up Butte Creek Canyon at 14.5 miles to the formal crossing site. Cross via a log if conditions are dry; wade if wet.

Upon reaching the west bank of Butte Creek above the Wenaha River, resume upstream alongside the river for another 0.3 mile to the Cross Canyon junction, marked by another small, weathered sign. Look for it on a forest flat after rounding a weeping wall—this side trail requires a river fording. The Wenaha River Trail continues upstream to Timothy Campground, with more jungle-like stretches in between.

Ford the river where the current appears lightest and be alert for deceptively deep spots; boots are required for the surest footing on the slippery rock bed. The trail emerges on the south bank near a couple of camp flats. A hefty 3.4-mile, 2,000-foot climb awaits; it is well-paced advancing via contours and switchbacks. Be sure to have a good water supply before leaving the river.

Along the lower canyon wall, pass alongside a deep ravine, touring amid trees for partial shade. The trail opens up as it climbs. Midway to the top (17 miles), a photogenic split juniper on an outcrop suggests pause. The view spans the rim-terrace setting of the Wenaha River Canyon. Looks north across the river find the Butte Creek drainage and Rattlesnake Ridge.

Next, alternate from the forest edge of the drainages to the open grassland slope. Loose rock can sometimes steal footing. Views continue.

A delicate sprinkling of wildflowers adds to the upper grassy slope. Lone-standing ponderosa pines deliver prized shade. At 18.7 miles, come out at trail information board and two-track near the road's end parking on FR 6217.

92 | SNAKE RIVER TRAIL

Distance: 17.5 miles one way *(Lookout Creek to Dug Bar, with boat-shuttle to Lookout Creek)*
Elevation change: 900 feet
Difficulty: Strenuous
Season: Spring through fall
Map: USFS Hells Canyon National Recreation Area
For information: Hells Canyon National Recreation Area

This is the most untamed, rugged, and adventurous trail of the book. Tracing the west canyon wall above the Snake Wild and Scenic River, it offers tremendous solitude, spectacular arid scenery, wildlife sightings, and a look at early homestead efforts.

Hot and remote, the hike explores Hells Canyon Wilderness, traveling grassland slopes dotted with prickly pear cactus and colored with wildflowers. The hike reveals the canyon scenery of both Oregon and Idaho. Raptors, deer, elk, and coyotes add to the excitement, but rattlesnakes can be a concern, especially when the trail is overgrown.

Because of the trail's condition and length (48 miles), chartering a boat trip to an upstream trailhead for a one-way hike back to Dug Bar offers the

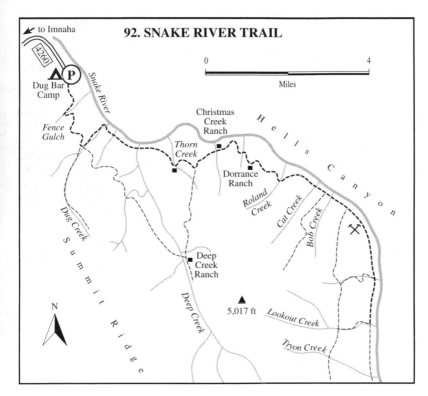

92. SNAKE RIVER TRAIL

best way to see more of the canyon and trail, including riverside segments. Charters stop for the hikers at Dug Bar and then drop them off at points upstream where the trail nears the river. Contact the recreation area head-quarters or the Lewiston, Idaho, Chamber of Commerce for the names of charter services.

To reach Dug Bar, from Imnaha, go northeast on Lower Imnaha Road, a slow, winding route not recommended for low-clearance vehicles. In 30 miles, pass through the gate to reach the Dug Bar boat launch and the Snake River Trail. From here, hikers may be picked up for their prearranged boat shuttle or strike uphill to the left of the corral, where the trail begins some 40 feet above a fence stair-stile.

For the selected 17.5-mile shuttle option, a downstream hike begins at the Tryon Creek–Snake River Trail Junction above the gravel beach at Lookout Creek. Traveling about 30 to 50 feet above the river, the often-overgrown path rounds rock outcrops and arid slopes.

River views feature slow bends, riffles, and a few rapids and eddies; the shoreline is mostly rocky, marked by a few gravel bars and beaches. At 2.7 miles, the trail tops a cliff overlooking the water for a grand Snake River view.

A cross-canyon view of the Snake River and the Idaho wall of Hells Canyon

Where the trail passes an old mining tunnel opposite the Getta Creek confluence on the Idaho shore, take the uphill path to skirt a private property; do not take the lower trail. Above the property, the trail crosses a grassy plateau. Keep a sharp eye as the path often disappears amid the tall grasses and sumac.

From the gate at 3.5 miles, cairns angle downhill pointing the way. In less than a mile, the route crosses Bob Creek. At the mouth of Bob, the gentle slope allows easy river access for the refilling of water jugs. The creeks to this point are unreliable.

Soon a tree-shaded table occupies a grassy bench above the river—a nice stop or campsite. The trail then pulls steeply uphill rounding a ranch, touring a grassland where the trail is again overgrown. At 5 miles, the more reliable waters of Cat Creek attract deer.

As the trail remains far above the river, the Idaho canyon wall shows a low rim of columnar basalt. After crossing Roland Creek at 5.8 miles, the trail heads left to climb the steep, open slope of the creek's north bank. Elk frequent this remote canyon. The grade eases as the trail rounds the left side of a low knoll.

By 7.4 miles, the trail passes the outbuildings of abandoned Dorrance Ranch. At the junction on the saddle, the Snake River Trail bears left staying uphill, wrapping across arid slopes and crossing unreliable creeks.

Beyond Thorn Creek, the trail tops a saddle at 10.9 miles and then begins a steep descent crisscrossing Trail Gulch. With the trail's grade and surface, it is easy to lose your footing; be careful. Poison ivy further complicates the going.

In another mile, the trail again tours a slope some 50 feet above the river. Here, the Snake River is much more gorgelike with rugged canyon walls. Deep Creek, a 15-foot-wide tumbling stream, requires fording. At 13 miles is another established campsite.

From the Dug Creek crossing, the Snake River Trail heads inland, zigzagging up Dug Creek Canyon. Overgrown, the trail requires bushwhacking. Nettles and poison ivy add to the burden.

Departing the creek canyon at 14.4 miles, the trail again tours a grassland, this time toward the saddle above Dug Bar. At the upcoming junction, the Lord Flat Trail heads left up a side canyon, while the Snake River Trail continues its climb east toward the saddle, often traveling alongside horse tracks.

After attaining the saddle, the trail begins a slope-rounding, slow descent. It crosses Fence Gulch and collects upstream views before leaving the wilderness at 16.3 miles. A steep descent then leads to Dug Bar Ranch. At 17.2 miles, a stair step over the fence at the end of the corral finds an open grassland, where the overgrown trail continues to the boat launch and the end of the tour.

93 | CHIMNEY LAKE HIKE

Distance: 10 miles round trip *(wilderness permit required)*
Elevation change: 2,500 feet
Difficulty: Moderate to strenuous
Season: Summer through fall
Map: USFS Eagle Cap Wilderness, Wallowa-Whitman; Imus
  Geographics Wallowa Mountains Eagle Cap Wilderness
For information: Eagle Cap Ranger District

The popular Bowman Trail (Trail 1651) launches this wilderness hike with a zigzagging tour up the west canyon wall of the Lostine River drainage. Travel high-elevation forest, crossing tributaries and collecting views. Marble Point, Eagle Cap, and the tinsel-like ribbon of the Lostine River are among the early images.

The trail skirts the picturesque alpine meadow of Brownie Basin and visits tranquil Laverty Lakes before reaching the shining beauty of Chimney Lake. The area also holds an invitation for outward exploration with Hobo, Wood, and John Henry Lakes, all within easy striking distance.

From OR 82 in Lostine (northwest of Enterprise), go 14.1 miles south on Lostine River Road/FR 8210, a paved and improved-surface road, which is signed for Lostine River Campgrounds. On the right, find Bowman Trailhead with parking for up to ten passenger vehicles. Locate horse-trailer parking 0.1 mile farther south at the Frances Lake/Bowman Trailhead.

Cross the concrete bridge overlooking the Lostine River, with its bouldery streambed and rock ledge, and then turn upstream. The well-used trail passes through a lodgepole pine–fir forest with a huckleberry understory.

Enter the wilderness, coming to a rock crossing (seasonal fording) of Bowman Creek. Long angling contours now advance the trail, for a comfortable measured ascent. Alternately tour forest and meadow, gathering the first open view—a cross-canyon look at Marble Point—after the initial switchback at 0.4 mile. Then, at the next switchback, overlook a racing chute (or late-season water slide) on Bowman Creek. An unnamed peak presides at the head of the creek canyon.

At 1.3 miles, a grassy opening funnels the line of vision up the East Fork Lostine River drainage to Eagle Cap for a first-rate presentation of this famous peak. Below the trail at 1.6 miles, a forested shelf holds a campsite with additional cross-canyon views of Marble Point.

Chimney Lake

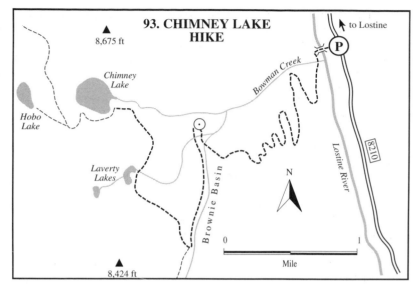

By 2.1 miles enter the "high country," with granite outcrops and cliffs, talus slopes, and fir, spruce, and whitebark pine. Next, cross the head forks of Bowman Creek and the outlet of Laverty Lakes, scenic cascading waters each. At 2.75-mile switchback, an outcrop point may waylay hikers for a breather. Glimpse Hurricane Divide and the top of Twin Peaks above the Marble Point Ridge, and admire the nearby ragged skyline and layered canyon walls.

The trail continues rounding over outcrop and across rock-studded slope to cross back over the Laverty Lakes outlet. The trail then traces the foot of the slope overlooking the long alpine meadow of Brownie Basin (3.3 miles). Jagged peaks, sweeping saddles, and Flagstaff Point frame this basin, which is parted by a shimmery stream.

At the marked trail junction at 3.8 miles, turn right for Chimney Lake on Trail 1659. Forward leads to Wilson Basin and John Henry Lake.

Ascending from Brownie Basin for Chimney Lake, the trail crosses exposed granite outcrops that serve up rewarding Lostine River canyon views. At 4.3 miles, it begins to round the main Laverty Lakes body, a serene mixed-depth mountain pool below a talus-skirted peak. To view the upper lake in the next higher basin requires cross-country travel up a rocky slope beside the inlet stream.

Cross the outlet and round toward Chimney Lake, again traversing exposed outcrop. By 4.7 miles, peer across a saddle at Eagle Cap and its high-peak gallery. Also, admire the sweeping vertical-relief of the Lostine River canyon.

At 5 miles, cobalt Chimney Lake measures 19 acres and is cupped by ragged peaks. A dark red dike streaks one wall above the lake. Steep talus slopes, alpine tree clusters, and a couple of rock islands add to the lake's charm.

Nearby lie a couple of inappropriate wilderness campsites; camp no closer than 0.25 mile to this fragile lake body or Laverty Lakes. The wilderness trail continues, rounding above and away from Chimney Lake, splitting off at a saddle for Hobo and Wood Lakes. The return is as you came.

94 | WEST FORK LOSTINE – BLUE LAKE HIKE

Distance: 15 miles round trip to Blue Lake
(wilderness permit required)
Elevation change: 2,000 feet
Difficulty: Moderate to strenuous
Season: Summer through fall
Map: USFS Eagle Cap Wilderness, Wallowa-Whitman; Imus
    Geographics Wallowa Mountains Eagle Cap Wilderness
For information: Eagle Cap Ranger District

This wilderness tour travels the forest and meadow habitats of the West Fork Lostine River drainage to visit Minam and Blue Lakes. Along the way, the hiker discovers the high mountain scenery: steep-flanked ridges, spired forests, snowfields, and seasonal waterfalls.

Minam is the larger lake, a long, oval water below the aptly dubbed Brown Mountain. A small earthen dam at its south end diverted its natural drainage, but little detracts from the overall lake beauty. Blue Lake, a pretty, midsized circular lake is nestled at the foot of a sharp-spined white ridge and offers the more intimate, tranquil retreat.

For this hike, at Lostine, turn south off OR 82 at the sign for Lostine River Campgrounds. This is Lostine River Road/FR 8210, a paved and gravel route; follow it south for 17.5 miles. The trail leaves the south end of Two Pan Campground.

Upon entering the Eagle Cap Wilderness, a right begins the West Fork hike. This trail crosses the East Fork Lostine River, gathers views of the West Fork, and then drifts inland, where it climbs parallel to but removed from the river. A dense forest of thin, tall Engelmann spruce, alder, white fir, western larch, and lodgepole pine frames the way. Aster, thimbleberry, twisted stalk, and bride's bonnet don the floor.

The trail passes granite outcrops, a boulder-littered slope with huckleberry bushes, and a mature forest stand. By 1.1 miles, it tours just above the West Fork.

A talus slope announces the 2.8-mile junction. A right begins the Copper

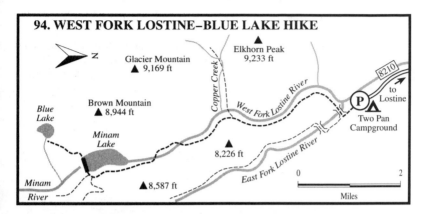

94. WEST FORK LOSTINE–BLUE LAKE HIKE

Creek Trail. Go left to continue the West Fork hike toward Minam and Blue Lakes.

From the junction, the West Fork Trail climbs and skirts a spruce-dotted meadow. It next traverses the granite boulder slope at the foot of the dividing ridge to the Lostine River forks. By 3.1 miles, the trail presents open views of the Copper Creek drainage, Elkhorn Peak, and the neighboring tree-studded, dome-shaped granite peaks.

With a fluctuating grade, the trail now passes in and out of the lodgepole pine–subalpine fir forest for sunnier trekking. Views come frequently. Touring a wildflower and grass meadow at 4.1 miles, the trail draws closer to the West Fork Lostine River.

Ahead, a string of stones normally allows a dry crossing of the now creek-sized West Fork; early-season hikers may have to wade. As it alternately passes through meadow and subalpine fir forest, the trail overlooks the slow-coursing upstream waters of the West Fork.

A couple of drainage crossings follow, before the trail crosses back over the West Fork at 5.3 miles to return to a forest tour. Soon after comes the first look at Brown Mountain. At 5.8 miles, the trail reaches Minam Lake at its outlet.

In the morning, Minam Lake's glassy waters reflect the ridge of Brown Mountain and the distant southern peaks. The large lake shows a varied shore with areas of forest, meadow, and white granite boulders. Much of the water is surprisingly shallow. The primary trail rounds the east slope well above the lake, while camper footpaths tour closer to shore. With the forest-meadow floor being soft and moist, avoid off-trail excursions.

Near the earthen dam at 6.5 miles, the trail forks in three directions: to the left leads to the popular Wallowa Lakes Basin; the route straight ahead leads to the long-distance Minam River Trail; and the chosen Blue Lake Trail crosses atop the dam and then bears left.

En route to Blue Lake, the trail climbs quickly away from the Minam Lake Basin, heading southwest along a similar steep, open-forested slope.

Blue Lake

At 6.8 miles, it crosses a small creek drainage. Beyond lies a swath of trees tumbled by either avalanche or wind storm. The trail continues climbing.

At 7.5 miles, Blue Lake presents its deep, shimmering waters. White granite boulders, pockets of subalpine fir, and a few weathered whitebark pines accent its shore. Retrace the way when ready to return.

95 | WEST FORK WALLOWA– LAKES BASIN LOOP HIKE

Distance: 30 miles round trip *(wilderness permit required)*
Elevation change: 3,900 feet
Difficulty: Strenuous
Season: Summer through fall
Map: USFS Eagle Cap Wilderness, Wallowa-Whitman; Imus
   Geographics Wallowa Mountains Eagle Cap Wilderness
For information: Eagle Cap Ranger District

Among Eagle Cap's prized system of trails, this hike stands out as the premier route for discovering the Wallowa Mountain majesty. The tour takes visitors along a deep, chiseled river drainage, through high-country meadows, past six magnificent high lakes, and up and over steep, rugged ridges. Granite domes, spired forests, snowfields, alpine wildflower fields, chilly stream crossings, and snowmelt falls pepper the way. Mountain goats, deer, elk, and coyotes may surprise. Despite the loop's popularity, the lakeshores remain remarkably uncrowded and pristine.

To reach the trailhead from Joseph, go south for 6.5 miles on OR 82 and Upper Power House Road. The trail begins opposite the South Day Use of Wallowa Lake State Park.

The route climbs and proceeds straight at the 0.25-mile junction to parallel the West Fork Wallowa River into Eagle Cap Wilderness. Because area concessions lead horse strings along the first 2 miles, the early route can be dusty. Mountain goats range the steep flanks of Hurwal Divide, rising to the west. Where the trail nears the river, side trails wiggle to its bank.

At the 2.8-mile junction, the West Fork Trail again heads straight, continuing up the river canyon. Beyond the Adam Creek–West Fork confluence, western views feature Craig Mountain. Travel is well above the river.

At 6 miles, the trail reaches extensive Six Mile Meadow and the Lakes Basin Loop Junction. Campsites occupy the forest edge, and a cliff rises to the east.

Going straight begins a clockwise tour of the loop, still following the clear-running West Fork upstream. At 7.75 miles, the trail affords looks at

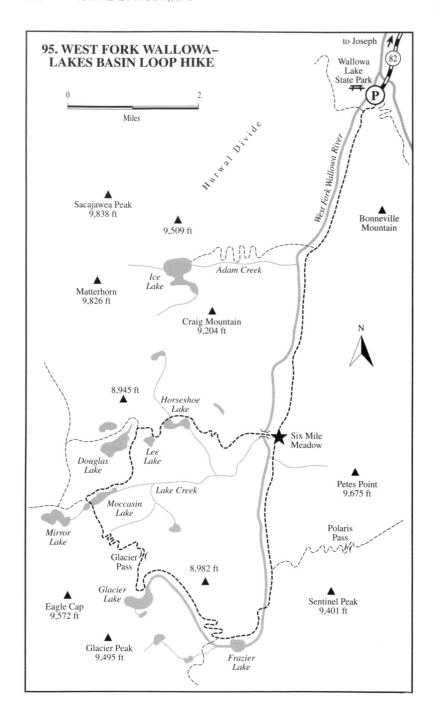

95. WEST FORK WALLOWA–LAKES BASIN LOOP HIKE

0   2

Miles

to Joseph

Wallowa Lake State Park

82

P

Hurwal Divide

West Fork Wallowa River

▲ Sacajawea Peak
9,838 ft

▲ 9,509 ft

Bonneville Mountain

Ice Lake

Adam Creek

▲ Matterhorn
9,826 ft

▲ Craig Mountain
9,204 ft

N

8,945 ft
▲

Horseshoe Lake

Six Mile Meadow

Douglas Lake

Lee Lake

▲ Petes Point
9,675 ft

Lake Creek

Moccasin Lake

Mirror Lake

Polaris Pass

Glacier Pass

8,982 ft
▲

▲ Eagle Cap
9,572 ft

Glacier Lake

▲ Sentinel Peak
9,401 ft

▲ Glacier Peak
9,495 ft

Frazier Lake

the light-colored peaks at the head of the canyon. The climb then picks up. Beginning at 8.5 miles, the trail switchbacks up slope to round a rocky ridge. It bypasses Polaris Pass Trail, skirts a cliff overlooking a West Fork gorge, and crosses the high meadow below the east canyon wall to arrive at a wet crossing of the West Fork at 9.75 miles.

The trail next switchbacks into forest as it journeys toward the canyon head. At 10.5 miles is Frazier Lake—a green, shallow pool in a scenic bowl framed by an impressive ridge. Thin chutes and snow patches mark the ridge; a smaller lake sits at its foot.

At the upcoming junction, the loop heads right, climbing toward Glacier Pass. It crosses granite boulder slopes with small tree pockets and overlooks the meadow drainage of the ribbony West Fork. Granite domes marking the ridges resemble the High Sierra. After 12.5 miles, Eagle Cap becomes a familiar tour landmark.

At 13 miles, the loop tags the shore of Glacier Lake below Eagle Cap Ridge. Fed by Benson Glacier, it is a heart-stopping beauty. Rock slides and snowfields spill from the cliff to its waters, while wildflowers sprinkle its meadow shore. As the trail climbs from Glacier Lake, a smaller, upper lake comes into view.

At 13.75 miles, the trail tops Glacier Pass, the high point on the trail. A sharp descent on a mostly exposed slope follows, offering down-canyon views of the East Fork Lostine River and Hurricane Creek along with Hurricane Divide, Matterhorn, and Moccasin and Mirror Lakes.

In another mile, the trail crosses a drainage to enter a series of downhill switchbacks, still steeply descending. After the next drainage, the trail strings through meadows of wildflowers and wild onion to top a rise at 16 miles. Where it again dips, find Moccasin Lake. Its blue depths drop sharply away from the rocky shelves of shore.

The loop continues with a crossing at the neck of Moccasin Lake's two watery lobes; an isthmus and walkway of rocks usually keep the feet dry. At the junction on the opposite shore, the loop curves right, rounding the northwest slope above Moccasin Lake. Cross-lake views feature Eagle Cap's fractured face and Glacier Pass.

The semiforested route then rolls between lake basins, bearing right at the junctions. It rings up visits to 44-acre Douglas Lake (18 miles), 9-acre Lee Lake (19 miles), and 40-acre Horseshoe Lake (20 miles).

After traveling the length of Horseshoe Lake, the trail begins another major descent. Branding the steep, forested slope, a series of switchbacks eases the going. Occasional views feature the West Fork Canyon. At 23.5 miles, the trail meets and follows Lake Creek downstream, passing through a stand of dead spruce. At the confluence, the route crosses footbridges over Lake Creek and the West Fork.

The trail then edges the north end of Six Mile Meadow to close the loop at 24 miles. For the return to the trailhead, go left, backtracking the West Fork Wallowa Trail downstream for 6 miles.

96

SUMMIT RIDGE TRAIL

Distance: 18 miles round trip *(to Lookout Mountain)*
Elevation change: 1,400 feet
Difficulty: Strenuous
Season: Summer through fall
Map: USFS Hells Canyon National Recreation Area
For information: Hells Canyon National Recreation Area

Traveling the ridgeline that marks the Hells Canyon Wilderness boundary for the western rim, this trail offers sweeping vistas of the deep-cut canyons of the Imnaha and Snake Rivers. The neighborhood is one of flat-topped bluffs; bald, furrowed flanks; and tree-lined drainages. In the distance, hikers can see the high Wallowas to the southwest and Idaho's Seven Devils (a high-peak chain) to the east. The hike ends at the Lookout Mountain summit (elevation 6,792 feet).

Much of the trail strings across arid grassland steppes sprinkled with wildflowers; peak blooms arrive in early summer. By autumn, asters and Indian paintbrush alone bring color to the russet-gold grassland gone to seed. Ponderosa pine and mixed firs patch the slopes.

Hells Canyon, wild and remote, requires hikers to exercise the full caution warranted by this rugged terrain, and beware of rattlesnakes. Always carry plenty of water.

From Imnaha, go 17 miles southeast on FR 4240, Hat Point Road, to find this trail's marked Jim Spring Trailhead on the right, past Granny Vista. Parking is to the side of the road or uphill at Saddle Creek Campground. The single-lane gravel road with turnouts is winding, narrow, and not suitable for low-clearance vehicles.

The Summit Ridge Trail, also known as the Western Rim National

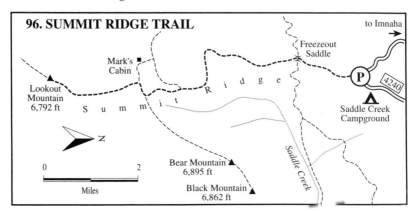

96. SUMMIT RIDGE TRAIL

to Imnaha

Freezeout Saddle

Mark's Cabin

R i d g e

P

4240

Lookout Mountain 6,792 ft

S u m m i t

Saddle Creek Campground

N

0   2

Miles

Bear Mountain 6,895 ft

Black Mountain 6,862 ft

Saddle Creek

Freezeout Saddle pack train

Recreation Trail, wraps around and down the ridge, offering early views of the Imnaha River and Freezeout Creek drainages. The open, dry slope features buckwheat, bunchgrass, and fireweed. A few fir and scenic snags dot the route.

By 0.4 mile, the view expands to include the Snake River Canyon. Keep an eye out at 0.8 mile, as the trail angles back to descend the east side of the slope overlooking the Snake Canyon. Do not take the path ahead.

At 1.5 miles, the trail crosses back onto the west side of the ridge to travel a beautiful native bunchgrass meadow to Freezeout Saddle and its junction (2.2 miles). The Summit Ridge Trail now proceeds straight along the ridge toward McGraw Lookout. The trail to the left follows Saddle Creek to the Snake River, and the one to the right reaches Freezeout Road. The southeastern view juxtaposes smooth-sided Bear Mountain with the rocky cliffs of Black Mountain.

The trail now travels a bunchgrass-wildflower slope just below the ridge on the Freezeout Canyon side. The trail is less rocky and canted for more comfort. At 2.7 miles, where the ridge dips to the trail, hikers can overlook two drainages and snare a peek at Hat Point Lookout.

The trail then contours and ascends the northeast side of the ridge. While more trees enter the setting, the route remains mostly open.

At 3.5 miles, the trail rounds a bend, exchanging views of Freezeout Saddle for views of the Freezeout Creek and Imnaha River drainages. The snowy-crowned Wallowas offer a striking skyline above the arid Imnaha rim. The trail continues, alternately touring grassland and a tree-shrub transition habitat.

As the trail is again about to change direction, a superb over-the-shoulder view peers straight down Freezeout Creek to its confluence with the Imnaha River. The rugged enclosing rims present a classic Hells Canyon image.

Beginning at 5.3 miles, the trail travels below an old burn, and later passes through a fence opening. At the 5.5-mile junction with Trail 1763, the Summit Ridge Trail continues straight ahead. Hikers find a prized view of Idaho's Seven Devils rising up behind Bear Mountain.

The trail then crosses over to the west slope, touring just below the ridge. The fire's impact here lingers with snags, downed logs, and the many sprouting groves of aspen. At the 6.6-mile junction, the Bear Mountain Trail heads left as the Summit Ridge Trail bears right. Below the junction, a seasonal spring feeds a greener area with false hellebore and buttercups.

Soon, an old jeep trail continues the journey, and at 6.9 miles, meets another jeep trail. Downhill to the right is Mark's Cabin (now sealed), 0.5 mile; the ridge route continues bearing left. By 7.5 miles, the rolling tour returns to an undisturbed grassland; high-elevation firs and spruce mark the edge.

With a gentle ascent, the trail claims the Lookout Mountain summit at 9 miles. A radio tower occupies this mostly tree-flanked site. Although the trees deny a 360-degree view, the top conveys a strong Hells Canyon impression. Return as you came or continue the ridge chase for another 9 miles to McGraw Lookout.

97 | EAST EAGLE CREEK – EAGLE CAP HIKE

Distance: 27.2 miles round trip (wilderness permit required)
Elevation change: 5,000 feet
Difficulty: Strenuous
Season: Summer through fall
Map: USFS Eagle Cap Wilderness, Wallowa-Whitman; Imus Geographics Wallowa Mountains Eagle Cap Wilderness
For information: Eagle Cap Ranger District

A southern gateway to the wilderness, this hike journeys up the splendid East Eagle Creek Canyon to top the granite crown of the wilderness skyline— Eagle Cap (elevation 9,572 feet). In one tidy, long-distance package, hikers will discover forest, meadow, ridge, sterling waters, and landmark peaks, but side trips are needed for any lake visits. Despite most of the area's high peaks going trailless, a surprisingly easy path leads to the top of Eagle Cap. Lofty reaches hold the potential for sighting bighorn sheep and mountain goats.

From OR 86 (6 miles west of Halfway, 47 miles east of Baker City) turn north on gravel FR 77; expect some washboard. Stay on FR 77 for 23 miles,

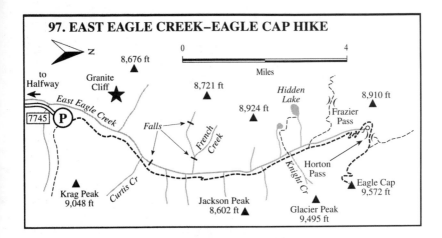

97. EAST EAGLE CREEK–EAGLE CAP HIKE

turning right on FR 7745/East Eagle Road. In another 5.2 miles find horse-trailer and spill-over parking on the right. Proceed 0.8 mile more to reach the actual East Eagle Trailhead, where parking is limited. Drive cautiously as the final 0.8 mile includes a vehicle fording of Little Kettle Creek, normal-to high-clearance required.

For the signed East Eagle Trail (Trail 1910), hike an old jeep trail west through an area of white fir, spruce, and huge ponderosa pines to follow the east shore of East Eagle Creek upstream. East Eagle Creek is audible but not visible. Granite Cliff leads off the views with its stark gray walls and a 4,000-foot vertical relief.

At 0.25 mile, veer right, now following a footpath. The trail alternates between rich woods and dry meadow habitats, shade and sun. Some of the firs along the trail exceed 4 feet in diameter. Before long, the trail crosses into Eagle Cap Wilderness.

The trail next rolls and ascends, passing some 50 feet above the remarkably clear East Eagle Creek. Intermittent tributaries mark off distance, while the cross-canyon views present the wooded mantle and rocky crest of the west ridge.

Where the trail traverses a rocky meadow drainage at 1.25 miles, view "the Box" (uphill to the right), Krag Peak, and the rugged, folded canyon. At 2 miles, cross the rocky bed of Curtis Creek to first admire a two-stage waterfall on East Eagle Creek.

Open, shrubby meadows now characterize the upstream tour, as strong red dikes punctuate the white peaks. At 2.4 miles, a gorge excites the water along East Eagle Creek. Ribbony falls streak the canyon walls. Before long, small aspen and evergreen pockets lend shade, and Eagle Cap joins Jackson and Glacier Peaks at the head the canyon.

At 3.5 miles, the broad meadow flat between Snow and Coon Creeks suggests the first place to camp. At 4.2 miles, the first switchback puts the

Glacier Peak from Eagle Cap

trail on a higher contour along the east canyon wall. Views present a hang-ing valley and falls on East Eagle Creek and the skyline white domes. The trail then rounds through granite outcrops and returns to meadow (5.1 miles). Here, it passes closer to East Eagle Creek, edging clusters of the full-skirted alpine trees.

Beyond intermittent Dodge Creek, alder thickets are common on the floodplain. At 6 miles, the trail crosses the rocky bed of Dennis Creek, and at 6.5 miles is the left turnoff for Hidden Lakes. Continue forward, again switchbacking to travel a higher line on the east canyon slope. Past Knight Creek, the views up-canyon are of Horton and Frazier Passes.

At the 7.5-mile trail junction post, bear right for Horton Pass and Eagle Cap, remaining on Trail 1910. The trail narrows with a rockier footing and continues crossing small streams. At 8.4 miles, an avalanche has tumbled trees. By 9.2 miles, the ascending trail switchbacks to and from East Eagle Creek.

At the headwall basin, cross East Eagle Creek (10.5 miles), and watch for elk. Before continuing, be sure to have enough water to complete the remaining journey to and from Eagle Cap.

The trail next traverses granite outcrops. A consistent moderate grade then leads to Horton Pass (12.1 miles). There find a cairn and commemora-tive plaque.

Looks northeast present the Lostine, Hurricane, and Wallowa drainages, their isolating divides, and Matterhorn. Below, admire a cirque and dimpled, scalloped snowfields.

From the pass, two options lead to Eagle Cap: The primary trail crosses over the pass, descends (often on snowfield), rounds the northern edge of the pond, and then bears right up a low side-ridge at the junction post where a left leads to Mirror Lake. Alternatively, a rocky secondary trail heads directly up the ridge to the right from the cairn at Horton Pass. This shorter route generally escapes snowfield travel and is commonly used by elk. Both summit routes merge in a short distance.

When opting for the latter, strike up the ridge from Horton Pass. The brightness of the snow and rock cries out for sunglasses. The meadow green that parts the cliffs of the East Fork Lostine River Canyon draws attention. This hike travels the ridge backbone to meet the primary trail (Trail 1805) in 0.2 mile. Another snowfield typically claims the main trail just before this meeting.

Summit travel now contours the western slope below the ridge and serves up views of East Eagle Canyon, Brown Mountain, and Blue Lake. Soon Eagle Cap appears. After attaining the saddle at 12.8 miles, switchbacks carry the tour skyward, reaching the summit at 13.6 miles.

From this top-of-world vantage, Seven Devils and the Elkhorns serve as east-west bookends for the sweeping panorama. Glacier Peak is front and center. On the return, backtrack out East Eagle Creek.

98 | NATIONAL HISTORIC OREGON TRAIL INTERPRETIVE CENTER TRAILS

Distance: 4.6 miles round trip
Elevation change: 400 feet
Difficulty: Easy to moderate
Season: Summer through fall
Map: Center brochure
For information: National Historic Oregon Trail Interpretive Center

This trail system explores the arid countryside of Flagstaff Hill, revealing remnants from the mining era, the legacy ruts of the historic Oregon Trail, and a side wagon trail that helped open up the western frontier. The often-parched landscape unveils sweeping expanses with distant farmlands and high peaks. The interpretive center stands out on its hilltop location.

The year 1843 brought the first pioneers west on the Oregon Trail. As part of the centennial celebration an obelisk was placed at the base of Flagstaff Hill along OR 86; look for it as you arrive at the historic site. When hiking, carry ample water, and wear a hat, sun lotion, and sunglasses.

From I-84 just north of Baker City, take exit 302 and go east on OR 86 for 5 miles. There turn left to follow the entrance road to the Flagstaff Hill National Historic Oregon Trail Interpretive Center. The gate and fee station typically open soon after 7:00 A.M., with the museum opening at 9:00 A.M. For the price of admission, receive a trail map and access to the center's trails and exhibits.

Start by following the paved all-ability trail where it rounds below the entry walk to the interpretive center. Stairways from the center also access the trail and cut down to its attractions, but for this tour keep on the 5-foot-wide paved trail.

As the trail rounds the center, hikers can survey the Flagstaff Mine. The claim dates to 1895, and placer mining and later hard-rock mining took place there. The restored native grasses growing alongside the trail hint at the habitat when the pioneers first crossed into this area. Past grazing altered the vegetation mix.

At the back of the center, come to a junction at 0.2 mile. To the right leads to Panorama Point and the Hard Rock Lode Mine display, which includes a mock adit, tunnel, vertical shaft, and stamp mill. A left leads back to parking and the covered wagons of Emigrant Camp. Go right for the full tour.

The trail descends with side spurs to the mining exhibits. Historic photos and word panels help unfold the mining tale. By following the Panorama Point Trail west from the center, overlook the treeless high desert to the farmland of Baker City and the Powder River Valley. Rising at their backs is the rugged Elkhorn Crest of the Blue Mountains.

Interpretive signs and benches suggest a slow stroll, while the sun sets a different pace. At 1 mile, reach an inviting shade shelter with slat sides

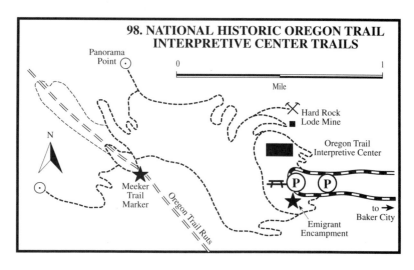

98. NATIONAL HISTORIC OREGON TRAIL INTERPRETIVE CENTER TRAILS

letting in the breeze. From the shelter's bench, glimpse the Oregon Trail monument on OR 86 across the way.

At 1.5 miles, spur right to reach Panorama Point in another 0.1 mile. This viewpoint shelter occupies an outcrop point for a fine vantage on the landscape and a perspective on the lichen-decorated rock. In this lonesome, treeless setting, the view sweeps 360 degrees. Search for the trace of the Oregon Trail; it arrives along the hillside south of the center and arcs northwest through the drainage.

Backtrack to the 1.5-mile junction (at 1.7 miles), and turn right to continue the counterclockwise tour, now on the Mountain Ash Trail heading for the ruts. The trail remains paved as it descends and passes between a couple of rock outcrops dotted by small trees that suggest the trail's name.

The trail soon overlooks the line of the Oregon Trail. Simple white concrete posts point out the historic wagon route. The trace is faint owing to a stock reservoir having covered it for many years. Past the Ascent Trail (the steep footpath returning to the center), the paved trail ends at the second shade shelter (2.4 miles).

At the shelter, view a covered wagon placed along the trace of the historic Oregon Trail at the granite marker commemorating pioneer Ezra Meeker's 1906 return visit. While better examples of the wagon ruts can be seen in other parts of the state and in other parts of the country, the Meeker marker and the open terrain that duplicates the historic landscape, if not the vegetation, distinguish this site.

A clockwise tour of the Oregon Trail Ruts Loop offers additional perspectives on the scene and accesses the Auburn–Burnt River Spur Trail in 0.1 mile. This spur (0.8-mile round trip) journeys across the desert plain to end at an interpretive board overlooking a wagon road that branched off the Oregon Trail to the gold mining town of Auburn.

Resuming the clockwise tour of the Oregon Trail Ruts Loop at 3.3 miles, hikers soon come upon the 0.4-mile Eagle Valley Railroad Grade Loop. This loop travels a section of a rural "feeder" line of the early 1900s that linked Baker City to points east, and it overlooks the Oregon Trail in the drainage below it. The trail can be overgrown.

For the cleanest wrap-up of the tour, forgo this side trip and cross back over the Oregon Trail, coming out near the shade shelter. At 3.6 miles, either follow the Ascent Trail back to the center or backtrack the paved walk. The Ascent Trail requires a sturdy shoe and is the steepest trail in the system. It follows a hardpan dirt trail that has some rock studding.

At 4.1 miles, nearing the top of the hill, the trail becomes rockier and passes among thistles growing 5 to 6 feet tall. Views east span Virtue Flat to the mountains at the Oregon-Idaho border. Upon meeting the Flagstaff Hill Loop at 4.4 miles, a left leads to the Emigrant Encampment and Interpretive Center; right leads to parking. Go left to round up the remaining history.

99 | UPPER LESLIE GULCH HIKE

Distance: 4 miles round trip
Elevation change: 500 feet
Difficulty: Moderate
Season: Spring through fall
Map: USGS Bannock Ridge, Rooster Comb
For information: Vale District BLM

Named for a pioneer struck by lightning here in 1882 (Hiram Leslie), Leslie Gulch enfolds the beauty of erosion-carved volcanic-ash cliffs and captures the isolation and romance of the wild. The canyon of Upper Leslie Gulch, a wilderness study area (WSA), provides a natural avenue for discovery. The drainage is also part of the greater Leslie Gulch Area of Critical Environmental Concern (ACEC). Leslie Gulch, along with its adjacent canyons, is known for its bighorn sheep viewing opportunities.

Massive flows, dikes, fissures, and elemental sculpting create a canyon rich in character. Many of the sheer walls and pitted towers represent the weathered formations of Leslie Gulch tuff—a solidified volcanic ash unique to the Owyhee region. In places, the tuff measures some 2,000 feet thick.

Camping and ground fires are restricted to the BLM's Slocum Creek primitive camp where Leslie Gulch Road dead-ends at the Owyhee Reservoir, 4 miles west of the trailhead. With no developed water systems in the area, bring what you will need. Recreational livestock is prohibited within the ACEC. As always in desert canyon country, be alert for snakes.

Attractive backcountry roads access this canyon hike; high-clearance vehicles are recommended. Winter conditions can preclude access; contact the Vale District Office for an update on road status.

From OR 201, 8 miles south of Adrian, go southwest on Succor Creek Road for 26 miles and turn right onto Leslie Gulch Road. Continue 8.9 miles on Leslie Gulch Road to reach the mouth of Upper Leslie Gulch Canyon and a parking turnout, both on the left. If you pass Dago Gulch Road and a cabin, you have gone 0.2 mile too far.

An intermittent, informal footpath travels the belly of the gulch, crisscrossing the wash. The drainage itself offers an alternative path; although near the mouth, it proves more difficult to follow.

The footpath weaves amid the 4- to 6-foot-high sagebrush, parted by rabbitbrush, sweet clover, and a few juniper. In May and early June, fleabane, phlox, paintbrush, milk vetch, geraniums, and balsamroot add their floral signatures.

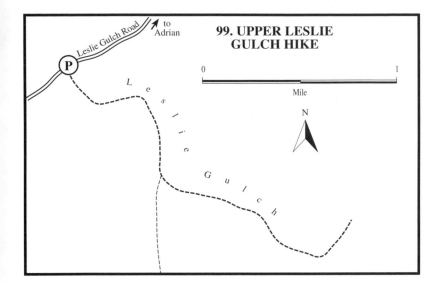

Where the canyon makes a gradual bend at 0.25 mile, the west wall features rounded, rock outcrop-dotted bunchgrass slopes. The opposite wall shows rugged, spire-topped cliffs rising some 300 to 400 feet above the canyon bottom.

Continue up the canyon drainage. Side drainages, mostly shallow and dead end in nature, invite additional exploration. The industrious may mount the gentler slopes for canyon overlooks.

By 0.75 mile, the route reveals the cone-shaped grassland hill topped by a lone chimney rock that isolates the canyon's two arms. Beyond it stretches a grassland ridge topped by protruding rock shields that conjures up the image of a platy spined dinosaur.

At the canyon-dividing hillside at 0.9 mile, go left to follow the main wash. It rolls out a bed of small rocks and coarse sand for easy walking. Heavy rains, however, may alter its condition over time.

At 1.4 miles, the route arrives below a mountain mahogany stand on the hillside. A great monolith reigns at the head of the canyon, while above and to the left sits a scenic hanging basin with a dark-varnished bottom.

At 1.8 miles, the route approaches the base of the slope housing the large monolith. Follow the main canyon as it curves left. Imposing rock walls now straddle the pinched canyon as the hike draws to a close. Where it dead-ends at 2 miles, return as you came.

100 | SLOCUM CREEK CANYON HIKE

Distance: 3.5 miles round trip
Elevation change: 400 feet
Difficulty: Easy
Season: Spring through fall
Map: USGS Rooster Comb
For information: Vale District BLM

Near the eastern shore of the Owyhee Reservoir, this hike up the Slocum Creek wash offers a fine look at the superb red-rock canyons of Southeast Oregon. Slocum Creek is part of the 11,653-acre Leslie Gulch Area of Critical Environmental Concern (ACEC); it is also part of the Slocum Creek Wilderness Study Area (WSA).

The BLM designated the greater Leslie Gulch area an ACEC because of the rare plant species and fragile habitat. Wildlife of the area include coyote, bobcat, reptiles, and a host of birds. The bighorn sheep that may be spied are California bighorns, reintroduced into this native range in 1965.

All camping is restricted to the minimally developed campground at the mouth of Slocum Creek Canyon. Bring water as none is available at the camp. Recreational livestock is prohibited within the ACEC. While exploring the desert, take the necessary precautions for sun and snakes.

Despite the long, winding route to camp, the attractive canyon settings

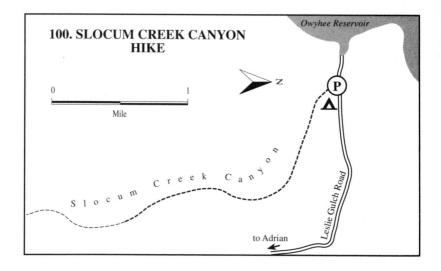

100. SLOCUM CREEK CANYON HIKE

N

Owyhee Reservoir

0   1
Mile

P

Slocum Creek Canyon

Leslie Gulch Road

to Adrian

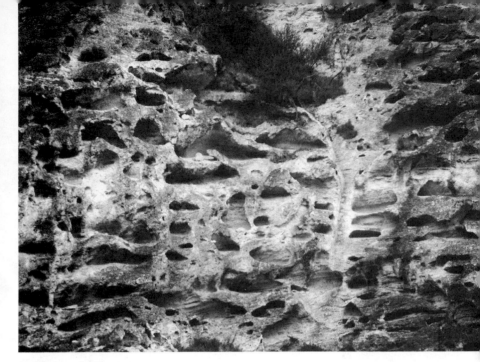

Honeycombed outcrop

make the trip worthwhile. High-clearance vehicles are recommended. Winter conditions can preclude access; contact the Vale District Office for an update on road status.

To reach Slocum Creek Campground, where the hike begins, from OR 201, 8 miles south of Adrian, go southwest on Succor Creek Road for 26 miles and turn right onto Leslie Gulch Road. Then, continue about 13 miles on Leslie Gulch Road to find the campground on the left. The boat launch is just beyond the camp entrance, where the road ends at Owyhee Reservoir.

The hike begins at the upper end of the campground, entering the canyon. An artichoke-shaped rock with folded plates of red and orange hues guards the canyon entrance. The sandy wash shapes the lane of travel, which slowly wiggles southeast into the canyon.

At 1 mile, the wash leads through a rich amber-gold canyon setting with honeycomb walls. Gases trapped in the volcanic rock create the unusual pocking and contribute to the eroded skyline windows. What first appears to be a unified wall later reveals itself to be a series of rock plates and shields separated by narrow gorges and channels. The best time to tour the canyon is early evening, when the soft lighting accents the golden hues. At 1.5 miles, the canyon arcs right.

The turnaround point for this hike comes at 1.75 miles, where the canyon splits, although both forks may extend the discovery. The return is as you came.

Metolius Wild and Scenic River, Deschutes National Forest

ADDRESSES

Baker Ranger District
3165 10th Street
Baker City, OR 97814
(541) 523-4476

Bend/Fort Rock Ranger District
1230 NE 3rd
Bend, OR 97701
(541) 388-5664

Big Summit Ranger District
33700 NE Ochoco Ranger Station
Road
Prineville, OR 97754
(541) 416-6645

Blue River Ranger District
P.O. Box 199
Blue River, OR 97413
(541) 822-3317

Bly Ranger District
Bly, OR 97622
(541) 353-2427

Bullards Beach State Park
P.O. Box 569
Bandon, OR 97411
(541) 347-2209

Burns District, BLM
HC 74-12533, Highway 20 West
Hines, OR 97738
(541) 573-4400

Burns Ranger District
HC 74, Box 12870
Hines, OR 97738
(541) 573-4300

Cape Lookout State Park
13000 Whiskey Creek Road West
Tillamook, OR 97141
(503) 842-4981

Cape Perpetua Interpretive Center
2400 Highway 101 South
Yachats, OR 97498
(541) 547-3289

Chemult Ranger District
P.O. Box 150
Chemult, OR 97731
(541) 365-7001

Clackamas Ranger District
595 NW Industrial Way
Estacada, OR 97023
(503) 630-6861

Collier Memorial State Park
46000 Highway 97 North
Chiloquin, OR 97624
(541) 783-2471

Columbia River Gorge National Scenic Area
USDA Forest Service
902 Wasco Avenue, Suite 200
Hood River, OR 97031
(541) 386-2333

Coos Bay District, BLM
1300 Airport Lane
North Bend, OR 97459
(541) 756-0100

Cottage Grove Ranger District
78405 Cedar Park Road
Cottage Grove, OR 97424
(541) 942-5591

Crater Lake National Park
P.O. Box 7
Crater Lake, OR 97604
(541) 594-2211

Crooked River National Grassland
Ochoco National Forest
P.O. Box 490
Prineville, OR 97754
(541) 475-9272

Detroit Ranger District
HC 73, Box 320
Mill City, OR 97360
(503) 854-3366

Diamond Lake Ranger District
HC 60, Box 101
Idleyld Park, OR 97447
(541) 498-2531

Douglas County Parks
P.O. Box 800
Winchester, OR 97495
(541) 957-7001

Dufur Ranger Station
P.O. Box 67
Dufur, OR 97021
(541) 467-2291

Eagle Cap Ranger District
88401 Highway 82
Enterprise, OR 97828
(541) 426-4978

Estacada Ranger District
595 NW Industrial Way
Estacada, OR 97023
(503) 630-6861

Galice Ranger District
200 NE Greenfield Road
Grants Pass, OR 97526
(541) 471-6500

Gold Beach Ranger District
29279 Ellensburg Avenue
Gold Beach, OR 97444
(541) 247-3600

Hart Mountain National Antelope Refuge
P.O. Box 111
Lakeview, OR 97630
(541) 947-3315

Hells Canyon National Recreation Area
88401 Highway 82
Enterprise, OR 97828
(541) 426-4978

Hood River Ranger District
6780 Highway 35
Mt. Hood–Parkdale, OR 97041
(541) 352-6002

Illinois Valley Ranger District
26568 Redwood Highway
Cave Junction, OR 97523
(541) 592-2166

John Day Fossil Beds National Monument
HCR 82, Box 126
Kimberly, OR 97848
(541) 987-2333

Klamath Ranger District
1936 California Avenue
Klamath Falls, OR 97601
(541) 885-3400

Lane County Parks Division
90064 Coburg Road
Eugene, OR 97408
(541) 682-2000

McKenzie Ranger District
McKenzie Bridge, OR 97413
(541) 822-3381

Medford District, BLM
3040 Biddle Road
Medford, OR 97504
(541) 770-2200

Middle Fork Ranger District, Lowell Office
60 South Pioneer Street
Lowell, OR 97452
(541) 937-2129

Middle Fork Ranger District, Oakridge
P.O. Box 1410
Oakridge, OR 97463
(541) 782-2283

Mount Hood Information Center
65000 East Highway 26
Welches, OR 97067
(503) 622-4822
If outside the Portland Metro
area: 1-888-622-4822

National Historic Oregon Trail Interpretive Center
P.O. Box 987
Baker City, OR 97814
(541) 523-1843

Nature of the Northwest U.S. Forest Service
800 NE Oregon Street, #177
Portland, OR 97232
(503) 872-2750

North Fork John Day Ranger District
P.O. Box 158
Ukiah, OR 97880
(541) 427-3231

North Umpqua Ranger District
18782 North Umpqua Highway
Glide, OR 97443
(541) 496-3532

Oregon Dunes National Recreation Area
855 Highway Avenue
Reedsport, OR 97467
(541) 271-3611

Paulina Ranger District
171500 Beaver Creek Road
Paulina, OR 97751
(541) 416-6643

Pomeroy (Washington) Ranger District
71 West Main Street
Pomeroy, WA 99347
(509) 843-1891

Portland Parks and Recreation Department
Hoyt Arboretum
4000 SW Fairview Boulevard
Portland, OR 97221
(503) 823-3655

Prairie City Ranger District
327 Southwest Front Street
P.O. Box 337
Prairie City, OR 97869
(541) 820-3311

Prineville District, BLM
3050 NE Third Street
P.O. Box 550
Prineville, OR 97754
(541) 416-6700

Prineville Ranger District
3160 NE Third Street
P.O. Box 490
Prineville, OR 97754
(541) 416-6500

Prospect Ranger District
Prospect, OR 97536
(541) 560-3400

Roseburg District, BLM
777 NW Garden Valley Boulevard
Roseburg, OR 97470
(541) 440-4930

Salem District, BLM
1717 Fabry Road SE
Salem, OR 97306
(503) 375-5646

Silver Falls State Park
20024 Silver Falls Highway SE
Sublimity, OR 97385
(503) 873-8681

Silver Lake Ranger District
Silver Lake, OR 97638
(541) 576-2107

Sisters Ranger District
P.O. Box 249
Sisters, OR 97759
(541) 549-2111

South Slough National Estuarine Research Reserve
P.O. Box 5417
Charleston, OR 97420
(541) 888-5558

State Parks and Recreation Department
1115 Commercial Street
Salem, OR 97310
(503) 378-6305

State Parks, Central Oregon Area
Empire Corporate Park, Suite B1
20310 Empire Avenue
Bend, OR 97701
(541) 388-6212

State Parks, North Coast Area
Ridge Road
Hammond, OR 97121
(503) 861-1671

State Parks, Portland/Columbia Gorge Area
P.O. Box 500
Portland, OR 97207
(503) 731-3293

State Parks, South Central Coast Area
84505 Highway 101 South
Florence, OR 97439
(541) 997-3851

State Parks, South Coast Area
10965 Cape Arago Highway
Coos Bay, OR 97420
(541) 888-8867

Summer Lake Wildlife Area
36981 Highway 31
Summer Lake, OR 97640
(541) 943-3152

Sweet Home Ranger District
3225 Highway 20
Sweet Home, OR 97386
(541) 367-5168

Tillamook County Parks
P.O. Box 633
Garibaldi, OR 97118
(503) 322-3477

Tiller Ranger District
27812 Tiller-Trail Highway
Tiller, OR 97484
(541) 825-3201

Vale District, BLM
100 Oregon Street
Vale, OR 97918
(541) 473-3144

Waldport Ranger District
1049 SW Pacific Way
P.O. Box 400
Waldport, OR 97394
(541) 563-3211

Walla Walla (Washington) Ranger District
1415 West Rose Avenue
Walla Walla, WA 99362
(509) 522-6290

INDEX

ABOUT THE AUTHORS

Over the past 18 years, this Oregon author team—Rhonda (a writer) and George (a photographer)—has collaborated on 10 outdoor guidebooks; sold hundreds of articles on topics of nature, travel, and outdoor recreation; and participated in environmental impact studies. This book brought them back to some of their favorite Oregon haunts and gave them an excuse to do some more exploring.

Other Mountaineers Book titles by the team include *50 Hikes in Hells Canyon and Oregon's Wallowas* (1997), *California State Parks: A Complete Recreation Guide* (1995), *Oregon Campgrounds Hiking Guide* (1991/1997), and *50 Hikes in Oregon's Coast Range and Siskiyous* (1989). See also their *Hiking New York* (1996), *Hiking Southern New England* (1997), and *Hiking Pennsylvania* (1997), all with Falcon Publishing (Helena, Montana).

THE MOUNTAINEERS, founded in 1906, is a nonprofit outdoor activity and conservation club, whose mission is "to explore, study, preserve, and enjoy the natural beauty of the outdoors. . . . " Based in Seattle, Washington, the club is now the third largest such organization in the United States, with 15,000 members and five branches throughout Washington State.

The Mountaineers sponsors both classes and year-round outdoor activities in the Pacific Northwest, which include hiking, mountain climbing, ski-touring, snowshoeing, bicycling, camping, kayaking and canoeing, nature study, sailing, and adventure travel. The club's conservation division supports environmental causes through educational activities, sponsoring legislation, and presenting informational programs. All club activities are led by skilled, experienced volunteers, who are dedicated to promoting safe and responsible enjoyment and preservation of the outdoors.

If you would like to participate in these organized outdoor activities or the club's programs, consider a membership in The Mountaineers. For information and an application, write or call The Mountaineers, Club Headquarters, 300 Third Avenue West, Seattle, WA 98119; 206-284-6310.

The Mountaineers Books, an active, nonprofit publishing program of the club, produces guidebooks, instructional texts, historical works, natural history guides, and works on environmental conservation. All books produced by The Mountaineers are aimed at fulfilling the club's mission.

Send or call for our catalog of more than 300 outdoor titles.

The Mountaineers Books
1001 SW Klickitat Way, Suite 201
Seattle, WA 98134
800-553-4453
mbooks@mountaineers.org
www.mountaineersbooks.org